The Ultima
Negotiatio

Peter Fleming,
Di McLanachan a
Mo Shapiro

The Teach Yourself series has been trusted around the world for
over 75 years. This book is designed to help people at all levels
and around the world to further their careers. Learn, from one
book, what the experts learn in a lifetime.

Peter Ronald Kellino Fleming is a Chartered Fellow of both the UK Chartered Institute of Marketing and the Chartered Institute of Personnel Development. He is author of numerous management books and has more than 30 years' experience as an International Management Consultant and Trainer (through his consultancy, PFA International).

With past negotiating experience in senior management roles in the Public Sector – and buying exposure in Retailing – he has continued his family's path of international travel (through The Kellino's acrobatic group) and built up his expertise in negotiating in Europe, the Middle East and Australasia.

His specialisms lie with business development through marketing solutions – and helping organizations improve their learning development programmes through his original work on the transfer of learning in the business setting (which brought him his MA/HRM). Apart from his authorship, he is also an active mentor working in both business and voluntary sectors.

Peter is married with two children and lives in Derbyshire, UK.

Di McLanachan is managing director of Learning Curves Personal Development Ltd. She is an international trainer, executive coach, a master practitioner of Neuro-linguistic Programming and author of the bestselling book *NLP for Business Excellence*. She has frequently been featured on both radio and television, and has been delivering training in customer care on a regular basis since 1993.
www.learningcurves.co.uk

Mo Shapiro, partner of INFORM Training & Communication, is a Master Practitioner in NLP and Coaching. She has an outstanding record as a communications and presentation skills coach and trainer and as an international public speaker. Mo contributes regularly to all broadcast media, has also authored *Interviewing People Successfully in a Week*, and co-authored *Tackling Tough Interview Questions in a Week* and *Job Interviews in a Week*.

Teach Yourself®

The Ultimate Negotiation Book

Discover What Top Negotiators Do, Master Persuasion and Influence, Build Rapport with NLP

Peter Fleming,
Di McLanachan and
Mo Shapiro

First published in Great Britain in 2020 by Teach Yourself, an imprint of John Murray Press, a division of Hodder and Stoughton Ltd. An Hachette UK company.

The right of Peter Fleming, Di McLanachan and Mo Shapiro to be identified as the Authors of the Work has been asserted by them in accordance with the Copyright, Designs and Patents Act 1988.

Based on original material from *Negotiation Skills In A Week; Advanced Negotiation Skills In A Week; Persuasion and Influence In A Week; NLP In A Week*

Database right Hodder & Stoughton (makers)

The *Teach Yourself* name is a registered trademark of Hachette UK.

British Library Cataloguing in Publication Data: a catalogue record for this title is available from the British Library.

Library of Congress Catalog Card Number: on file.

Paperback ISBN: 978 1 473 68880 3

Ebook ISBN: 978 1 473 68881 0

1

The publisher has used its best endeavours to ensure that any website addresses referred to in this book are correct and active at the time of going to press. However, the publisher and the author have no responsibility for the websites and can make no guarantee that a site will remain live or that the content will remain relevant, decent or appropriate.

The publisher has made every effort to mark as such all words which it believes to be trademarks. The publisher should also like to make it clear that the presence of a word in the book, whether marked or unmarked, in no way affects its legal status as a trademark.

Every reasonable effort has been made by the publisher to trace the copyright holders of material in this book. Any errors or omissions should be notified in writing to the publisher, who will endeavour to rectify the situation for any reprints and future editions.

Typeset by Cenveo® Publisher Services.

Printed and bound in Great Britain by CPI Group (UK) Ltd., Croydon, CR0 4YY.

John Murray Press policy is to use papers that are natural, renewable and recyclable products and made from wood grown in sustainable forests. The logging and manufacturing processes are expected to conform to the environmental regulations of the country of origin.

Carmelite House
50 Victoria Embankment
London EC4Y 0DZ
www.hodder.co.uk

Contents

**Part 3: Your Persuasion and
Influence Masterclass**

PART 1
Your Negotiation Skills Masterclass

Introduction

There was a time, not that long ago, when negotiation was seen, in the main, as the province of industrial relations folk and car-sales advisers. But, no longer!

Repeated financial crises have squeezed profit margins and, in some markets, discouraged buyers from making marginal purchases or continuing habitual expenditure. Managers have found themselves in the frontline of the expectation to achieve better value for money, and the starting point for this is to shop around and explore the offers made by new suppliers, and/or to negotiate better deals with existing suppliers.

Becoming an effective negotiator is certainly within the scope of the majority of people. At its simplest, it involves thinking out what you want, planning how you'd like to get it and developing your powers of persuasion to convince other people that you are simply being reasonable.

This Part will help you to plan to become a better negotiator through:

● being better prepared for meetings
● planning clear and realistic objectives for a negotiation
● maintaining concentration
● making logical proposals that create agreement in the other party.

It is important to remember that negotiating may not be essential (or even desirable) in every situation. Alternative approaches or outcomes could include:

● **acceptance** by the other party
● **consultation** of the other party (this could result in erosion of possible objections)
● **selling the idea** (a simple but effective method of persuasion)
● **imposition** (not nice – but sometimes necessary in a crisis situation)

- **arbitration** by another, mutually acceptable and appointed, party (the result is usually binding)
- **mediation** through a neutral third party (who provides an additional communication channel)
- **alternative dispute resolution** – which is useful when all else fails and the parties want to avoid recourse to the law.

CHAPTER 1

Creating the right environment

You are more likely to be successful if you know how to create the right environment for negotiation to take place.

Before setting out on a negotiation strategy, it is important to review your motivations for wanting to negotiate in the first place.

Did you identify strongly with the ideas expressed in the Introduction and now want to put them into practice? Or, maybe, you are planning a new 'attack' on your department's objectives (cost controls, sales revenues or even reorganizing work routines) and you fear that there might be some negative reactions.

This chapter will help you to set up the best environment for a negotiation, so that you avoid distractions and negative factors that can reduce the chances of a successful outcome. This includes:

- reviewing your own attitudes to a negotiation
- creating the best atmosphere for the meeting
- selecting the best time
- selecting the best place.

Reviewing your own attitudes

Let's look at an example. Your manager has told you to cut back your team's hours, and the best way to do this would be to make someone redundant. You are concerned that this will cause negative attitudes or even conflict among your team, making you feel that you have to be more insistent and take a more hard-line attitude. This, in turn, might make change more difficult and result in a bad working atmosphere.

Alternatively, you could take a softer, more consultative line, which might bring constructive ideas from the team and engender a better atmosphere. It may even lead, for example, to everyone agreeing to a cut in their hours to 'save' their colleague.

Creating the right atmosphere

Experienced negotiators recognize that there are four possible outcomes to a negotiation:

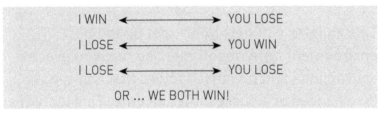

```
I WIN      ←————————→   YOU LOSE

I LOSE     ←————————→   YOU WIN

I LOSE     ←————————→   YOU LOSE

        OR ... WE BOTH WIN!
```

Most people would prefer not to be losers – unless they have unusual motives – and the risk of 'losing' divides negotiators into three categories – those who are:

- **competitive** and want to win at everything
- **collaborative** and want to achieve the best deal for both or all parties
- **consensual** and want to put the importance of maintaining good relationships above any issues which could threaten to divide the parties.

If your role or aim is the continuing development of your business, goodwill or relationships, the collaborative style will bring better, long-lasting relationships and results.

So, the right atmosphere will be affected by:

- how you feel about the situation
- how you feel about your 'opponent'
- the relative power of the two parties
- your ability to cope with stressful situations
- your composure – especially with emotional pressure
- how much you trust each other
- your degree of open-mindedness
- your aspirations (Are you the sort of person who would wish to achieve better-than-average results?)
- how prepared you are to listen (as well as to speak)
- your charisma.

Incidentally, our use of the word 'opponent' does not mean 'pistols at dawn'! It is simply a shorthand word to describe the person with whom we are negotiating.

 Remember that, if you want to achieve a win/win deal, your opponent needs to want to arrive at a satisfactory agreement, too. You can influence this by the way you use the ten factors listed above.

Choosing the right time

The 'right time' to negotiate is probably when you have least need for a deal and your opponent's need is greater. However, collaborative negotiators minimize the 'fallout' from such relationships. Otherwise, the opponent may feel 'beaten' and determined to beat you next time. Warfare of this kind can go on for years!

Skilled negotiators:

- choose their timing carefully (avoid the 'bull-in-a-china-shop' approach)
- patiently draw reluctant opponents to the negotiating table (it could take time)
- avoid spontaneous negotiation sessions (if at all possible!)
- prepare their case carefully

- weigh up what they think may be on their opponent's agenda
- know their own limitations and those of their opponents (for example, are you 'sharper' in the mornings or in the evenings?).

Selecting the best place

The right place to negotiate is any place where you feel most comfortable and, as important, most confident.

This comfort factor involves more than just feeling at home. There may be times when your 'home territory' could provide you with disadvantages as well as advantages.

For example, you would prefer not to:

- be distracted by minor queries while trying to concentrate on the negotiation
- be interrupted by telephone calls
- allow your opponents to see the state of your workplace if it is chaotic or somewhat luxurious in their eyes (this might not impress them!).

These factors may help to heighten your opponent's confidence and lower yours. On the other hand, witnessing these things on your opponent's home ground may help you.

Meeting in neutral territory is often suggested by negotiators as an appropriate way of avoiding any bias in the meeting.

However, you should beware of:

- neutral territory which subsequently turns out to be your opponent's home ground
- being 'landed' in a situation in which you do not feel comfortable.

Social situations can put some negotiators at a disadvantage, for example being invited to a more upmarket restaurant than they might have visited previously for a business negotiation – or vice versa!

Perhaps having to work in very cramped conditions, or with bold furnishings, might unsettle some people.

Summary

So, let's summarize our progress. You should think carefully about how to build a partnership with your opponent.

Look inside your heart and ask yourself:

- Am I really seeking a win/win outcome?
- When will be the best time to negotiate?
- Are we / is our opponent in a hurry?
- How can we use time to our mutual benefit?
- What advantages are there in going to the other party to negotiate or in asking them to come to us?

These questions may seem obvious, but the art of negotiating lies in applying them to your own situation.

Try to relate them to a current project or need. For example, you may be thinking of changing your car. Which of these points might be of greatest help to you?

Atmosphere	Time	Place

Negotiation is not a 'dark art' which should be avoided at all costs! It provides a useful skill that often enables a manager to achieve desirable outcomes with minimal disruption or expenditure.

Setting the scene is a vital part of this process – one which should not be minimized – and in the next chapter we will work on more preparations that should contribute to a successful outcome.

Now try our multiple-choice questions to see how you have progressed.

For each question, choose *one preferred answer* (tick the box), then go to the answers at the end of the book to score your choices.

If you chose second (or even third) best answers, then think about why these answers are not as good as our 'top-rated' one(s).

Fact-check (answers at the back)

1. How do you feel when you read of a major negotiation that has achieved an outstanding result?
   a) There must have been some 'fiddling' going on ❑
   b) I'd like to have been around to see it because I bet it wasn't that easy! ❑
   c) If they can do it, I'm sure I should find out more and give it a try ❑
   d) I bet they don't have all the constraints that are put on managers here ❑

2. You have a supplier whose representative is very competitive; their product range is good but you only buy 'necessities' from them as the rep 'winds you up' by trying to make you buy things you don't think you need. Should you:
   a) Continue to keep the rep at a distance and minimize the orders? ❑
   b) Avoid the rep by ordering on line? ❑
   c) Get the problem 'off your chest' and give the rep a piece of your mind? ❑
   d) Politely, but firmly, explain to the rep that you might be prepared to place bigger orders but only on the condition that you will not be pressurized into purchasing items you do not need or want? ❑

3. Where will you have this conversation?
   a) At a local hostelry at the rep's invitation ❑
   b) In your busy office where there are witnesses to record the conversation ❑
   c) In your quiet meeting room where you can both concentrate on making a 'new' start ❑
   d) In a personal letter addressed to the supplier company ❑

4. You experienced bad traffic conditions on the way to work this morning and were an hour late. When you arrived, your assistant told you that your director had called to talk to you about a customer complaint and seemed very cross. Should you:
   a) Call on the phone and try to resolve the problem – starting with an apology for being late? ❑
   b) Go straight to the director's office and try to resolve the problem – starting with an apology for being late? ❑
   c) Ignore the situation and wait for the director to call again? ❑
   d) Delegate your assistant to deal with the problem? ❑

5. You are experiencing a very pressurized work period and are struggling to keep on top of things. You want to take on a new supplier but know little about them, as their base is at the other end of your country. Should you:

a) 'Bite the bullet' by prioritizing the time and task; and learn about the supplier by visiting them before placing the order? ❏

b) Ask for their Annual Report, placing the order if all seems in order and putting off the visit until things are quieter? ❏

c) Ask them for the name of a referee or satisfied customer to gain an independent report? ❏

d) Seek a third-hand report from your (independent) trade body? ❏

6. On your way into work today you noticed that one tyre on your car is almost flat. You had intended to book it into your regular service garage but forgot, and they are 'too busy' to collect it today. You called out an alternative 'emergency service' and the operative has removed the wheel (reporting that the tyre is dangerous) while he prices a replacement. You believe that the quoted price is twice the real cost. Should you:

a) Pay up and put it down to experience? ❏

b) Have a staff member block his vehicle in with the company van, to 'even up the playing field'? ❏

c) Telephone your motoring club to check the normal cost and, if it is lower, tell the operative that that is what you believe the cost should be? ❏

d) Stop taking risks with your own personal safety? ❏

7. You are naturally extrovert, preferring to deal openly with colleagues and team members. One of your team has just been elected by union members as a staff representative and you are worried about how this development might affect relations in the team. Would you:

a) Warn the individual that you will not tolerate your team relations being 'contaminated' by extremist propaganda? ❏

b) Check how many team members are also members of the union and warn any that are not members not to join? ❏

c) Seek advice from your boss? ❏

d) Welcome your colleague's preparedness to represent their colleagues in meetings/debates and offer your 'counselling support' if it should become necessary? ❏

8. You are visiting a customer in his office and are surprised that all the visitors' chairs are low chairs while the customer has a high adjustable chair. You feel that you would be at a disadvantage sitting on one of the low visitors' chairs. Would you:

a) Politely refuse to sit down, claiming a bad back and only relenting if your host can provide a higher or high-backed chair? ❏

b) Reluctantly sit down on the low chair and hope that it will not put you at a disadvantage? ❏

c) Explain that this can only be a quick call as you are expected elsewhere, but you'd like to invite the customer to lunch down the road? ❏

d) Leave as soon as it seems polite/decent? ❏

9. Your boss asks you to attend a meeting in the office to agree a cost-saving plan – with a hint that redundancies may result. You are anxious to argue strongly against this but worry that your case will lose impact because of the constant interruptions that are common in the office. Would you:

a) Refuse to attend unless a quieter venue is found? ❏

b) Book the boardroom, which is quiet and confidential? ❏

c) Hide your doubts and determine to struggle on regardless? ❏

d) Start looking for alternative vacancies in case someone in your team needs them? ❏

10. At the cost-saving meeting your boss accuses you of closing your mind to ways of improving productivity, over-identifying with your team members by defending their interests. Would you:

a) Seek support and advice from the local union organizer to protect your own position? ❏

b) Present a case for recovery that involves a stronger marketing plan to improve revenue and margins, with milestones for monitoring progress (and with the aim of avoiding impetuous cuts)? ❏

c) Propose a 'no replacement' policy, supposing that individual staff members might decide to chase better opportunities with your competitors? ❏

d) Suggest an in-depth research project of methods used by competitors, which you could then emulate? ❏

CHAPTER 2

Researching your objectives

How do you take decisions? Are you a person who relies on instinct, feelings and emotion, or are you a person who chases down real facts and evidence to support your decisions?

Experienced managers may tell you that they just 'know' the best way to go with a strategy or plan because business goes in cycles and 'what goes around, comes around'! Is this a safe approach? Or should experienced personnel check their facts like anyone else?

Relying on instinct (or even 'luck') may work out well as much as 80 per cent of the time – but is that good enough? Probably not, especially if an incorrect decision could blow a hole in the organization's budget and lead to even more drastic action. And how long do you have to wait before you have enough experience to back 'instinct'?

Managers often find themselves having to take (or influence) decisions that involve deploying resources internally, or committing the organization to external action. In either instance, it is probable that a commitment to the action will be needed from other people – and this may well mean a meeting involving a negotiation (even when there is no buying or selling intention). So, in this chapter, we are going to look closer at your negotiation objectives.

Have you ever considered when the worst time for doing the week's food shopping might be? Is it:

● when the store is busiest?
● when stock is running out?
● when you are in a hurry?

If concern about impulse purchasing is uppermost in your mind, the answer has to be:

● when you are hungry!

Of course, you might always prepare a list before starting the shopping expedition – some people do, but many others do not. If you stand and observe your fellow shoppers at the checkout, you can quickly identify those who probably did not bring a shopping list!

There is nothing wrong with buying products we like, but was this a conscious decision or did the final bill come as a shock? The objective shopper starts out with a checklist and then consciously avoids buying any items that are not on the list.

Similarly, the skilled negotiator always prepares a checklist of objectives – a 'shopping list' – and uses it to compare actual results from meetings with those expected. Any move away from the original plan is then a conscious decision and a target for trading off concessions from the opponent.

Skilled negotiators rarely negotiate without any kind of plan – and most produce detailed plans on anything but the back of an envelope or cigarette packet!

Preparing your own 'shopping list'

Preparing for a dinner party you are going to host may involve some or all of the following:

● deciding on a menu
● preparing a list of ingredients
● making a list of jobs to be done (and by whom)
● drawing up a seating plan
● sending out invitations.

Similarly, a decision to move house should lead us to prepare an objective plan. For example, you may have decided to move to a larger house – three-bedroomed, semi-detached with a garage – from your present two-bedroomed terraced house. You will probably start with a 'wish list' for the 'new' house which might read as follows:

- two double bedrooms, one single
- two reception rooms downstairs
- a downstairs cloakroom
- separate garage – close to the house
- gas-fired central heating.

Of course, these items either exist or they do not – but their priority may vary and your view may be very different from that of your partner!

When house hunting we rarely find exactly what we want and this listing will probably provide an important basis for negotiation at home before you even visit a prospective vendor. The result of these discussions will be a baseline of standards or objectives, against which various possibilities will be screened. You will probably not want to visit properties that do not come up to your expectations (although this is by no means certain – did your present accommodation exactly match your 'minimum' standards?).

Preparing your negotiation brief

Once you have selected a property you find attractive, you will need to produce a negotiating brief for both your purchase and your sale (if you have a property to sell). This will be two-dimensional and encompass:

- your objectives
- your best assessment of your opponent's objectives.

Planning your objectives

Establishing your own objectives will be relatively easy. Taking price as an example, the buyer's objective will be to obtain good value for money bearing in mind the need not to exceed 'market value'. The buyer's parameters for price will be determined by the following:

- At the 'upper end':
  - available funds – from the sale of a current property
  - any bridging finance available
  - a personal loan from your favourite aunt
  - how much you really want the property.

- At the 'lower end':
  - the lowest price you feel the vendor might consider without insulting him/her and causing the withdrawal of the property
  - the price which you feel correctly matches current market activity
  - a price which enables the vendor to meet his/her plans.

Assessing your opponent's objectives

Assessing your opponent's objectives means carrying out some research – at best – and guessing – at worst!

The process requires the ability to put yourself in your opponent's position. For example, a vendor may have chosen to advertise a property at £180,000. It would be surprising (and unusual) if this did not include a 'fall-back position' which would allow for the agent's advice and the fact that some (if not all) potential buyers may make a lower offer.

So, the parameters for the sale may vary between:

(a) Price

Base limit	Ideal position

£ 162,000 ⟷ £180,000

The 'base limit' here represents 10 per cent discount on the asking price and could be lower if the vendor is desperate to sell, or if some fault is discovered in the building survey.

(b) Timing

Base limit	Ideal position

5–14 April ⟷ 3–31 May

(This would allow for a holiday between 16 and 30 April.)

Of course, there is a lot more at stake when we buy a house, such as how well our own furniture will fit into it and what it will 'feel' like when we are living there. Vendors are often keen to sell items of furnishings such as carpets and curtains and this can be very helpful if the move is a strictly budgeted affair. Expensive mistakes can be made here, too:

(c) Furnishing and fittings

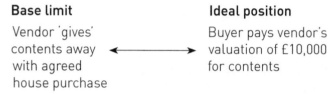

Base limit	Ideal position
Vendor 'gives' contents away with agreed house purchase	Buyer pays vendor's valuation of £10,000 for contents

As we shall see later, goodwill between buyer and seller may have quite an effect in arriving at the most appropriate point of 'balance' between the two extremes on the three charts. Any breakdown or loss of confidence between the parties can lead to a lose/lose outcome.

Examples of lose/lose results could be:

- either party changing their mind and withdrawing from the transaction (leaving one party, or possibly both, with considerable professional fees to pay – and nothing to show for them)
- carpets and curtains (etc.) put into store rather than being given away (leading to increased costs for the vendor)
- some items 'taken' by the vendor when the buyer expected them to be included in the price (leading to a rearguard action for restitution).

The effect of time

Time can have a crucial effect on the negotiation process. A vendor who is being moved by his company (with a tight deadline) may be prepared to consider a lower offer if he is convinced that the contract can be speeded up (e.g. by a cash sale).

Equally, the vendor who is able to put his house contents into storage (bearing in mind his firm's willingness to pay the bill) may be prepared to meet the buyer's timetable, especially when sales activity is depressed.

How do you find out about such levers?

At its simplest, you need to ask:

- friends, family members and so on
- professional advisers (e.g. solicitors, agents)
- people who have moved recently
- your opponent/his or her family/friends/staff, etc.

'My opponent? Surely he or she will not tell you the truth,' you may say. That may be so, but exaggerations or understatements can easily be checked and being 'economical with the truth' may risk the breach of all trust between the parties.

The broader the issue on which you need to negotiate, the more valuable it is to consult a wide range of people.

In commercial negotiations the following consulting checklist may prove useful:

- past users of the product/service   ☐
- other experienced buyers/sellers   ☐
- present referees   ☐
- comparison agencies/publications   ☐
- advisers   ☐
- other people in your own organization (the Japanese use this method to great effect – especially with new business contacts)   ☐
- your opponent's own staff.   ☐

So, your negotiation brief should include:

- an agenda of issues to discuss   ☐
- your objectives expressed in terms of parameters   ☐
- questions to ask to reveal information about the negotiation or your opponent's position.   ☐

A negotiation brief is not paper for the sake of paper – a systematic approach will pay for itself over and over again!

Pre-meeting planning

The following checklist may help you avoid any loose ends.

Opening

- How should I open the meeting?
- How interested is our opponent in the meeting?
- What needs might exist?
  - Theirs
  - Ours
- What areas of common ground exist between us?

Authority

- Whom am I meeting?
- What is the history/track record of the relationship?
- How much authority does my opponent have?

Power and influence

- What is their 'power' over us and/or our competitors?
- What is our power in this situation?
- How can we exploit our strengths for mutual benefit?

Commitment

- How interested is our opponent in the meeting?
- How badly do they need an agreement?
- Do we want/need an agreement today?
- Will a negotiated agreement stick?

Competition/exclusivity

● How might market forces affect the negotiation?
● What leverage might be used?

Innovation and promotion

● What concessions are we likely to have to make to ensure
that the deal is successful?
● How innovative are the proposals under discussion?
● Who will contribute what to help?

Summary

Researching and planning your objectives (and supporting facts) may not, on their own, produce a convincing argument. However, a negotiation plan – based on a reality that has been carefully and systematically compiled – should give the manager both confidence and a 'winning hand' (especially if your opponent is not as well prepared).

You will still need to prepare to introduce the facts as persuasively as possible, and, even then, you may need a fallback position – especially if your opponent decides to play 'hardball' or is rigidly attached to his/her position. There is a risk of a lose/lose outcome (perhaps no loan agreed, or the probability that your target property will be sold to someone else).

Now that you have worked through this chapter, why not try out your own plans for a car change or a house move or perhaps where you would prefer to spend your summer holidays? The following template could help you with your planning:

Your objectives	Opponent's position
1 _____	_____
2 _____	_____
3 _____	_____
4 _____	_____
5 _____	_____

Concessions you can give	**Concessions you seek**
1 _____	_____
2 _____	_____
3 _____	_____
4 _____	_____
5 _____	_____

Questions I need to ask

1 _____

_____

2 _____

_____

3 _____

_____

4 _____

_____

5 _____

_____

Fact-check (answers at the back)

1. How much importance would you give to the following factors (if you were following the example of high-performance negotiators)?
   a) Your own negotiating position on the current topic ❑
   b) Your opponent's position ❑
   c) The venue for the negotiation ❑
   d) All of the above are equally important ❑

2. If you can choose the time and place for negotiating a 'significant' case, would you choose:
   a) The preferred time/venue of your opponent? ❑
   b) A location by mutual agreement? ❑
   c) Your preferred time/venue (where you believe that you will be on your top form)? ❑
   d) Anywhere and any time – it shouldn't matter! ❑

3. If your opponent's role is to try to agree a wide range of topics/items with you at the meeting, how should you protect yourself from being tempted away from meeting your own needs?
   a) Be open-minded and prepared to discuss anything ❑
   b) Postpone the meeting until you have a definitive list from the other side ❑
   c) Prepare a definitive list of subjects and your own goals with supporting arguments ❑
   d) Don't do anything ❑

4. Your negotiating brief should concentrate on defining:
   a) Your least favourable positions – every other result would be a 'win' ❑
   b) Some desirable results – taking into account any known outcomes that are defined ❑
   c) Your most favourable position – every other result would be a 'lose' ❑
   d) All of the above ❑

5. Which constraints should be considered when preparing your brief?
   a) Predictions for financial/trade/world markets ❑
   b) Any likelihood of political pressure ❑
   c) Legal and/or social constraints ❑
   d) All of the above ❑

6. Outcomes of a negotiation are mostly affected by:
   a) How people feel at different times of the day ❑
   b) The amount of effort both parties put into their preparation ❑
   c) When the participants receive their 'pay' ❑
   d) Timing of the economic cycle ❑

7. The suggestion that you could have a (better) offer from your opponent's competitor could be viewed as:
a) An unacceptable insult ❏
b) A powerful tool that always get results ❏
c) A perfectly acceptable 'lever' ❏
d) A one-way tactic which gives the 'user' an edge over the opponent ❏

8. In negotiation, an agenda:
a) Helps to provide a template for the topics for discussion ❏
b) Provides a 'straitjacket' for what would otherwise be an interesting, free discussion ❏
c) Could reduce opportunities for discussing new or additional needs ❏
d) Should be prepared by the boss ❏

9. A concession is:
a) Something you give to make your opponent feel happier ❏
b) A demand you make to 'weaken' the other person's position ❏
c) A factor which you can exchange for a similar concession from your opponent ❏
d) A gift or 'sweetener' to ease agreement ❏

10. Building flexibility into your negotiation brief:
a) Helps ensure that the meeting will not result in a breakdown if either party 'digs in' ❏
b) Gives confidence to both parties ❏
c) Helps the parties explore alternative options leading to agreement around those that are acceptable to both ❏
d) Enables another 'deputy' to take over if one negotiator is unable to conduct the negotiation ❏

CHAPTER 3

People and places

Have you ever met someone with a 'magnetic' personality – someone who, whatever the situation, seems to carry other people with them?

While this characteristic may not be common, there is no doubt that people who have it can make highly effective negotiators! No matter what the issue or situation, they seem comfortable and persuasive and, most important, engaging.

We may not be able to copy such qualities, but we can develop some of the ways of behaving which can have a similar impact. For example, do you show an interest in others? Are you a good listener, but also someone who has an interesting point of view?

These qualities are valuable if you are planning to persuade other people to agree with you or do something for you – important features of the work of the negotiator.

Salespeople have plenty of opportunities to practise persuading others. The best salespeople are those who have found a natural and acceptable way of selling themselves, which makes selling their product or proposals much easier.

Negotiation is not about having blazing rows with opponents, nor creating an icy atmosphere (although in some circumstances this might prove a useful tactic!). To be successful, negotiators need to be able to persuade other people to agree with them and/or take action, and the successful salesperson undoubtedly has a head start over the rest of us.

Who am I?

Success in negotiation is affected by our ability to demonstrate the following skills and attributes. Rate yourself on this checklist by circling the figure which you feel represents your present skills:

FACTOR	LOW	HIGH
I am the kind of person who:		
1 presents myself as a person who likes people	1 2 3 4 5 6	
2 is positive (Who wants to work with a negative person?)	1 2 3 4 5 6	
3 is persistent ('No' can nearly always be turned into 'Maybe' and 'Maybe' into 'Yes')	1 2 3 4 5 6	
4 is open-minded (There is always more than one way of achieving an objective)	1 2 3 4 5 6	
5 has a good sense of timing and tact	1 2 3 4 5 6	
6 has high aspirations for deals (skilled negotiators have high aspiration levels and tend to search for above-average agreements)	1 2 3 4 5 6	
7 presents the case assertively (i.e. without waffle)	1 2 3 4 5 6	
8 chooses the most persuasive words (use of vocabulary)	1 2 3 4 5 6	
9 thinks clearly under stress	1 2 3 4 5 6	
10 influences the emotional atmosphere of meetings	1 2 3 4 5 6	
11 maintains self-control	1 2 3 4 5 6	
12 is decisive	1 2 3 4 5 6	

You may not be good at *all* these things but, as we progress, awareness may encourage you to experiment... and practice makes perfect! However, be careful not to experiment in live negotiations which could have a significant effect on your organization's objectives – well, not yet, anyway!

Our next topic is about your personal effectiveness in relations with others and how to identify the strengths and weaknesses of your opponents.

Personal communications and negotiations

One facet of personal effectiveness, when it is applied in negotiations, is the use of an appropriate communications style. There are two specific styles that are used by us all in everyday communication:

- the **extrovert** style
- the **inductive** style.

As may be readily deduced from the names, the first style relates to our attempts to persuade the person to do something by giving them lots of information – in effect, seeking to persuade by 'pushing' your opponent into a position.

The inductive style is concerned with trying to encourage your opponent to do something, by 'pulling' him or her towards that position. Clearly, this approach is more about manipulation and is more subtle than the extrovert style.

The extrovert style

Obvious characteristics of this style are shown below. The person using this style:

- always has a say
- produces lots of ideas and suggestions
- may enjoy a discussion and argument
- quite likes to stir things up in a discussion
- may reveal inner thoughts regardless of the circumstances
- frequently gets his/her own way in conversations.

The style also has a downside which may dilute its effectiveness – especially in extreme cases. If opponents are to be persuaded rather than bludgeoned into submission, these characteristics need to be kept under control. The person may:

- take an aggressive approach to others
- be bluntly honest

- give as good as they get in an argument
- having expressed a point of view, sticks to it
- criticize others
- look for all the snags and problems in new ideas.

This style will be most successful, in the short term, when negotiators are working in a powerful situation (i.e. power is on their side) and in a competitive climate. However, if the relationship is dependent on goodwill for its continuing success, there may be a greater likelihood of bruised feelings resulting from the negotiation. This, in turn, may lead to more aggressive tactics being used by the opponent next time (i.e. 'tit for tat').

Characters of the 'old school' who have developed a reputation of being strong negotiators – with a measure of charisma in their personal make-up – may attract a high level of respect from other people. This is particularly noticeable in competitive organizations and in sales-oriented negotiations.

However, the style may not always transfer readily into non-aggressive environments and may lead to the isolation of the negotiator if the style is not appreciated by staff, senior managers, trade unionists or, indeed, customers.

The inductive style

As we have seen, this is the opposite communications style to the extrovert style and, as such, tends to be rather less predictable.

Its relative success is based on the principle that the more you are able to test out the attitudes and arguments of your opponents, the more likely it is you will be able to pinpoint weaknesses in their arguments. Indeed, the weaknesses may become clearer to them, thus enabling you to induce them to move towards your position.

This style will involve the following conversational skills:

- putting others at ease
- encouraging them to come up with lots of ideas
- being able to extend and develop those ideas

- fostering a warm and friendly atmosphere
- giving credit and praise to others
- taking care to avoid upsetting others.

Do you know people like this? How do you feel about being in discussions with them? Can you imagine your probable response if they were to ask for your help? Most of us would probably be predisposed to help them.

This effect is enhanced further if you are also able to use clarifying behaviour in interactions with others, to ensure that there is a minimum of misunderstandings. This will involve:

- listening carefully to what others say
- checking that you have understood what they have been saying
- finding out what others are saying
- asking lots of open questions (i.e. those that start with 'What', 'When', 'Who', 'Why', 'Where' and 'How').

Your effectiveness will be further enhanced if you are the sort of person who:

- admits to mistakes readily
- conciliates when things get heated
- admits to your weaknesses.

Finally, these skills should enable you to:

- obtain the information from others which you need in any negotiation situation.

The inductive style demonstrates the advantages of co-operating rather than competing with others.

Choosing a style

There is no perfect style that will work in every situation. Both styles have advantages – for example, a sales representative will need to be reasonably extrovert to survive the various 'knocks' from clients, especially when involved with canvassing!

Similarly, a negotiator involved in a much longer-term negotiation spread over, say, several months (e.g. the purchase of natural gas from the Norwegians), will need to adopt a softer, inductive role.

We should also bear in mind two other influences:

1. Making the relationship work

If your opponent is a natural extrovert who fills the time with lots of communication, you may find yourself in competition for 'air time'. If this were to continue unabated, it could lead to increasing frustration, talking over each other and, eventually, conflict.

If two negotiators whose natural styles lie in the extreme areas of the inductive style were to meet to discuss a case, there could be many questions asked by one party only to be met with more questions from the other!

In practice, people tend to use a mix of both styles, with plenty of give and take. In fact, the skilled negotiator will aim to develop expertise in both areas, so that he or she has complete flexibility and can move in and out of either approach depending on the needs of the opponent.

2. General cultural influences

Over the past decade, there has been a general move towards the inductive style in management and society in general. This may be attributable to a variety of influences:

- political neutralizing of some of the aggressive influences in the field of industrial relations
- increased awareness of the importance of meeting the needs of others
- effects of the human relations school of management theory
- increased effects and support of management training.

TIP

Negotiators who are working in cultures other than their own need to adapt their style to suit the local customs and culture.

Who is my opponent?

We have seen that knowing something about your opponent before the meeting will be an advantage to any negotiator. If we have met the person before, we will be able to predict some of the possible levers and arguments which might be successful in the next round of discussions.

Aspects of communication style have already been discussed and we will now consider possible pressure points that could be applied to the debate.

All negotiations take place against a background of 'needs'; if needs did not exist, then there would be little point in meeting to negotiate. To help you prepare for the meeting, it would be useful to consider the needs of your opponent in more depth. There may also be a hidden agenda which will help you select a negotiation strategy.

The famous psychologist Abraham Maslow (1908–70) identified a **hierarchy of needs** to explain why people are motivated to work in a modern environment:

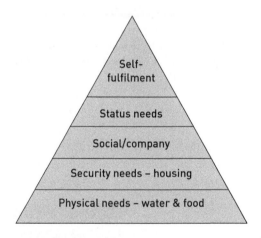

The broad concept of the triangle is that we all need to survive, by satisfying the needs at the base of the triangle. Having satisfied these **physiological** needs our attention turns to the need for **security**, satisfied through the provision of adequate housing/accommodation. Both these factors may be satisfied through the earning of money, but the higher motivators such as **social needs**, **status** and **self-fulfilment** are not usually satisfied in this way.

The model is shown as a triangle to illustrate the fact that not everybody reaches the higher needs – indeed, some people become hooked on one particular need.

For example, your opponent may have a particular liking for good food and, therefore, may be a lot more malleable after a good meal (at your expense, of course!). Others may be especially 'hooked' on status symbols and quickly identify your deal as a way in which they can be successful and earn a bigger company car or a status jump in the firm's hierarchy.

Equally manipulative is the industrial-relations negotiator who holds a little in reserve to allow an opponent to feel victorious just when the union branch is about to re-elect its representatives or the management is considering the regrading of personnel professionals.

So where should we meet?

At first sight, this is a common-sense matter. Sales representatives might say that they always expect to go to visit the buyer, and the management side of a joint industrial council might always expect to hold meetings in the boardroom.

Actually, the place of the meeting can make quite a difference to its 'comfort factor'. Some people seem to be able to fit into any environment and still behave confidently in business meetings. Others are intimidated by the very thought of having to negotiate on the opponent's ground.

So, playing 'home' or 'away' may have advantages to you and your opponent:

'Home' advantages
- You can control interruptions.
- You can orchestrate recesses.
- Back-up support is available should you need it.
- You can choose the office/location/layout to suit you.

'Away' advantages

- You may have the moral advantage in cases of late arrivals, etc.
- You have the chance to assess your opponent's workplace.
- Your opponent may make allowances as you are not on home ground.
- You can pressurize your opponent by suggesting that senior staff get involved to break any deadlocks.

Another alternative is to choose neutral territory. But, once again, there may be some hidden advantages. For example, the lobby of a hotel may appear to be neutral until you discover that your opponent is a regular visitor there and is personally known to the manager, the restaurant manager, the head porter, the barman and even the waitress. This can be most impressive – and is intended to be!

Will any of this make any difference to the meeting? It could do. After all, if you are dependent on your opponent for a crucial piece of information on which to base the negotiated agreement, would you mistrust someone who is so obviously credible in this sophisticated environment?

Summary

Developing our 'people skills' may need time and patience, but the payback will be really worth the effort and the progress steps suggested below may help you achieve better results:

● Try to develop a greater interest in other people – what they have to say, and their experiences.
● Build up your own self-confidence as you show you are a good listener.
● Learn how to reveal a little more of your own personality.
● Develop your questioning skills, especially those 'open' questions – the 'Whats', 'Wheres', 'Whens' and 'Hows', but not too many of the 'Whys' as they can seem confrontational.

You will find that, as people respond better to your conversations, they will talk more openly about their needs, making it much easier for you to show ways in which these can be met.

Use the following sheet to help you plan your style and negotiation venue:

PLAN YOUR STYLE AND NEGOTIATION VENUE

What do you know about your opponents?

_____
_____
_____
_____

Who will be involved?

_____
_____
_____
_____

Their preferred style:

_____
_____
_____
_____

Your preferred style:

_____
_____
_____
_____

Possible venues

Home: _____   Away: _____

Neutral ground: _____

Who will need to be briefed?

1 _____
2 _____
3 _____
4 _____

Fact-check (answers at the back)

1. Negotiation issues may be centred on the past or present but the results of the meeting will be most important to:
   a) Present issues and activities ❏
   b) Settlement of past difficulties ❏
   c) Future relationships ❏
   d) Past, present and future ❏

2. Talking persuasively in negotiations is best achieved by:
   a) Becoming a good listener ❏
   b) Improving your questioning skills ❏
   c) Concentrating on being positive ❏
   d) Exploiting an irresistible personality ❏

3. Having high aspirations in negotiation means:
   a) Trying to achieve win/win deals that are better than just 'average' ❏
   b) Being positive – even when there seems little to be positive about ❏
   c) Thinking clearly under stress ❏
   d) Being prepared to be 'pushy' ❏

4. An extrovert personality will be most effective in negotiating with an opponent who:
   a) Uses an inductive communication style ❏
   b) Enjoys stirring things up in a conversation ❏
   c) Uses an extrovert style ❏
   d) Is able to extend the ideas of others ❏

5. The application of a typical extrovert style in negotiating can result in:
   a) A 'tit-for-tat' competition in successive meetings ❏
   b) Opponents concentrating on all the negative aspects of a proposal ❏
   c) Outstanding results – especially if power is on that person's side ❏
   d) 'Bruised' feelings on the part of the opponent if feeling obliged ❏

6. Inductive-style negotiators benefit from:
   a) Revelations of focused information which may contradict the claims of the extrovert/uncontrolled negotiator ❏
   b) More thorough exploration of options ❏
   c) A general shift away from the extreme extrovert style in business culture ❏
   d) Shorter, but open, conversations with opponents ❏

7. The style of communication you choose to use in a negotiation should be determined by:
   a) The personality you have developed over the years ❏
   b) The outcomes you are trying to achieve ❏
   c) The communication style of your opponent ❏
   d) Your skills in asking/answering questions ❏

8. Self-knowledge
a) Makes it more difficult to influence the other person because you over-identify with their 'problem' ❏
b) Enables you to get your own way in a negotiation ❏
c) Guarantees that you know when to 'back off' ❏
d) Enables you to recognize when you are in the presence of a rather better opponent ❏

9. An analysis of the underlying needs of your opponent may reveal:
a) Weaknesses in their case ❏
b) Needs which you could satisfy with the current offer ❏
c) 'Pressure points' which may persuade them into a deal ❏
d) Opportunities to build the relationship over a longer time ❏

10. The venue of the meeting should always be:
a) Agreed as part of the planning for the negotiation ❏
b) On 'home' territory ❏
c) Alternate – home or away – to be fair ❏
d) Somewhere both parties are comfortable ❏

CHAPTER 4

Breaking
the ice

As with many other business functions, negotiation results are influenced considerably by your planning effort (and, conversely, disappointing results are often caused by inadequate preparation).

In the past three chapters' study we have explored the foundation plan of the meeting. Now it is time to open our meeting and begin the communication (talking, listening and non-verbal communication) which we hope will ultimately lead to an agreement.

Sometimes these foundations may seem to be ignored by experienced operators, who still achieve good results. However, for the less experienced, it would be a mistake to jeopardize or compromise good results by cutting corners when planning a negotiation.

It is a mistake to undervalue the part that good presentation can play in setting the scene for the meeting and in making proposals, and it is easy to see why good communicators might believe that the preparation stages are less important. However, it has been said that, if you fail to plan, you risk planning to fail! This can come as quite a shock to a persuasive communicator.

The way in which negotiators 'break the ice' at the start of a negotiation can have a big effect on the later stages of the meeting – so we are going to explore the twin aspects of:

- opening the meeting
- communicating.

Skills assessment

Results from the opening and the development of the early stages of a meeting will be affected by the following factors. Before working through this chapter, you might like to rate your current skills in each of these areas by circling the rating that you feel applies (and you might consider obtaining a comparison with the ratings of someone who knows you well):

Factor	Rarely used				Always used
Establishing rapport – verbal and non-verbal	1	2	3	4	5
Establishing common ground	1	2	3	4	5
Exploring mutual objectives for the meeting	1	2	3	4	5
Building a joint agenda	1	2	3	4	5
Getting comfortable	1	2	3	4	5
Clarity of speech	1	2	3	4	5
Assertive behaviour	1	2	3	4	5
Avoidance of bias and tunnel vision	1	2	3	4	5
Maintaining flexibility	1	2	3	4	5
Listening for overtones and signals	1	2	3	4	5
Questioning skills	1	2	3	4	5
Controlling and reading body language	1	2	3	4	5

Your performance in each of these areas can be improved and will affect your results.

Opening the meeting

Creating the right atmosphere for the meeting will be important if it is to end in agreement. Tough issues can be sorted out without necessarily establishing an ice-cold atmosphere at the start; equally, if the players have not met before and the stakes are high, quite some time may be allocated to establishing an atmosphere of trust.

Case study

Two parties of two negotiators from businesses in the finance sector met recently for the first time to discuss transfer charges between their two organizations. Millions of pounds were at stake and from the start it was obvious that both sides were nervous about the possibility of making expensive mistakes.

To the surprise of both teams when they met in the hotel meeting room, all the participants looked similar, were of similar ages, were dressed alike, and came from similar backgrounds. All this became increasingly evident in the first 45 minutes of the meeting, which covered almost any topic except that which the meeting was about!

At this point, almost instinctively, the parties felt they had built up a feeling of trust, and they started on the agenda. Progress was then rapid and, to everyone's surprise, the meeting concluded in 1.5 hours with a win/win agreement and a celebratory lunch! The agreement endured for a year and provided a sound basis for subsequent renewals.

Establishing rapport

The initial contact between people who are meeting for the first time – or, indeed, who have met before – is normally accompanied by an appropriate choice of words and actions.

However, the way these things are done can be significant. Passing the time of day and, as important, using your opponent's name, are accepted customs in greeting – just as shaking hands provides an acceptable way of expressing warmth to the other person. We make some hidden judgements on the basis of these greetings:

- the firmness of the handshake – the 'crusher' or the 'wet fish'
- the distance between the parties when they shake hands
- the formality or informality of the greeting – varying from 'Good morning' to 'Hi' or 'G'day'
- the warmth of the facial expression when meeting – for example, smiles can be open or, perhaps, cynical
- the extent of eye contact – open and level, or hooded and uncertain
- the appearance of the parties – the manner of dress and so on.

The golden rule in the area of appearance – for the best results – is to try not to breach any areas of known preference on the part of your opponent.

Common ground

It is always easier negotiating with someone you have met before because you will have some knowledge of that person's domestic circumstances, leisure interests, last holiday and/or drive or motivation. The early stages of a meeting provide an excellent opportunity to catch up with what has been happening in your respective lives – domestically and, probably more importantly (from the point of view of the negotiation), in business – since you last met.

This episode should help both parties to rebuild common ground, which may be especially valuable if (or when) the going gets tough later in the meeting.

Obviously, a new contact needs careful nurturing, and the opportunity should be taken to find out a little about them without creating the impression of being either nosy or pushy.

The agenda

It is surprising how often negotiators get together with a mutual interest in meeting but without having established a common agenda at the start. This is probably because each negotiator tends to think of their own agenda as of paramount importance and superior to the other person's.

If the meeting is to be collaborative, then it is important to provide the opportunity for both participants to air their own agenda. Apart from anything else, it is quite a challenge to check your opponent's agenda against the items you expected to be raised when you prepared for the meeting!

This does not mean that every agenda item or objective has to be revealed at the start of the meeting, but failure to do so in a collaborative atmosphere will invite scepticism: 'Why was this item concealed? Was it really a slip of the memory or has some advantage been sought by failing to reveal the topic?'

Physical comfort

The physical conditions of the meeting will also influence how comfortable (and possibly how co-operative) either party may feel, and this can be transferred readily to comfort with the deal itself. A variety of tactics may be adopted to win 'unfair' advantage over the opponent.

These usually work only when they are not too obvious, and, by virtue of their exposure, they tend to become less effective the more they are used. Examples are:

● your opponent's chair set at a lower level than yours
● your opponent having to look into the sun (or bright light)
● orchestrating interruptions when the going gets rough
● manipulating the temperature of the meeting room
● choosing a venue for the meeting which has distracting furnishings (e.g. walls decorated in, say, a vivid blue can affect some people and may account for an opponent disagreeing with proposals)
● prominent positioning of a clock, which may give discussions a sense of time pressure.

How should you deal with these tricks if and when they arise?

In short, the best method is to let your opponent see that you have noticed the tactic and seek his/her approval to remove the influence. You can do this by correcting or neutralizing the influence and commenting on it to allow your opponent to understand that you have noticed the use of the tactic.

Communicating

The most obvious skills are sometimes those which cause most difficulty in meetings. The effectiveness of the talking and listening process is affected by a variety of factors:

- self-discipline in allowing your opponent to speak (giving them some 'air-time')
- the style you use in speaking (e.g. not too biased or self-opinionated)
- quality of listening, which is affected by factors such as interpretation and concentration
- your body language.

Talking

From our earliest years, talking is essential to our well-being, but how we talk in a negotiation meeting can have quite an effect on how we are perceived by those we meet. For example, the following request to the boss would probably be greeted by a simple 'No!':

> 'I suppose it wouldn't be possible – I know this is probably not the best time to ask – to maybe find five minutes to get together to see if you could find your way clear to, perhaps, pay me an extra £10 per week?'

A great deal of work has been done recently on helping people develop assertiveness skills – the example above demonstrates non-assertive behaviour: vague, apologetic and almost defeatist. Few skilled negotiators would contemplate using this approach.

Equally, making the following demand:

> 'If you don't pay the yard staff an extra £10 per week, you will be looking for a new team!'

could result in the response:

> 'If that's your attitude, then perhaps that is the best thing for us to do!'

Skilled negotiators are more likely to use the following approach:

Negotiator 1: When will the Board be looking at this year's pay review?

Negotiator 2: It is scheduled for consideration in March.

Negotiator 1: How much are you proposing to include in the budget?

Negotiator 2: We will be under great pressure to find anything – given the present state of the market. How could the staff side make a contribution?

Negotiator 1: If you are talking about productivity improvement, the staff need money on the table! However, if you have something to offer, there may be scope for discussion.

Assertive expression is based on our needs, and the use of 'we' is better than 'I'. In fact, self-opinionated negotiators who use an egotistical approach often find it difficult to persuade others to change their minds or adopt their proposals.

Similarly, emotional responses are best kept under control. The use of anger, for example, can make a short-term point in a meeting, but if it is overused it can obstruct a negotiated settlement – with a 'lose/lose' result.

 The golden rule is to keep cool, avoid rhetoric and provocative language and maintain self-control.

This can be difficult if your opponent is hyped up and determined to cause maximum disruption as a deliberate tactic. In such cases, a good defence is to slow down interaction, make a conscious effort to avoid reaction and concentrate on non-confrontational language.

Listening

To say that it is essential to listen to interaction in negotiation meetings is to state the obvious. However, this can be harder than it seems. For a start, the process in any conversation can be difficult for some people, and when we are seeking a negotiated bargain it is complicated by the additional demands on our brain in the meeting.

Case study

Negotiator 1 makes a proposal to Negotiator 2, who listens carefully to the point. However, as the statement is unfolding, Negotiator 2 seeks to comprehend the point made – checking it against prior knowledge and experience and listening for the overtones in the expression – while also beginning to form a suitable reply and use an appropriate method (e.g. 'Shall I ask a question, make a statement or what?'). It is hardly surprising that points are missed in such circumstances – and sometimes our response may be totally irrelevant! (How well do you listen to your partner at home?)

How else can 'listening' go wrong? People have a habit of 'tuning out' – especially if they do not want to hear what is being said (try telling your teenage children to tidy their bedrooms, for example!). Others turn a deaf ear, making the right sounds while their brain is not really engaged and without having a real commitment to change.

And, lastly, we take the power of vocabulary for granted – especially the importance of using comprehensible language. Jargon, for example, needs to be avoided and it is essential that any words that are not understood by the opponent are immediately clarified. Here, again, is another valuable use of assertive questioning.

Tips for improving your listening skills include the following:

- Watch your opponent's lips while they are talking (and watch their eyes while you are talking – to gauge their reaction to what you are saying).
- Try to concentrate on the overriding message in their contributions, rather than becoming bogged down or distracted by individual words.
- Take notes to aid your concentration.

- Avoid trying to second-guess your opponent's statements or trying to finish off their sentences (even in unison!).
- Categorize contributions received from your opponent (e.g. 'Is this contribution a question, summary or proposal?') and plan an appropriate response.

These approaches will improve your concentration and enable you to spot opportunities for discussion and for bargaining. For example, an innocuous discussion during the earlier part of a meeting with a client might reveal some interesting snippets of information:

1   'Yes, things have been pretty busy – we have just changed our computer system.'
2   'What kind of pressures has this brought? Strings of noughts on payslips?'
1   'No, but our bought ledger system came to a halt...'

If you are proposing to supply this customer with a service or goods, be careful. You may decide on a contract easily enough, but may then have problems encouraging them to pay up! So, this signal should be followed up when it comes to agreeing terms of the contract at the end of the meeting.

Non-verbal communication

There are many other ways of communicating.

Body language, and the skill of reading it, has recently become a very popular topic among the business community. The reasoning goes something like this: 'If we could read the minds of our opponents and be able to work out exactly what they are thinking and planning, we could achieve much better deals!' Unfortunately, it is not as easy as that because analysing body language is an imprecise science.

That said, there are some simple signals that are useful to observe in negotiation, although the novice should be careful not to apply the meanings too literally in every situation.

Face touches

In a conversation about, say, the price of a service or goods, if the speaker accompanies a price quotation with a typical statement such as 'This is my best offer' with a rub of the nose, a scratch of the chin, a wipe of the eye or a tug at the collar, it may be an untruth! The chances of this being so increase if a chain of these actions occurs one after the other.

However, it should always be remembered that the speaker may have a cold (causing a constant nose irritation) or be feeling uncomfortable in a hot environment (hence the tug at the collar).

The moral here is that, while it is sensible to observe and try to read your opponent's body language, it is best not to allow your hands too near your face while negotiating!

Eye gaze

Level eye contact is often taken as an indication of honesty and, therefore, an interpretation could be that the negotiator may be trusted. However, if a gaze is held in one direction too intently, it may be interpreted as staring! Negotiators need to vary their use of eye contact, but it is essential when looking for reactions to ideas or trial proposals. Failure to make eye contact may protract a meeting simply because the signals showing that your opponent is prepared to accept your position go unnoticed. What signals? The occasional frown or flicker of a smile; the raising of an eyebrow or even the sharp return of a glance. We take many of these actions for granted, but, if observed, they may help us interpret progress in the negotiation.

Mirroring

Two people who are anxious to make a good impression on each other with the aim of a win/win deal may mirror each other's body position and movements. The explanation for this is that each party is sending signals to convince their opponent that they are very similar in terms of attitudes, values and aims.

This approach can have a significant effect, although it may only be subconscious. So, if your meeting is rather cold and you wish to try to relax your opponent, mirroring their body positioning may have a positive effect.

Hand movements

Many people speak with their hands and, while this is quite natural, it is important that such movements do not become extravagant or distracting to your opponent. A pen or pencil can provide a useful means of underlining a point – especially if the meeting has become emotional – but aggressive movements should be eliminated. Anything which causes irritation in an opponent is to be avoided as it may lead to non-acceptance of your proposals.

In general, open-handed expressions may be taken to underpin the sincerity of the speaker, whereas pointing or closed fists may reveal aggressive undertones in your opponent.

Summary

This chapter has explored the foundations of communication between the two parties in some detail.

We tend to take communication skills for granted and recognize that we could improve them only when we come across an opponent who is significantly better at it than we are (or when there is a major misunderstanding with our nearest and dearest!). Why not revisit the self-assessment at the beginning of Chapter 3 to check whether you need to update those grades, adding crosses against the target numbers (above your previous scores).

Fact-check (answers at the back)

1. Opening a meeting or discussion will be much more effective if there is already an agreement about:
   a) Its purpose ❏
   b) The agenda ❏
   c) Who should attend ❏
   d) The venue for the meeting ❏

2. Confirming the purpose of the meeting at the start will help:
   a) Make everyone feel welcome ❏
   b) Ensure that everyone is at the right meeting ❏
   c) Enable additional items to be added to the agenda ❏
   d) Ensure that everyone knows the range of contribution they should be making ❏

3. Establishing rapport means:
   a) Concentrating on speaking the same 'language' as your fellow attendees ❏
   b) Getting on the same 'wavelength' as your colleagues at the meeting ❏
   c) Reading other people's body language ❏
   d) Being able to look one another in the eye ❏

4. How you open the meeting can have a big impact on the level of trust you are able to build up and, consequently:
   a) How open your colleagues might be to accepting new ideas or refining/improving established ones ❏
   b) How long the meeting will take to reach its objectives ❏
   c) The acceptability of any new ideas proposed at the meeting ❏
   d) The level of agreement everyone is prepared to give ❏

5. Building common ground with your opponent involves:
   a) Ensuring that you are wearing clothes that will not offend the other person ❏
   b) Avoiding any extreme language or subject matter that might offend your guests ❏
   c) Concentrating discussion on the main agenda subject ❏
   d) Sitting close together so that everyone feels committed to the meeting's objectives ❏

6. Listening to your opponents in a negotiation is easier if you:
   a) Like them ❏
   b) Are committed to the subject they are talking about ❏
   c) Achieve a balanced talk/listen ratio ❏
   d) Are able to ignore the distractions around you ❏

7. The agenda is the main guide for discussion topics at a negotiation meeting, and the main negotiators should:
a) Avoid all other topics ❏
b) Listen carefully for any new information which could have a bearing on outcomes/relationships between the parties ❏
c) Be prepared to add in their own (additional) topics, especially if it seems likely they will be agreed upon ❏
d) Avoid any discussion without a complete written agenda being agreed at the start ❏

8. It is best if the negotiator takes the lead by dominating the discussion and doing most of the talking
a) Wrong – both parties need to have their say ❏
b) It is better to aim for a fair/natural balance (e.g. 55 to 45 per cent) ❏
c) Correct, as being dominated could mean 'losing' ❏
d) It is best to leave the conversation to take its own course ❏

9. Analysing non-verbal communication (or body language) is overrated
a) Wrong – it can indicate issues which need clarifying or tackling ❏
b) Correct – people should feel that they can behave naturally and not worry about being misread ❏
c) Sometimes – uninhibited behaviour can be more persuasive ❏
d) It requires expert training and disciplined observation ❏

10. Negotiators who use hand movements to emphasize speech in negotiation meetings:
a) Can distract the listener and mislead them ❏
b) Should always be encouraged to behave naturally ❏
c) Provide additional information which may signal issues for greater exploration ❏
d) Should be encouraged to sit on their hands ❏

CHAPTER 5

The agenda

Having opened our negotiation and made some inner judgements about the other party, we need to make some progress in discussing our agenda. Of course, this should be in the other party's interest too, and if this does not seem to be the case then the need for the meeting should be reassessed.

Could it be that you have a reluctant partner to this negotiation – and, no matter how hard you try, the outcome will be a 'lose/lose'? The 'loss' may just be some time and effort – salespeople sometimes describe unwilling clients as 'time-wasters', although their failure to 'qualify the customer' (ask questions to determine their interests, needs, preferences, timing, budget, etc.) in the first instance may have led directly to this situation.

Needs

We know that negotiation meetings are about resolving (or meeting) mutual needs. For example:

- you need to buy a new car and the dealer needs to sell one

or

- you need to obtain the reinstatement of a suspended work colleague and the management needs to obtain staff support for overtime to meet a rush order.

In the previous chapter, we found that discussion meetings provide the opportunity for us to present our side of the case – to promote and defend our interests, to sell our position and the advantages of accepting it to the other side.

We will also have tried to draw from our opponent a description of their position so that we can begin to debate it, undermine it and make it seem impossible or unreasonable. While this is going on, our opponent may be trying the same tactic on us!

Example

A standard tactic when surveying a second-hand car is to fault the car by referring to the high mileage, worn tyres or rust-marked body. This softening-up process is designed to precede the making of a proposal or offer (often a rather low one!), but this tactic may be easily rebuffed if the vendor is prepared to cite the 'large number' of other potential buyers who have been in touch about the car. Is the buyer really interested, or not?

Assertive questions such as 'How can you justify this position?' may draw your opponent to reveal his or her arguments and aims in the negotiation. With persistent questions, difficulties in arriving at a mutually agreed strategy on his or her side may be revealed, thus enabling you to take the high moral ground or express the stronger (more persuasive) argument.

Dividing your opponent from his or her side becomes easier once you know that there may have been some difficulty on their part in arriving at an agreed negotiating strategy.

Of course, such debating points are reversible and you must be careful not to lay yourself open to the use of this approach by your opponent. So, in our example outlined above, any attempts by the vendor of the car to sell it to your partner – who is loudly proclaiming enthusiasm for the vehicle – may cause you some difficulty when it comes to obtaining the best price or terms.

In reality, it is unlikely that your opponent will make any major moves for nothing, so you will need to demonstrate your preparedness to move in some way as a means of obtaining movement from your opponent. These signals should have been sent and received before beginning to form the proposals or offers that will lead to the final bargain.

Proposing

This chapter describes how to maintain progress in the meeting by making appropriate proposals. We will consider:

● timing
● encouraging proposals
● the best formula
● defending principles
● meeting inhibitions.

 All your preparation will prove its value in this vitally important stage.

Timing

There is a right time for proposals in a negotiation meeting, and experienced negotiators sense when the moment is right. This sense of timing is akin to the salesperson's ability to choose the right moment to close the sale. How we find this out, other than by trial and error, is analysed below.

Exhausting every avenue of discussion will eventually lead you to a stage when you have to make progress in the meeting, and making proposals is the next obvious step. However, this approach can feel overcautious and pedestrian, and may lead your opponent to become exasperated owing to the lack of progress. (This can, of course, be turned to an advantage if your opponent is very anxious to conclude the meeting – a process which might be speeded up if he or she makes some quick and major concessions.)

When your meeting concerns an urgent issue and either or both negotiators have a strong sense of destiny, there will be an irresistible force moving the discussion towards agreement – especially if the parties have already expressed a strong desire to reach an agreement. In such a situation, proposals will flow naturally almost as a summary of each party's position.

The reverse of this natural progression rests in the truism described by Professor Parkinson (referred to as Parkinson's Law) – that time taken for decisions is in inverse proportion to the costs incurred. Committees have been known to spend hours taking decisions about the replacement of canteen cups but only minutes on major decisions which few members understand! The same can be true of negotiation: when small issues combine with ready quantities of time, progress in the meeting can be very slow – with as much attention given to the social objectives as the deal itself!

Finally, beware of the use of time as a major tactic in the meeting. Logical movement through the early stages of the meeting may be unattractive to so-called skilled negotiators, and this may lead to one of them suggesting a jump from base square to final square in one move. A simple, innocuous question might be asked:

- 'We are both busy people and I am sure we could close this deal very quickly – if you agree, of course?'
- 'Yes, that seems like a good idea.'
- 'So, what is your bottom line?'

Revealing this position may make it difficult for the opponent to trade movement once the base position has been revealed. There will then be little alternative to agreeing to the initiator's proposals without breaking off negotiations altogether.

Encouraging proposals

If you feel that the time is right for proposals to be made but are not sure whether this feeling is mutual, you can always ask! Hand-holding skills (i.e. encouraging the opponent to feel that you are trustworthy and are not trying to lay a trap) are valuable in negotiation. Apart from giving the other side the opportunity to drive the meeting, encouraging them to make leading proposals in an open atmosphere will help progress to be made.

Such a step needs to be accompanied by appropriate non-verbal signals – warm smiles, gentle nods and a high level of attention (eye contact and slightly laid-back body position but facing the opponent).

Who should make the first proposal – and what that should be – is an issue which can give the inexperienced negotiator some concern. After all, there is little pleasure in feeling that your first 'bid' was too high and, having seen the speed with which the other party accepted, that you are paying more than you needed to!

A major aim of the early discussion stage in the meeting is to tease out the other party's position on each agenda item – and the arguments used to defend them. This may well indicate that, say, the vendor's preferred price is going to be totally beyond the resources of the buyer and some concessionary proposal is necessary to keep the buyer in the meeting. (A similar argument can be advanced for the buyer who tries to introduce a very low offer – risking insulting the vendor.)

So, the opening stance is recognized as the position that would bring most benefit for the proposer's party – the debate will doubtless seek movement towards the opponent's position – and the best format for this is when both parties move towards each other, trading concessions.

The best formula

Phrasing of proposals is crucial. The best formula is to present your proposals using a conditional approach. For example:

> '*If* you will give us payment terms of 30 days, *then* we will meet your price request.'

Now, this proposal may seem rather bald – especially without the context of the earlier conversation. When a bridge is needed between the discussion part of the meeting and concluding the bargain, either party may introduce **trial proposals**. These will suggest tentative ways forward without necessarily burning boats and risking earlier agreement by suggesting something which is not acceptable to the opponent.

A typical example would be:

'I'll tell you what we might be able to arrange: *if perhaps* you could find a way of speeding up payment – say, in 30 days – *then we might* be able to find a way of reducing the price.'

If this approach brings a constructive response, then it is likely to be followed swiftly by a formalized proposal along the lines of the first example above.

Defending principles and meeting inhibitions

It is at this stage that you may find your bottom line under attack or under threat of being compromised. For example, the UK government made it clear after the Falklands War in 1982 that sovereignty was not even on the agenda for peace negotiations with Argentina, and that this would be a precondition for any future discussions.

There could be a risk that, while such a condition might be agreed, your opponent may reintroduce that element in the meeting itself, with the expectation that the constructive atmosphere might persuade negotiators to allow discussion of the issue. This clearly should not be accepted and the team would have to make it clear that approaches to put the subject on the agenda would jeopardize agreements on other issues.

At the same time, you must remember that your opponent is not an entirely free agent. He or she is representing another organization or party, with interests which may differ from your own. These interests will overlap – or there will be no point in attending the meeting – but it is obviously in your opponent's interests to persuade you to move from your ideal position.

Example

A client complains about one of your service engineers whose behaviour on his premises has been the source of complaint from several of his staff. His initial approach may be to demand the withdrawal of that person ('Never send him here again!'), and this may be readily countered with an apology and a convincing promise to hold a full and thorough internal inquiry.

However, if we were to think through our opponent's position we would see that his organization has in it several people who would also like to see the back of the engineer. Failure on his part to sort out the issue could lead to a significant loss of face and credibility for your opponent. Such inhibitions can lead to apparent obstinacy and may make a win/win agreement more difficult to achieve if the client's inhibitions are not addressed.

Summary

We have seen in this chapter that proposals are vital to a negotiation, no matter how fundamental or extreme the issues under debate happen to be. There are many examples on record of negotiation teams becoming 'comfortable' in debating the issues, and conversation then seems to go round and round without any agreement or solution – except, maybe, an agreement for the location and timing of the next meeting!

If you find yourself to be a willing party to such a travesty, remember that senior management/leadership can always exercise its right to change the delegated negotiators. How might it feel and look to be one of the people who have been replaced so peremptorily?

So, proposals are what make the negotiation move forward, and they need to be carefully planned and thought through; not arrived at in desperation without any concern for how they might be implemented.

Fact-check

1. The only way a negotiation can progress is through the use of:
    a) Signals ❏
    b) Collaborative relationships ❏
    c) Proposals ❏
    d) Summaries ❏

2. When is the 'right' time to start making proposals?
    a) Any time, discovered through a process of trial and error. ❏
    b) When the issue, which needs resolution, is urgent ❏
    c) When your 'opponent' starts proposing ❏
    d) When you have a good idea of the needs of the other party ❏

3. The statement 'Supposing we were able to offer a discount of 5 per cent, if you committed to this purchase today' is a:
    a) Dream ❏
    b) Signal that your opponent is ready to make a move ❏
    c) Proposal ❏
    d) Trial proposal ❏

4. Conditional proposals are based on the principle of:
    a) Something for something ❏
    b) Collaborative bargaining ❏
    c) Win/lose ❏
    d) 'If..., then...' ❏

5. If your proposal is rejected by the other party, this means:
    a) They want you to improve your offer in some way ❏
    b) The negotiation has failed. ❏
    c) You may have misunderstood their position and you need to clarify it ❏
    d) The other party has a better proposal of their own ❏

6. A very low offer or proposal could result in:
    a) Insulting your opponents, and their withdrawal ❏
    b) Beating your own objectives, if it is accepted ❏
    c) A breakdown in relationships between the parties ❏
    d) A great reputation as a principled negotiator ❏

7. Revealing that the value of a proposal lies outside your authority to accept shows that:
    a) Your opponent is talking to the wrong person ❏
    b) You have no better arguments ❏
    c) You have prepared a negotiation plan ❏
    d) A real obstacle exists to any agreement at this level ❏

8. People who prefer to make the first proposal invariably:
    a) Lose through revealing their hand too soon ❏
    b) Should be given a quick counter-proposal ❏
    c) Are surprised when it isn't accepted ❏
    d) Win through leading the argument ❏

9. Debating what seem to be minor points (and in considerable depth):
a) Risks frustrating both parties and the withdrawal of one party (i.e. lose/lose) ❏
b) May reveal a lack of confidence (or knowledge) ❏
c) May hide a hope to win by causing the opponent to give in ❏
d) May lead to the opponent complaining to your boss ❏

10. How should you react if your discussion reveals that your original preparation was inadequate?
a) Call a natural recess/break to enable you to catch up ❏
b) Seek help from your boss ❏
c) Quickly change the subject ❏
d) Withdraw from discussion to avoid making an expensive or embarrassing mistake ❏

CHAPTER 6

Conclude
the deal

In the previous five chapters we have learned:

● about key aspects of negotiating
● how to move towards agreement
● how to conclude a negotiation successfully.

This may seem over-complicated when a street market negotiation may be concluded in a matter of minutes! Doubtless, the location and complexity of the topic can have a big effect on the speed of progress in negotiating, but the skills we employ in street trading are closer to 'haggling' than to the professional style of debating the issues, seeking mutual movement and benefits, and ensuring that the agreement is worthwhile and long-lasting.

Few experienced negotiators can claim to have a totally trouble-free record in the deals they have arrived at (and then had to live with!).

Experience can be an expensive teacher and this fact is what makes this last stage in the negotiation so important – the need to be able to close the meeting with agreements that are satisfactory to both sides (and with both parties clear and committed to the next stage – implementation).

Closing skills

There is little point in investing time in negotiation meetings if we cannot close them with satisfactory agreements. However, there are many people in the commercial world who make presentations with a view to selling a product or service, or buyers who invest time in meeting with sales representatives without those meetings resulting in a contract.

The question is: do those involved ever discover why their closing rate is not higher? And can they do anything about it? In staff-relations meetings there is less priority given to immediate results – they are often broken by recesses and adjournments, consultations between staff representatives and their members, and between personnel staff and their managers. But the same discipline applies here – if time is invested in meetings, then agreement must be the ultimate objective.

So, what are the skills we need to develop to close off a negotiation meeting satisfactorily? The following checklist may provide useful insights:

- Summarizing progress ☐
- Resurrecting earlier issues for agreement ☐
- Linking issues in the agreement ☐
- Using concessions to improve the agreement ☐
- Listening for concessions ☐
- Using appropriate closing techniques. ☐

Mistakes at the 'last fence' can be very expensive and frustrating. Make sure that you are able to clear the last few hurdles cleanly so that you are satisfied with your performance!

Summarizing
One little word!

It is not possible to do too much summarizing in a meeting. The fact is that many people become confused during negotiations and, even though one party has a clear belief in what has been agreed, it often happens that the opponent has a very different view of that same agreement! Both people were at the same meeting and yet there is still confusion and little unanimity – and this is very dangerous when the agreement is actually implemented.

Examples of things going wrong after the negotiations have stopped are legion. Buyers select colours of merchandise and plainly state the colours they do not want – and yet, somehow, those colours still arrive in deliveries! Similarly, sales representatives inform buyers about discount terms, and yet buyers still claim, once the invoice arrives, that they were not told about them.

Summaries help to clarify proposals and the terms of agreement. You cannot have too many of them! Remember the one little word which provides the signal of a summary – **'so'** – and try to use it:

● whenever the meeting stops making progress
● when you are not sure what has been said or agreed
● when you feel that the time is right to begin to close the meeting.

Accuracy in summaries

When summaries are used in a meeting they can have an extraordinary effect. First, a summary often seems to fix the points stated and agreed – even though both sides know that the discussion is not yet finished. This can be very helpful when seeking to make speedy progress, but it is important for the summary to be accurate. If you include in your summary something that has not been agreed – even if you feel that you are taking artistic licence – there is a risk that the relationship between the two parties will be broken and trust breached.

Similarly, it is very important to listen to summaries given by your opponent. There is always a risk that something you believe has been agreed is left out or changed in the opponent's summary. If this happens, it is important that the person who spots the error speaks out straight away, otherwise the change may be accepted into the agreement by default, and could cause major disruption towards the end of the meeting. This might not affect the ultimate agreement but it may leave either or both parties with a bad feeling and have a knock-on effect on future meetings.

Resurrection

By virtue of the fact that a strategic summary will be seen as a means of bringing the meeting towards a close, it provides a last opportunity to raise any items on which no progress was made earlier.

In Chapter 3, you will have rated yourself on persistence. This is an important quality for negotiators. The fact is that people who refuse to move earlier in a meeting may be a little more flexible when the end of the meeting is in sight. Also, the presentation of your case and the subtle temptation of concessions may encourage your opponent to be more flexible on issues which were sticking points before.

Linking

Linking one item with another is another method of obtaining movement on difficult issues. Most negotiators see their agenda as consisting of a variety of separate issues or objectives – indeed, many commercial deals involve the sale and purchase of several products or items, each of which needs to have been negotiated. It would be quite normal for the negotiators to achieve different deals on each item on the list, but it is also likely that either side may resist giving way on one particular item. A way out of this is to link one issue with another.

Example

A buyer may have agreed to pay a wholesaler $11.00 for a box of five reams of photocopying paper with an order of 100 boxes. He is pleased with this agreement as the price agreed is 50 cents a box less than he had expected to have to pay. Another item on his shopping list is some specialized bond paper for use in preparing and presenting reports. The wholesaler has offered a price of $18.00 per box, to which the buyer is not prepared to agree – his counter-offer is $16.00. On the basis of negotiating the same quantity of paper, the buyer offers to increase the price on the copy paper by 25 cents per box if the vendor will agree to a price of $16.00 for the bond.

Using concessions

Concessions may provide a way of obtaining additional movement towards the end of the meeting. Skilled negotiators know to keep additional concessions up their sleeves to use in closing the meeting. These will be most effective where the concessions are cheap for you to give but very valuable to your opponent.

Example

If you have just sold your car – and therefore have cleared the cheque – you may be able to persuade your garage to extend the warranty on a new car for the all-in price which you agreed earlier, but now with the additional concession of a cash transaction.

Closing

Salespeople are frequently trained in how to close the sale, and a variety of methods exist to help achieve just that. However, if negotiators have done their job well, the meeting will close itself. The best resolution of the meeting is when both parties have achieved what they set out to achieve (i.e. within the parameters of their objectives) and all that is left to do is to formalize the agreement.

This may not always happen, so it is sometimes necessary for the meeting to be nudged towards closure. Some common ways of achieving this are:

- calling a recess
- imposing a deadline
- threatening to pull out or call time
- asking for agreement
- the summary close.

Calling a recess

Making a decision about, and therefore committing to, the agreement that has been discussed often requires a little time and space. Reluctance from your opponent to agree to the deal may be overcome by planting the seeds of satisfaction in his or her mind and then allowing time for thought (with a view to allowing the seed to mature and flourish). If you have covered the ground well and summarized the areas of agreement, a short recess at this stage should bring a positive decision.

Imposing a deadline

If there is any doubt about the result of the recess it might be prudent to lay down some rules about the time for which the current offer will be valid. Clearly, this approach may be viewed as pressurizing your opponent, but is quite justifiable when the time period is fair.

A typical example could be a quotation for a construction task that is dependent on the supply of the materials, for which the quotation assumes no price rises for the materials. Therefore the quoted price can be valid only for, say, one month.

Threatening to pull out

If one party believes that the other party needs the agreement, then a bluff to pull out of the meeting may work.

However, such orchestrated tactics can easily rebound on the bluffer if the timing or style of the threat is poor. You might easily find that you are allowed to go and are not called back! On the other hand, it has been known for creative answers to be found to situations when the time has run out on the negotiating.

For example, when international negotiators spent 18 months trying to negotiate a Strategic Arms Limitation Treaty, and the self-imposed deadline was reached, the parties agreed to stop the clock for 36 hours – just sufficient time for the final agreement to be transacted. When they finished, the agreement was backdated to fit the original deadline!

Asking for agreement

A simple way of closing the deal is to ask for your opponent's agreement! At first sight, this is such an obvious approach that it may be unclear why everyone doesn't use it all the time. 'Asking for the order' is a classic technique taught on most sales training courses. However, salespeople do not often use the approach, simply because of the risks of being turned down.

Actually, a rejection might not be the disaster it may seem. It may be possible to rescue the deal even at a late stage simply by asking 'Why?'. The answer may clarify your opponent's objections, giving you one last chance to bring the negotiation to a satisfactory conclusion.

The summary close

Finally, the closing point for the meeting should be summarized. The skills for this have been described earlier.

> ## A cautionary note!
>
> Don't forget that your opponent enjoys the freedom to agree or not to agree! Even though you may have worked hard and concluded a good deal, your opponent is still acting for his or her reasons, not yours. This may be worth bearing in mind if you are feeling euphoric when you start to evaluate the deal.

Confirming

Even when your meeting seems to have closed with a whole-hearted agreement, there are still risks that the implementation of the agreement will be faulty. The success of the negotiation lies in this process and it is probably hard – with the euphoria of a successful outcome – to turn your mind to what can go wrong.

However, things do go wrong, often for no sinister reason. The parties' recollection of what was agreed may be inadequate, but if the performance of the agreement does not meet either sides' expectations it would be quite understandable if underlying motives were questioned.

Solutions to avoiding these problems include:

- taking and exchanging notes
- getting the agreement in writing
- checking that minutes and opponent's notes agree with your notes
- taking care with the small print.

Taking and exchanging notes

It isn't easy to contribute to a negotiation meeting – talking, listening and making notes – but working notes of the meeting will be an essential foundation for any subsequent agreement or contract. In the commercial world, it is quite usual for a representative's memorandum of sale and a buyer's order to be drafted during the meeting and exchanged at the end. This provides the first check that both sides have a common understanding of what has been agreed and, with experience and trust built up over time, one side may be prepared to accept the other's notes.

In staff-relations meetings it is common for both parties to nominate their own secretary to take minutes of the meeting, and the notes are then used to form the ultimate record of the meeting.

Get it in writing!

Even when notes have been exchanged at the end of the meeting, it is still important for a formal record of the agreement to be exchanged. Most negotiations commit two organizations as well as the various players, and formal records will need to be exchanged.

Confirmations may take the form of:

- purchase requisitions
- sales order notes
- minutes of meetings
- letters of confirmation
- revised proposals (bringing letters of acceptance)
- formal contracts
- joint communiqués or treaties
- procedural agreements and bargains.

A cautionary check is to ask yourself: 'Am I covered in law if anything should go wrong? Who could I sue?' This is not to say that you would wish to sue – most disputes between contractors are resolved by negotiation. But skilled negotiators will not put themselves in a position where they have no recourse if the opponent should renege on the agreement.

Check minutes agree with your notes

How often have you attended meetings and failed to recognize the minutes when they have been released some time later? Unfortunately, those who have the responsibility to prepare the notes are sometimes tempted to misuse that power to rewrite them to suit their preferred position – subsequent to the meeting. Even if deception is not intended, subtle changes may take place to meet the political inhibitions of the boss, the organization or even some of the people present. Where changes have been noted, and where these affect the letter or spirit of the agreement, a loud complaint should be made, officially. Any apathy here may be taken as acceptance of the new situation.

Take care with the small print

One major company in the north of England employs a whole department of lawyers whose main task is to check buying agreements and ensure that their own terms and conditions are supreme over those of their suppliers. The consequence of this is that any small supplier is unlikely to be able to achieve any variation to those terms and may be faced with the stark choice of contracting on the buyer's terms or not at all.

We would all prefer that contractual breakdowns did not lead to recourse to the law – this can be very expensive in time and money – but the larger the contract the better it would be to ensure that the worst consequences of failure do not leave you totally exposed to losses. For this reason, penalty clauses are often found in construction contracts, restraint of trade in personal contracts and even clauses allowing actions for damages against trade union bodies where the continuity of supply of a service is affected by a trade dispute.

Summary

A 'win/win' result is usually the objective of every negotiator who is aiming for repeat business and the building of goodwill. It matters not whether the sums or issues are small or gargantuan – alliances are built by mutual trust and benefit for both parties, and can be reflected on with mutual pride and trust.

This may sound trite, but it is not difficult to find cases where one party's greed or 'sharp practice' has led to the breakdown of trust, loss of repeat business or even court action (to say nothing of all that appalling publicity). No one in their right mind would want that, but the consequences of getting it wrong are what makes this negotiation skill so important (and the negotiator highly responsible).

It has been said that the combination of an industry-leading strategy and excellent negotiators can bring world-beating results. Unfortunately, the opposite is also true!

Fact-check (answers at the back)

1. When you hear the word 'so' you should:
   a) Ignore it – only your summary is important ❏
   b) Insist that what is said is put into writing before you agree ❏
   c) Listen carefully, as your opponent is about to summarize and you will need to reject it if you disagree with it ❏
   d) Be prepared to reject the proposal ❏

2. Resurrecting earlier issues towards the end of the meeting:
   a) Risks spoiling the whole agreement ❏
   b) May lead to a fuller agreement if the atmosphere is more constructive ❏
   c) Should be avoided for fear of causing the other party to walk out ❏
   d) Provides a way out of an impasse or stalemate ❏

3. When facing potential deadlock, a recess will:
   a) Be a waste of time ❏
   b) Enable both sides to relax ❏
   c) Create a solution for the final agreement ❏
   d) Provide an opportunity to do some creative thinking and maybe seek further information or advice ❏

4. When recognizing a degree of uncertainty/nervousness in your opponent's reluctance to reach agreement, the best option is to:
   a) Impose a time deadline ❏
   b) Threaten to put the matter to their senior management ❏
   c) Give specific reassurances on how any 'losses' will be mitigated (e.g. through guarantees) ❏
   d) Threaten to escalate the case to your senior management ❏

5. Forcing further concessions from the opposition after agreement has been reached (and on an issue that has been overlooked in discussion) would most likely:
   a) Enhance the final deal for one party at the expense of the other ❏
   b) Risk the whole agreement being cancelled ❏
   c) Cause the other party to 'lose face' ❏
   d) Achieve a great winning result ❏

6. A good measure of success in a negotiation is the number of concessions that could have been made but which remained unused.
   a) True ❏
   b) True if both parties become aware of the total picture ❏
   c) Totally untrue – it's the quality of the outcome that's important ❏
   d) Untrue – it's the level of goodwill that has been further enhanced by the agreement ❏

7. A satisfactory deal can sometimes be further improved by:
a) Meeting on neutral territory ❏
b) Exploring concessions that might not have been used by either side and that could be exchanged with mutual benefit ❏
c) Negotiating over a meal (the other side paying the bill) ❏
d) Having two different negotiators ❏

8. However good – and complete – the negotiation, the proof of its success lies in:
a) The tactics used in the meeting ❏
b) The way the deal sounds to the 'boss' ❏
c) Both parties' understanding of the agreement ❏
d) The written record ❏

9. Successful implementation of a negotiated agreement is nearly always dependent on:
a) Both parties' commitment to the deal ❏
b) The size of the deal ❏
c) The degree of trust that has been built up between the negotiators ❏
d) The scale of the risk of failure of implementation ❏

10. The 'best pairing' of negotiators occurs when:
a) Both are committed to a win/lose outcome ❏
b) Both are highly rated as effective negotiators and they recognize this in each other ❏
c) Their styles of interaction are very similar ❏
d) Their styles of interaction are fully compatible ❏

CHAPTER 7

Learning from your experiences

If life provides experiences from which we can learn and develop, this must be more true of negotiating than most other activities! However, human nature (being what it is) does not bring a guarantee that all of us learn from our experiences and apply those lessons. We have all met people who keep on repeating the same mistakes, even when those errors are blatantly obvious and pointed out to them. Is there anything we can do about this if it is in our nature?

Yes! When it comes to negotiating, there are things we can (and should) do – starting with self-reflection, better preparation and more self-discipline in developing the skills outlined in this book.

Evaluating performance

Consider the following checklist, which may help you pinpoint your own strengths and weaknesses.

Preparation

1 Do I spend enough time preparing to negotiate?
2 Have I discussed the case with other people in my organization?
3 Have I researched my opponent's case?
4 Is there any additional information I may be able to collect from my opponent's organization?
5 Which outcome do I really want: win/win, win/lose or lose/lose?
6 Have I prepared a negotiation plan/brief?
7 What is on my objectives/shopping list?
8 What are the parameters for each objective?
9 Have I prioritized my objectives?
10 What concessions can I give?
11 Where will we meet?
12 Have I analysed the relative power positions of our two organizations?
13 When will be the best time to meet?

Know yourself

14 In what circumstances am I:

  - most comfortable?
  - least comfortable?

15 How easy do I find it to:

  - take decisions?
  - persuade others?
  - be positive and persistent?
  - choose the most persuasive words?
  - think clearly under stress?
  - control myself?

16 What motivates me? What 'Achilles' heels' (weak points) might exist in me?
17 Am I a disciplined listener?
18 Am I tempted by a win/lose opportunity if I will be the winner?

Opening the meeting

19 How good am I at putting others at ease?
20 How good are my presentation skills?
21 Can I control and read body language?
22 How able am I to probe others for information?
23 Can I respond to others' probing without giving away anything of value?
24 How well am I able to develop a collaborative atmosphere in a meeting?
25 Have we established a common agenda and identified common ground?

The meeting

26 How well can I balance talking and listening?
27 How can I make the meeting layout work for me?
28 How good are my concentration and listening skills?
29 When might a recess be useful?
30 How can I make good use of interruptions?
31 Who is in control in the meeting?
32 Have I identified the best time to make proposals?
33 How good am I at introducing trial proposals?
34 How can I formulate counter-proposals to overtake my opponent's proposals?
35 Am I using 'If... then' and 'So...' successfully?
36 When my opponent blocks my proposals, am I able to unblock them again?
37 How able am I to use the following closing skills?

- hand-holding
- summarizing
- using late concessions
- linking.

Continuing to grow

Negotiation is a practical skill. It is subject to the same characteristics as other skills – it gets rusty if it is not used and improves when used frequently. So, there are a number of steps which you as a negotiator can take to increase these skills:

- Take every opportunity to negotiate
- Talk about negotiation with experienced people both inside and outside your organization
- Read about negotiation. Look at:

  - newspaper articles for recent cases
  - trade magazines for technical sources
  - books and articles.

- Review your deals carefully and thoroughly
- Attend a training course that enables you to obtain some feedback about your style and skills (preferably through the use of video).

The truth is rarely pleasant, but the review process will be pointless if you indulge in self-deception. Check your objectives and those of your opponent which you know about – and make sure that you do not make the same mistakes twice!

7 × 7

1 Seven tips for new negotiators

- Negotiation is now part of everyday life – judging the opportunities and applying the best methods is all important or the results may be disappointing at best and a waste of effort at worst.
- Initially, work within your comfort zones (which means place, time, people and topics), especially when building your confidence. Outcomes will be affected by past experiences – and the more positive these are, the more likely you will be able to repeat them and 'grow'.
- Identify your own weak areas of knowledge or facts – and give extra time and effort to these so that you have more positive information and persuasive arguments on hand to increase the chances of acceptance.
- Timing is crucial – the most productive atmosphere is when both parties are anxious to achieve change. This should be built upon and exploited. (Rolling a heavy 'scheme' downhill is easiest; pushing liquid uphill is well-nigh impossible. So, be prepared to drop everything else when an opportunity for change presents itself.)
- Make it easy on yourself by identifying and reducing any barriers. If you are invited to 'play away' (on your opponent's ground), build your strategy around winning tactics for that meeting. Don't give your opponent any excuses for rejecting your proposals or schemes by appearing to be 'stand-offish'.
- Listen carefully to what is said (and what is *not* said), to your opponent's needs and to their response to your proposals. Seek clarification rather than mount an attack, and be persuasive with incontrovertible evidence to support your full scheme.
- Be sensitive – use top 'people skills' in persuasion and avoid giving any impression of pressure, desperation… or weakness.

2 Seven best personal resources

- Gavin Kennedy, *Negotiate Anywhere: Doing Business Abroad* (Hutchinson, 1986)
- Dale Carnegie, *How to Win Friends and Influence People* (Vermillion, 2006) – a 'classic' and essential reading for all who seek to negotiate win/win deals.
- Terry Gillen, *Positive Influencing Skills* (Institute of Personnel & Development, 1995) – offers alternative approaches to command and control – especially 'pulling' rather than 'pushing'
- Thomas A. Harris, *I'm OK, You're OK* (Arrow, 2012) – a record-breaking US bestseller. Climb out of the cellar of your mind!
- John E. Tropman, *Making Meetings Work: Achieving High-quality Group Decisions*, 2nd edition (SAGE, 2003)
- Geoff Ribbens and Greg Whitear, *Body Language: How to Read People, Understand Office Politics and Uncover Deception* (Hodder Arnold)
- Peter Fleming, *The Negotiation Coach* (John Murray Learning, 2015) – aspire to a higher-level understanding of the power of negotiating through this self-learning guide

3 Seven things to do

- Revisit some recent deals and consider what created the differences between those that you would consider were win/win, win/lose or lose/lose.
- How might the results have been made different? And how will you work differently as a result of this assessment?
- Work out the relative bargaining power you have with another party – taking care that, if you use power to get your own way, sooner or later they will do the same to you. How else will you negotiate?
- Develop your own method of backing your proposals with sound justification and arguments (e.g. using discreet notes in 'code' or 'shorthand').

- Practise your listening – rather than talking; your questioning skills should be as strong as your 'selling' skills. (Yes, non-sellers need to be able to sell ideas, too!)
- Try to develop your summarizing skills – regular summaries show that you have heard and understood what has been said. Skilled negotiators tend to emphasize the points that are helpful to their 'cause' while playing down other party's points which would not be so acceptable.
- *And an important 'don't'!* Don't show triumph! Especially when you think you have the better end of a deal. It could lead to your 'opponent' to become determined to gain revenge next time round.

4 Seven behaviours to avoid

- Before you start: 'Don't talk yourself out of a deal!', so advises Carol Frohlinger of www.negotiatingwomen.com. This is good advice! It is your opponent's job to convince you that your scale of objectives is unrealistic.
- When trying to be flexible – take care! Bill Coleman advises us: 'The worst thing you can say is "I want £x for this job," leaving no opening for negotiation by the other side. Better language is "I hope to earn between £X and £Y". That gives the other party more flexibility.' BUT: it may also be taken to have revealed your 'limits'. Wouldn't any buyer immediately 'attack' the bottom figure? And wouldn't any self-respecting salesperson 'attack' the top one?
- Dangerous words: 'The single most dangerous word which can be spoken in business is "no"! The second most dangerous word is "yes"!' says Lois Wyse. It is possible to negotiate without saying either! However, 'shadow-boxing' can be very frustrating. Don't overuse this strategy or the meeting may end in turmoil.
- Lies: a presumption that lies will underpin negotiation encourages the thought that it will all be based on the win/lose culture. This could be very unhelpful in the case of building a long-term trading relationship.

- Kidology: when things are going well, it is easy to assume that we might just be able to 'walk on water' and fix any negotiation! Success will come from a variety of factors – for example, the reputation of your product/service/company. Try to maintain a sense of balance – enjoy your success, but don't overlook the fact that your 'opponents' always have a choice.
- To musician Marvin Gaye is attributed the saying: 'Negotiation means getting the best of your opponent.' Does it? This is a 'win/lose' strategy and very likely to rebound next time around.
- 'The most important trip you may take in life is meeting people halfway' is a commonly heard phrase. Halfway sounds fair enough but this depends on either party's limits – have these been disclosed?

5 Seven preliminary issues – your coach's suggestions

- 'In my "world" negotiation just doesn't happen... If I tried, I fear I would be made to look stupid, naive or even in the wrong business.'
  Coach: 'Don't be negative... even if this were true, for most people any "wins" are likely to be a closely guarded secret. Otherwise, everyone would be encouraged to negotiate and make life harder for their opponents! So, build your case (be prepared with a fallback position in case of an outright rejection) and be as persuasive as you can – to achieve just a small concession. Once the "door" is opened, even better results could follow!'
- 'I wouldn't want people to think that I cannot afford the product or service...'
  Coach: 'Don't worry about what people might think. Negotiating is more common than you might think and terms are often set with some room for manoeuvre by vendors or purchasers. If you don't try, you'll never know if you could have achieved a better deal!'

- 'How do you know when your "opponent" is prepared to negotiate?'
  Coach: 'They'll probably send a "signal". For example, when discussing a price they may say "price depends on the quantity that you order". In other words: "We may discount the price if the quantity is sufficient." Ignoring such a signal can prove costly.'
- 'My contacts try to negotiate over everything. Am I doing something wrong or should I be working a different way?'
  Coach: 'Their senior management may have imposed tough expectations as the economy has toughened. Once this is explained and proved, both buyers and sellers can usually find ways of helping each other with new ideas/proposals. If there are no good reasons established for seeking flexibility in prices/quantities, any negotiator has the right to refuse.'
- 'Isn't success in negotiating dependent on the relative power between the parties – and the small/weak party is likely to "lose" by making all the concessions?'
  Coach: 'Not necessarily – "small" can mean exclusive and highly desirable as a partner; many businesses started out with this strategy and quickly gained support from other organizations with similar marketing strategies. This approach can lead to impressive growth in the marketplace!'
- 'Time is money in my setting. I don't have lots of spare time to sit down and negotiate – even if it became a priority.'
  Coach: 'This could mean that you are losing out with higher costs, lower profit margins and costly work practices which could be streamlined. Perhaps you should delegate negotiation tasks to colleagues – but do ensure that they are professionally trained first!'
- 'I tried to negotiate an initial deal recently but when it should have been implemented my "opponent" denied that we had set it up. What is the point?'
  Coach: 'Wasn't there an agreed record of the meeting? Relying on memory and the "good nature" of the parties can be a big mistake – even when the parties have an established track record.'

6 Seven planning issues – more support from your coach

- 'I have heard it said that "failing to plan could really mean planning to fail!" Aren't top negotiators born, not made?'
  Coach: 'The best negotiators are those who may appear to be negotiating off the cuff but you can be sure that, "off camera" they will have been: researching, making notes, checking track records, taking stock, assessing costs and/or market projections and preparing easily accessed notes for use in the meeting.'

- 'Why do some "authorities" recommend going to the other party's base for a meeting?'
  Coach: 'There are no "rules" about where negotiations should be located. Skilled negotiators may have private preferences but, clearly, revealing them could prejudice the psychological comfort factors applying – and possibly the outcome, too!'

- 'I am most comfortable negotiating at my "home base". Why should I risk feeling uncomfortable by negotiating "away"?'
  Coach: 'We can learn a lot about our "partners" or "opponents" when we see them in their own environments – and how they are viewed by their colleagues. This organization may become a significant "partner" for your organization – how well organized is it? How likely is it that their implementation of the deal you'll be making will be trouble-free, from what you have seen and heard?'

- 'I always try to host meetings with other negotiators on "neutral territory". Is that a "better" idea?'
  Coach: 'It can be if it is genuinely "neutral" and if there are no obvious distractions!'

- 'I am told that I tend to talk too much. Is that a disadvantage in negotiations? And how could I change it?'
  Coach: 'If there are two people involved in the meeting, you should try not to talk for more than 50 per cent of the time! You could achieve that by trying to ask more questions and, when receiving questions, avoid *over*-answering.'

● 'People sometimes use anger when negotiating about a complaint. Is that acceptable behaviour?'
Coach: 'It is very important to practise self-control when negotiating! Discuss what has gone wrong objectively and calmly, and ask your contact what they can do to put things right. Never use personal insults or bad behaviour.'
● 'Why do some negotiators try to pretend they are something they are not?'
Coach: 'Some people may do this because they have low confidence or self-esteem. Let them see that reaching good deals is the best way of achieving a reputation as a trusted and effective negotiator.'

7 Seven powerful behaviours to practise in your next negotiation round

● Don't start negotiating without preparing first (at least identifying the least and most desirable outcomes).
● If misunderstandings should occur, check whether you could be to blame. If so, apologize, take personal steps to correct the position and ensure that it is not repeated.
● Ask more questions – and listen carefully to the answers (seeking clarification when you are unsure what has been said/agreed). Do not close until your needs are satisfied.
● Ensure that you build up and maintain your personal trust and integrity – for example by not withdrawing an offer made (especially when it has been accepted unambiguously).
● Identify 'sticking points' carefully and encourage open discussion to find practical ways around them (or by balancing them with alternative concessions).
● Practise summarizing and confirming actions to finalize a deal (ensuring that there are no errors and omissions which could lead to yet more negotiating later).
● Don't dwell on 'might-have-beens' when negotiations have not been conclusive (or a 'cooling-off' period has elapsed without agreement). Set some new personal goals to continue this self-development process.

PART 2
Your Advanced Negotiation Skills Masterclass

Introduction

So, you are now an experienced negotiator. But what do you understand by that description? Are you a 'fixer'? An intermediary? A person to whom others turn when they need solutions to difficulties with others? Whether or not you see yourself in these situations, your interest in this book indicates that you have more than a passing interest in the topic. More importantly, you want to improve the results you achieve from the negotiating process.

When you think analytically about your most recent experiences, you will probably be wondering how to measure your levels of success. After all, a deal done must surely satisfy both sides, or it would have broken down. And perhaps you are feeling 90-per-cent sure that you could not have achieved more.

That last elusive 10 per cent is probably the source of some lingering doubts – and might lead you to kick yourself if it is ever revealed that you could have done better.

But don't panic! The aim of this Part is to help you to balance these dilemmas with the need to close deals that will benefit your organization and those you are working with. 'Win/win' is still our principal aim in negotiating, even if it seems a hard standard to achieve!

CHAPTER 8

Preparation: a hard taskmaster

Most negotiators are kept busy pursuing their objectives with little opportunity to:

- 'stop the clock'
- revisit their methods and approaches
- set some realistic development goals.

Even when self-reviews are second nature, the sheer pace of business can make such activities difficult (and, possibly, unattractive).

In this chapter we are encouraging you to begin a self-development journey with a view to handling more demanding projects and achieving an even higher level of success by negotiating even better deals.

After each chapter, try to develop your Personal Action Plan (at the end of this Part) and implement it.

Now you will achieve the following tasks:

- Rate yourself as a negotiator and your relationship with others (and consider the strengths and weaknesses of each approach)
- Obtain some feedback from someone who knows you well (possibly confirming those ratings)
- Learn which styles are most common among top 'win/win' negotiators
- Show that you can produce a negotiation plan with clear goals and objectives
- Reassess your personal communication skills – both verbal and non-verbal – and identify some improvement points.

Have you ever met a *real* expert? No, not a self-proclaimed one but someone whose expertise is well known and valued by many people. Would you dare to question this person's word or advice? Probably not, unless you wanted to test their expertise. If this is the case, then read on.

Recognizing someone's expertise should make a negotiation easier – but sometimes it can simply raise the stakes. 'Why don't we let our two experts meet and sort this thing out and we'll simply agree who pays what and when?' Such a proposal should be a simple way out of a difficulty, but there are still enormous pitfalls to avoid – for example:

- **Trial of expertise:** the experts enter into an academic form of arm-wrestling (to prove or disprove theory, academic learning, or even practical common sense)
- **One-upmanship:** one expert promotes their own theories as supreme, with all others deemed worthless
- **Research awareness:** there is a reluctance to recommend a particular route for fear that someone else is already working on this project and is more likely to achieve a successful result more quickly
- **Long grass:** one party seeks to kick the negotiation into the long grass with the aim of delaying any decision until events make the original scheme or idea redundant.

In a theoretical sense, a negotiation takes place between two people or parties who start out in the belief that their knowledge is sufficient for them to debate proposals and arrive at a deal that will benefit both sides (or at least their own!).

How would you feel if your opponent is a novice or has little knowledge of the task in hand? Relaxed? Excited? Suspicious? Sympathetic? Or simply concerned?

After all, it should be easy to achieve a deal in such circumstances, but could that deal be implemented to everyone's satisfaction? What might happen further down the line? Could the other party withdraw, default or go into liquidation? Or just decide to fail to deliver?

This might result in a protracted and expensive legal case – with an ultimate result of lose/lose: on one side the original need still exists while on the other the 'consideration' (money or benefit) remains uninvested.

There is a much better chance of achieving a good deal when both parties are well prepared. This means understanding:

- the technical features
- the 'deliverables'
- the overall terms and conditions
- each party's track record on delivery or implementation
- safety nets in case of future difficulties
- relative power factors (both real and perceived).

If this sounds like a tall order, think how you might feel if, in the process of a negotiation, you suddenly realize that you had shortcomings in your own preparation? What action would you take?

There are four main factors that contribute success to a negotiation:

1 knowledge of the subject/processes involved
2 the relative starting positions of the negotiating parties
3 any levers/benefits that could be applied to bring the parties towards an agreement
4 the skills involved in influencing/persuading the other party to reach agreement.

Confidence comes from sound knowledge, which results from thorough preparation.

So why start this Part with yet more exhortations about preparation? In a way, the more experience negotiators have, the greater the risk that they will cut corners in the belief that thorough research, reading and analysis are no longer so essential. It is certainly time-consuming, but expertise is maintained only if it is constantly topped up.

Preparation is a hard taskmaster – unprepared negotiators are vulnerable to making expensive mistakes; they may be clever at improvising or covering them up, but serious errors have a way of resurfacing when the agreement is implemented. Will the 'guilty' party have escaped? Possibly, but their reputation may be sullied. The message is clear – don't let this be you!

This may seem obvious, but negotiations can come to grief when some of the key factors listed are missing and especially when new relationships are being formed. Remember, too, that what is obvious to you may not be obvious to your opponent. What is worse, they may be using a competitive style to encourage you to throw caution to the wind and negotiate spontaneously, with the assumption that this tactic might benefit them considerably more than you.

One solution

If you feel that your opponent does not have the necessary skills to reach a deal with you, then it is always possible to escalate the topic or project to someone at a more senior level, with agreement from your client or supplier that they do the same. To avoid your opponent losing face, you could suggest that your two bosses come to the next meeting to help with the agenda. You cannot, however, make too much of a habit of using this tactic – your own organization may begin to worry that you are not up to the job!

One way of exploring these potential difficulties in advance is to implement an internal dummy run, or role-play, with a senior manager or colleague. The objective is simple – to pinpoint any unidentified obstacles or barriers to an acceptable agreement.

Who should I be?

We shall return to the preparation theme a little later. But first of all, let's conduct a self-examination task of our own values and approaches to negotiation.

TASK 1: RATE YOURSELF – WHAT KIND OF NEGOTIATOR AM I?

Please rate yourself on the following profiles by choosing the number that you believe you portray in all your relationships with others, inside your organization and externally. (1 = does not apply to me and 9 = applies to me most of the time in business deals.)

Role 1: SAFETY FIRST
Your rating: 1   2   3   4   5   6   7   8   9

If you fall into the **Safety First** category, you might err on the side of safety with every decision and negotiation you undertake. In the extreme, you have an extremely cautious approach to risk-taking – always sticking to the verifiable truth and a safe ground that will work out equally satisfactorily in both the short and the long term.

Role 2: OPPORTUNIST
Your rating: 1   2   3   4   5   6   7   8   9

At the other end of the scale, you might be an **Opportunist** – quick to reach a deal that you instinctively know will be welcomed by your own organization, even if you are unsure whether it will achieve much for your opponent.

Role 3: COMPLETER/FINISHER
Your rating: 1   2   3   4   5   6   7   8   9

A **Completer/Finisher** is someone who aspires to have all the *i*s dotted and *t*s crossed and sets out from the start to ensure that everything promised can be delivered exactly as agreed. Fine detail is important to this negotiator as an indicator of both good faith and precision, which is essential for full completion of the contract/agreement.

Role 4: ESCAPOLOGIST
Your rating: 1   2   3   4   5   6   7   8   9

An **Escapologist** boasts that he or she never relies on the 'crutch' of logical thought and instead prefers to cut deals on the basis of instinct. A thrill is gained from living dangerously and the Escapologist may well be tempted to make promises that are just on the right side of the law. Unsurprisingly, these people do experience difficulties with deals, but thrive on the skill of being able to 'pull another deal' that promises to correct the earlier one. They always seem able to recover without any taint to their short- or long-term results... or they move jobs quite frequently! Are you tempted to think like this?

Role 5: POLITICIAN
Your rating: 1   2   3   4   5   6   7   8   9

The **Politician** is very concerned about ensuring that the deal reached meets current standards of acceptability – in terms of preferred status, rules, descriptive terms and/or political norms. These aspects can be allowed to take precedence over what is practical.

Role 6: EXPERT/TEACHER
Your rating: 1   2   3   4   5   6   7   8   9

A true **Expert** is often self-effacing and quiet about their expertise (whether publicly acknowledged or not). Experts can also present themselves as people who know a great deal about most topics and are not reluctant to share their supreme knowledge in everyday conversation as well as in negotiating sessions. They can often be heard explaining things with sentences starting with: 'You know why that is, don't you?' (which precedes a detailed explanation that is mostly accurate but of little interest to the audience because of the manner in which the information has been introduced).

Role 7: EXTROVERT
Your rating: 1   2   3   4   5   6   7   8   9

Warm and sociable, the **Extrovert** enjoys the company of other people and, at the extreme, will only happily negotiate awkward or difficult issues when they can predict that an existing comfortable client relationship will not be compromised.

Role 8: PESSIMIST
Your rating: 1   2   3   4   5   6   7   8   9

A **Pessimist** generally does not make a good negotiator as negotiation is mainly about the future. At the extreme, pessimists appear not to be optimistic that there is even a future ahead. In reality, the pessimism may be a front to minimize opponents' expectations.

Role 9: NAIVE PERSON
Your rating: 1   2   3   4   5   6   7   8   9

You may think that, if your opponent's organization is foolish enough to delegate negotiations to such **Naive** people, then why should you worry if they let you gain a significant win? The issue is that, once a big problem has been solved, the blame games follow. This may lead to attempts to renegotiate or take some spoiling action, making it impossible for the deal to go ahead. In effect, the deal becomes a lose/lose agreement.

Role 10: CONTROLLER
Your rating: 1   2   3   4   5   6   7   8   9

A **Controller** feels the need for personal control of all aspects of a negotiation and, at the extreme, the preparations for, and implementation of, the agreement as well. This may exist through an innate insecurity and fear of the likely repercussions if the deal should go wrong: loss of income/ security or tarnished reputation. The Controller will believe that the ends justify the means.

The experienced negotiator will have recognized some – if not all – of these ten styles in colleagues and past opponents. In their extreme forms, each may have a frustrating effect on other people, but can you make them work?

TASK 2: CHECK YOUR RATINGS WITH A COLLEAGUE OR PARTNER WHOSE JUDGEMENT YOU TRUST

The need remains to check our own perception and to set some goals to improve our approach and therefore our results. Ask a colleague to review your self-rating by choosing the rating they feel is most appropriate for you and offering you examples to support any significant variations (of two grades or more).

TASK 3: RATE YOURSELF – WHAT KIND OF PERSON WOULD YOU *LIKE* TO BE?

Is it possible to be all these things all the time? Having rated yourself on these scales, I now urge you to revisit the listing and think about the score you would like to achieve in the future. Given your environment and role, they may not all be higher than your present rating and some of the gaps between current and desired ratings may be rather small, although important all the same.

TASK 4: REFLECTION: 'ALL THINGS TO ALL PEOPLE?'

Another mark of highly skilled negotiators is that they are adept at adjusting their style and technique to fit those of their opponent. To be able to do this successfully, it is necessary to identify typical styles of people with whom you have negotiated. This next task is therefore to revisit Task 1 and identify past negotiators you have worked with. Use the same criteria to rate them on the scale. (It would be best to use pseudonyms if you write their names down!)

We know that any negotiating interview aims to achieve a clearly understood agreement that both sides are committed to implementing. It is sometimes argued that enjoying these meetings is something of a luxury and that the main measure should lie in the resulting agreement and its implementation.

A meeting is usually measured by the objectives that have been achieved, and both parties will be using their skills of influencing and persuasion in order to get a result. So, finally, let us consider the best methods of responding to the challenges offered by some of the extremes of negotiating style that are listed above.

You will have style preferences for all the negotiators you meet from the above listing, but, for the sake of simplicity, we can classify them as follows:

● Class A: Behaviours and styles that are most likely to bring best results
● Class B: Behaviours and styles that may limit your results to just average.

Class A

Role 1: Safety First
One way of breaking this down is by helping the other person to recognize the advantages of a proposed step through highlighting its good points and diluting any objections by expressing the unlikelihood of them occurring and the simple steps that could be taken to get back on track. This style might also be recognized as 'hand-holding'. As negotiators gain more experience and achieve some successes, this style tends to be overtaken by other styles.

Role 2: Completer/Finisher
People in this category generally seek the highest results from regular negotiations, in the sense that their results are usually sound, with rare errors or exceptions. Their agreements are usually fulfilled 100 per cent and, should any 'failures in implementation' occur, they are corrected (or compensated for) very rapidly. Natural reactions may include Safety First or even Controller.

Role 3: Expert/Teacher
Resist the temptation to compete with this strategy, keeping conversation factual and based on the current case. If necessary, ask how examples quoted relate exactly to the deal under discussion, indicating where factual evidence departs from the parallels quoted. If progress is being made, reinforce the benefits of arrangements that are proposed.

Role 4: Controller
Even if you find this style irritating, the best reaction is Safety First as it seeks to convince the opponent that all requirements have been, or will be, met.

Role 5: Opportunist
Taking a Safety First style with an Opportunist can generate considerable frustration because the Opportunist may see any obstacles (even open questions) as being used as a barrier. The Opportunist may be motivated by timing and will respond to phrases such as 'It's now or never' or 'We'll miss the boat if we have to go through the fine detail'. If you fear that your preparation is not 100 per cent, then seek to delay the meeting until it is. Try to neutralize the pressure by asking careful questions and demanding factual answers that compare with your preparation favourably. In extreme, rigid cases, walk away.

Class B

Role 6: Escapologist
The preferred response would be Safety First or Controller. However, experienced Opportunists may take some risks with Escapologists, especially where the risks are strictly limited and could be readily recovered (in a retail setting, for example, where an inexpensive product could bear a considerable reduction to its selling price as a crowd puller for the first day of a sale).

Role 7: Politician
The role of Politician is a tempting opposition role to take but this may result in a considerable investment of time and patience in pursuit down various blind alleys. Resist the temptation to try to change the accepted modus operandi: go along in the role as another Politician – while learning from the process and making careful note of opportunities for streamlining it.

Role 8: Extrovert

Notable for the style of talking too much, the Extrovert may unwittingly give away vital bargaining information without obtaining anything in return. Ask more questions with the aim of restricting the conversation to the negotiation in hand, and try to resist engaging in storytelling and socializing: fun and laughter should not play a significant role in the negotiating process. The best move is to agree to take time out to celebrate the deal *after* it is achieved, not before.

Role 9: Pessimist

Use the Expert role to illustrate the benefits to be gained and provide protection in the Completer/Finisher role.

Role 10: Naivety

An obvious reaction is the Expert/Teacher role but, if you choose this, avoid the dangers of adopting a patronizing tone, which might generate considerable resistance.

How can we progress from Class B to Class A in our negotiating tactics and style?

We can do this, first, by recognizing the temptations of Class B behaviours and then seeking Class A disciplines where these will be more appropriate and productive. If your organization constrains your behaviour, then either seek to change it through setting a better example or, if that fails, consider moving to a better/more professional environment elsewhere.

Build a reputation for your negotiating skills through a track record of significant success.

Preparing the case

We have seen that unprepared negotiators can be vulnerable to making mistakes; they may be skilled at covering them up but any serious errors will be discovered when the contract or agreement is implemented. In the previous Part we developed a thorough list-based approach to a case or project. This style has great strengths in 90 per cent of potential deals, as it lends itself to logical sequences, with positions, values and/or qualities that can be justified in the face of counter-proposals from an opponent. Rather more difficult are negotiations that involve:

- politics
- strategic choices
- long-term factors
- matters of principle
- 'what if?' issues.

Setting objectives and goals

A common preparation technique is using a grid that enables negotiating objectives to be identified and charted as follows:

Most favourable position $\longleftarrow$----------$\longrightarrow$ Least favourable position

A principal benefit of this approach is that offers that lie outside the grid should, at least, trigger a review of your preparation and, on occasion, lead to the rejection of any deal that is not part of your team's aims.

Clearly, the more information that can be gained before the meeting the better; this should enable you to prepare a matrix that might give a clearer indication of where common ground might lie – and the scope for settlement. So, research is vital – for example collecting information from anyone else in your organization who might have some involvement with your intended partner. It is amazing how much of this kind of information can be gleaned. For example, you might get to hear of an internal instruction to line managers to clamp down on expenses claims because of a 'short-term cash-flow problem'. This might trigger an offer to include extended credit (or, indeed, the complete opposite).

A quality plan for negotiating a service contract could look like this:

Initial negotiating plan or grid

Our 'shopping list'	Negotiation objectives		Their 'shopping list'
	US Most Favourable THEM Least Favourable	US Least Favourable THEM Most Favourable	
Buyer e.g. price	£72,000–£77,500 £72,500–£80,000		Vendor e.g. price
Objective 2: e.g. delivery	US MF THEM LF	NOW! 6 months	US LF THEM MF	Objective 2: e.g. delivery
Objective 3: e.g. payment terms	US MF THEM LF	3 months' credit 1 month	US LF THEM MF	Objective 3: e.g. payment terms

121

TIP *The challenge for quality standards in such a grid should focus on the following:*

- **Precision:** *in being able to define a standard*
- **Parameters:** *the need to establish parameters and priorities*
- **Realism:** *not asking for the moon!*
- **Aspirations:** *building in motivational targets to lift standards.*

Personal communication skills

One of the key fascinations with the task of negotiating is that success is dependent upon two vital functions: planning, then debating. The best results are achieved when attention is paid to both functions. Here is a reminder of the key skills that will repay the effort put into developing them over and over again:

- vocabulary
- speak/listen ratios
- comprehension
- non-verbal behaviour.

Vocabulary

Native English speakers are exceptionally fortunate that English is spoken in so much of the world. Like any language, the vocabulary is full of subtle nuances that convey different shades of meaning. For example, a negative situation can be expressed with a significant variation in strength, anywhere from 'a little local difficulty' to 'a complete disaster'. Either may be appropriate depending on the perception and mood of the speakers involved as well as the impact they would like to have on their fellow negotiator. There is an enormous power in the use of the right words when seeking to persuade your listeners – as all debaters understand!

However, those involved in the meeting must take care not to use an excess of technical vocabulary and jargon, as this may easily lead to confusion. Plain speaking should be the preferred style wherever possible.

Speak/listen ratios

Similarly, the best use of time in any meeting also needs careful consideration. A negotiation is unlikely to meet the true meaning of the word (or the aspiration needs of the participants) if one negotiator dominates most of the meeting time and speaks *at* the other party instead of talking *and* listening.

Maintaining the best balance will be affected by:

● the emotions involved
● the personal communication style of the people attending the meeting
● the seriousness of the issues
● the personality of each person attending
● the occupation of each person (salespeople, for example, are generally rather more extrovert than buyers).

Comprehension

Each of us has a variable speed at which our brain can comprehend what is being said – which is also affected by the speed of our opponent's communication style and language used. When we come to analyse the potential for misunderstandings, we need to recognize the potential for mistakes and exceptions – indeed, it is remarkable that more don't occur!

Concentrate hard on the content of what your opponent is saying, as well as the manner of its delivery. Never agree to anything that you do not fully understand – always seek clarification regarding WHO will do WHAT to WHOM and who will enforce this.

Non-verbal behaviour

Behavioural scientists have developed frameworks on how to read the body language of others. The result is that we are more sensitive to signals sent by our opponents, whether they were intentional or not. Is this significant? Perhaps! A misread signal is potentially just as dangerous as one that was deliberately sent but ignored or missed.

A possible safety net may be provided where an additional observer attends your meeting who has the sole task of observing non-verbal signals sent during the meeting. Time would then be taken in a recess to feed back on any body language observed – together with an analysis of the possible meanings. A particularly fruitful use of this approach may be where the meeting includes a team of three or more people on your opponent's side.

Developing your personal negotiating style

Negotiating brings out very different reactions from people, sometimes leading them to put on an act (on the principle that emulating the style or behaviour of their favourite actor or entrepreneur is the best way of achieving top results). This is not a recommended strategy and certainly not one favoured by highly skilled negotiators.

However, a negotiation is usually dependent upon the exchange of information and some negotiators will seek to uncover as much as possible while attempting to reveal as little as possible. A healthy meeting is one in which relevant information is exchanged without any notion of 'gamesmanship' (which may risk the outcome agreement).

The processes in use in a meeting will be affected by two control issues:

1 Use of push/pull techniques

An example of this approach might involve one person trying to control the exchange of information by talking more or most of the time. This is rarely an effective control method. Better results are achieved through the use of controlling behaviours, which can be categorized into:

● Push
  - revealing facts/information
  - communicating feelings.

● Pull
  - seeking answers to questions (especially open questions)
  - summarizing a discussion – encouraging agreement or revealing difficulties.

Push techniques tend to be used by salespeople, on the basis that sellers have to 'persuade actively' – otherwise, why would they exist? Pull techniques are traditionally used by purchasing people, who recognize potential problems that might occur if buying decisions were based simply on what salespeople want to declare. Critical factors may be those that the supplier would rather not answer. Of course, this example is an oversimplification, but your use of control techniques in a negotiation may well affect the value of the outcome.

Behaviours to practise

Push		Pull
Giving information	INFORMATION	Seeking through questions
Speaking	PROPOSALS	Listening
	BUILDING IDEAS	
Offering ideas	EXPRESSING SUPPORT	Bringing in
	COUNTER-PROPOSAL	

Think before speaking

How you get your point across is as important, if not more so, than *what* you say because of the impact it may have upon others at the meeting.

Much as it may be interesting – and even entertaining – to work with 'high reactors', their extrovert nature can both create a barrier and generate exhaustion.

Top negotiators are skilled at:

- talking economically and purposefully
- listening attentively
- observing and analysing accurately
- speaking sensitively.

Sound preparation requires more than learning a script about needs or supplies; it also requires a commitment to, and understanding of, the strategy of our business and a personal determination to succeed with measurable outcomes.

Summary

This first chapter has reinforced the importance of:

- systematic, sensitive and accurate preparation *before* attending the meeting
- analysing the situation objectively
- thinking through the issues – those that are explicit, and
- seeking evidence to support those that are only implied.

In real life, most negotiators will claim that they do this. If/when their preparation turns out to be faulty or insufficient, they 'blag' it (while also claiming that this lack did not show or affect the outcome!). But haven't you noticed when your opponents have fallen into that trap?

Next, we will explore the issues that contribute to longer-term growth and success.

Fact-check (answers at the back)

1. For best long-term results, negotiators should aim to achieve a deal that:
   a) Meets all objectives that satisfy their own organization ❏
   b) Meets their own 'shopping list' ❏
   c) Comes close to the objectives of both organizations ❏
   d) Meets all 'must achieve' objectives for both organizations ❏

2. It is good to achieve a reputation as a highly effective negotiator because:
   a) This will create an aura that will be off-putting for all other prospective negotiation partners ❏
   b) It will keep time-wasters at a distance ❏
   c) It is likely that most future deals will qualify as win/win arrangements ❏
   d) It is likely to bring early recognition and promotion ❏

3. Top negotiators:
   a) Talk more than they listen ❏
   b) Balance equally the time invested in preparation with time spent in debate ❏
   c) Use openly provocative statements to obtain top results ❏
   d) Are careful not to dominate by talking too much ❏

4. The 'pull' style is typically used by:
   a) Negotiators who have long experience in sales and marketing roles ❏
   b) Negotiators who think before they speak ❏
   c) Mainly negotiators who work in purchasing or procurement roles ❏
   d) Those negotiators who are really unsure of the case they are having to negotiate ❏

5. Misunderstandings in a negotiated agreement are a sign that:
   a) The deal will fail in the implementation stage ❏
   b) Insufficient preparation was carried out ❏
   c) One of the sides failed to clarify all the issues before reaching a deal ❏
   d) There could be genuine mistakes in the final record. ❏

6. For best long-term results, negotiators should aim to achieve a deal that:
   a) Meets all objectives that satisfy their own organization ❏
   b) Meets their own 'shopping list' ❏
   c) Comes close to the objectives of *both* organizations ❏
   d) Meets all 'must achieve' objectives for *both* organizations ❏

7. You have a client whose evident negotiating style is as a Naive/Introvert. Which style/tactics would be most appropriate for a productive and long-term relationship based on repeat business?

a) Adopt a Safety First role to avoid attracting blame if/when the proposals fail to meet their expectations ❏

b) Invest time to build up their trust and knowledge in your organization's expertise and proposals ❏

c) Build up trust by using the Completer-Finisher/Opportunist role ❏

d) Mirror their Naive/Introvert style to build their confidence ❏

8. Your new opponents' proposals already fit into the acceptable zone for most of your objectives. How would you respond?

a) Readily accept them – saving on time and energy ❏

b) Check all the finest detail to ensure there are no 'traps' ❏

c) Call a recess (e.g. coffee break) while you assess what could go wrong ❏

d) Build in progress checks to ensure that all commitments are fulfilled ❏

9. Your 'opponent' seems to 'tune out' in the conversation (with glazed eyes!). How would you respond?

a) Ask more questions – to test their concentration and understanding ❏

b) Suggest a recess or 'comfort break' in case they are experiencing a major distraction ❏

c) Introduce some new proposals to gain more interest ❏

d) Bring in a colleague to reinforce your impact ❏

10. You recently concluded a negotiation with a new 'opponent' and have already started to implement it as the deal is making a significant contribution to your objectives. However, you have now received their suggestion that it could be enhanced significantly and you fear that their interest is to recover their own 'lost ground' rather than help you. How would you respond?

a) Reject the suggestion outright, explaining that an urgent work commitment means that your time cannot be 'stretched' for another two months ❏

b) Request more written details before committing to any action ❏

c) Delegate the task to a colleague with strict instructions not to concede anything ❏

d) Agree a date as a priority as it will provide another opportunity to conclude another deal ❏

CHAPTER 9

Negotiating growth through partnering

Most highly successful organizations owe their success to repeat business; a large element of this will have arisen from successful relationships with their partners (i.e. trusted suppliers, loyal clients and so on). Top negotiators are those who seek out such partnering opportunities and then build and develop them.

In this chapter we will explore how to build a partnering relationship through:

- identifying best opportunities
- tuning in to partners' business culture and needs
- managing the challenges provided by project teams and specialists
- understanding how the partner's stage of development can affect trust, behaviour and the use (or misuse) of power.

Whom should I seek as a partner?

Negotiators can face challenges in working out whom best to approach for their proposals. Is the first person we approach the right person to handle all subsequent contact? This chapter explores the basics of individual contact and also how your approach may need to change as the client organization and its way of handling key decisions develops. Understanding these processes is vital to a senior negotiator who is handling big contracts.

In simple terms, we need to be able to work with someone who has the freedom and authority to reach agreement – and then to see the fullest implementation of the agreement. That may sound simplistic but in reality it poses numerous challenges.

For example, a sales representative for a fashion house needs to identify and approach someone who is probably identified by a retail client as the fashion buyer. A door opens, an appointment is arranged and a presentation is made. However, it then transpires that the buyer is about to hand over responsibility for the budget to a new person who is yet to be appointed and therefore cannot commit that budget in the meantime. This is a frustrating situation, and one that should have been identified earlier.

At its simplest, ALL negotiators need to find the right people who have:

- *a recognition and knowledge of needs*
- *the necessary resources*
- *the time to meet*
- *the authority to negotiate*
- *the self-confidence to commit.*

Accessibility

Senior job titles are used to ascribe seniority (e.g. Buying Director, Credit Controller or Sales Manager) and from this we may be led to believe that the job holder has accountability for resources such as budgets, time and people. However, an additional commitment may not be in the budget and the board may have embargoed any additional spending in the current trading period. So, here are the key factors that need re-examination:

Authority and self-presentation

Interestingly, the nearer one gets to the top of an organization, the higher the risk of prevarication (or even reluctance to commit). This can be a painful lesson to learn – both inside and outside the chain of command – and may help to explain why seemingly simple issues are delayed while an internal negotiation has to take place to agree an appropriate way of handling the issue. So, job titles provide one route for communicating levels of authority, but this is not a foolproof rule.

Direct sales staff are taught that they should 'qualify the contact' – in other words, ensure that the person they are talking to fulfils the five criteria cited in the above tip. This is not easy, but it avoids investing a lot of time and effort in trying to influence people who simply do not have the authority to make the decision.

This dilemma may be eased by adding a Key Account Manager role into the normal hierarchy or by ensuring that directors are more accessible to support their sales teams when they have to negotiate issues that are outside their normal authority levels.

The next challenge is that business can only be transacted through people being accessible, authoritative and mindful of the need for persuasive self-presentation.

Organization to organization or person to person?

Email and texting make it far easier to communicate with business contacts and, because nowadays there are fewer personal secretaries who act as gatekeepers to their bosses' diaries, personal requests for interviews are more likely to be at least read, even if they are not always granted.

Looking at this process from the viewpoint of the 'target', is it really possible to manage in today's environment if you spend your life in an icebox? Accessibility is very important, even if it is for no other reason than to keep up with ever-changing possibilities and potential threats.

Towards a better understanding – the case for partnering

As organizations succeed and grow, so their market position changes. For example, the small local specialist may, quite quickly, become one that is multicultural and even multinational. With that growth comes greater challenge: an increased risk of competition both from existing competitors who need to defend their position in the marketplace, and also from other new entrants.

The risk of things going wrong also increases because of the sheer scale of the operation or because of promises made that may not always be fulfilled. How the organization reacts in such situations can give a pretty clear indicator of the style with which it operates and – even more crucially – the way in which it exercises its power over weaker partners.

The **'power-over' complex** assumes that the other party's business exists only because 'our organization allows it' – an exaggeration that, in some instances, might be accurate.

A 'power-over' relationship may be domineering, even mean-spirited – especially when it comes to dealing with matters such as profit margins ('the more you make the less there is for me'). Good relationships in such a climate can quickly become competitive in the extreme, and may even lead to a complete relationship breakdown as alternatives are sought to break the 'power trap'.

The **'power-with' relationship,** on the other hand, assumes a more supportive partnership in which both parties aim for a genuine win/win outcome regarding matters such as shared profit margins, cost investment, market research and even technology development. Failures may still occur occasionally but they are dealt with in a non-punitive way, and parties seek to ensure that lessons are learned from the failure so that it does not recur.

Tune in to the business culture

Understanding the culture of your partner's business (and that of your own organization) can make a huge difference to the success of a negotiation and subsequent relationships:

Pioneers

The stage of development of your partner's organization may have less to do with size than state of play. In a sense, pioneers are easily recognized; their organization may be relatively new and their pioneering spirit can be witnessed at first hand.

Imagine this example: you wait in line for an interview with the MD of a company in the retail sector for, typically, half an hour before being granted a very short meeting – ten minutes or even less – punctuated by frequent telephone calls from suppliers and the MD barking out instructions. In such an environment it may be difficult, if not impossible, to develop a proposal for a longer-term case that may have a significant effect on the company's development.

The predominant negotiating style would appear to be one more commonly found in a street market and, unless something crucial changes, the same constraints are imposed on everyone.

The behaviour of pioneers can also be readily witnessed in their use of power over the people around them; this may not be pleasant to see (for example, if employees are publicly berated), but the picture conveys something of the reactions and punishment that may be exacted if someone fails to match expectations. Understanding that such an outcome is possible is as important as developing an approach that is time-economic and that conveys the key messages and potential benefits in an attractive and tempting way.

Remember, too, that the real power of pioneers might actually not lie within themselves; hidden behind them somewhere may be a family relative who exercises the real control and your normal contact is very reluctant to reveal this. This might explain lengthy periods of inaction, persuasion but no actual decision. In one case I know of, the 'frustrated persuader' learned about such constraints only from a chance discussion with another 'persuader'. 'The MD is not master of his own house,' he was told. 'The real power lies with his sisters who outvote him at every board meeting.' This piece of advice changed future negotiating strategy and more effort was put into persuasion strategies that the MD could use at board meetings.

Specialization

Once through the pioneer phase of business development (which in today's world may not take long), organizations tend to departmentalize their activities and authority levels. This can mean the freeing up of access and decision-making outside the bottleneck constraint of the pioneer. Setting up and operating budgetary controls is one obvious need, but another, more important, one is ensuring that key decisions on organization policy and commitment are followed by all players. This can lead to quite slow decision-making as access to the collective forum may still be controlled by the pioneer, who can use this political control to limit the freedom of colleagues to move the business forward.

Sharing responsibility through a group (typically a board of directors or management committee) ought to improve decision-making. However, if five-year plans, two- or three-year budget outlines, and an agreed trading policy do not exist, the new forum may not enjoy much effectiveness and, therefore, any opportunities for achieving agreement may still be restricted to the pioneer.

So, understanding how delegated authority is exercised is a vital point. Negotiations on everyday matters may be delegated, but a deal may become so large or so crucial to the future of the organization that a negotiator may need to adapt to a shift in the opponent's authority. For example, the negotiator could say that a particular issue needs to be dealt with by the board because of its potential impact on other divisions, which might be interpreted as 'I do not have the authority to negotiate that at the moment'.

A benefit here would be the learning possibilities derived from involvement with seniors, and gaining wider influence. A less positive aspect might be that the outcome could be considerably more time-consuming as meetings may be rather more dynamic, with more people involved and a mix of less predictable bargaining, management styles and objectives.

Integrated decision-making

As organizations grow and their structure becomes more complicated, decision-making may be conducted in 'committees'. High-performance organizations that are able to make this structure work have been known to avoid such distractions by adopting a different vocabulary – for example, a 'committee' may become a 'project team', 'sourcing team' or 'divisional board'. The presumption here is that the team shares authority and uses a more consultative management style before making properly costed recommendations.

Negotiating with project teams benefits from:

- *political sensitivity about the structure of the organization*
- *comprehensive briefing on a full scheme (not just a single purchase or sale)*
- *a persuasive approach for the verbal presentation (backed by a succinctly written paper)*
- *patience and sensitivity when dealing with questions/ key issues voiced by interested parties represented in the group*
- *personal belief in the scheme*
- *the ability to commit the time needed to develop full understanding and trust.*

Failing to arrive at a consensus in recommending a single forward decision or route (and thus incurring public criticism) can be an obvious hazard. Similarly, 'political' preferences may be allowed to supersede factual analysis. Such structures therefore require astute leadership from a trusted team leader who is also able to keep other power players in the organization informally briefed (an important ingredient in ensuring that a final recommendation does not come as a nasty surprise).

Organic structures

From time to time a negotiator may come across a more advanced organization structure where the client or supplier has a less usual way of incorporating individuals' skills into decision-making, even though the needs and benefits might seem to lie outside their own direct areas of responsibility. This approach is worth remembering when having informal discussions with people who appear to work in just one division of a business: their input, expertise and internal influence may extend well beyond their immediate 'paymasters'. As a consequence, potential suppliers of software might find themselves confronted with some very astute questioning in any sales presentation to the project team, and the credibility of the whole tendering process could be jeopardized by the way in which such discussions are managed and resolved.

TIP

Sensitive behaviours without which outcomes might be jeopardized include:

- *understanding organizational behaviour*
- *recognizing and impressing key influencers*
- *importance of maintaining confidentiality*
- *developing and maintaining 'partnership behaviours'.*

Power

No analysis of influence in negotiation would be complete without some reflection on the use (or misuse) of power. It can, of course, be reflective of the status of the individual, but in the majority of cases that individual power is delegated to us by an organization – which backs us. So, for example, an army officer has considerable authority over the soldiers in a particular division, but very little over the general population in peacetime (except, perhaps, in emergency situations). Negotiators need to understand the extent of an organization's power, as represented by a negotiator in whom trust may be placed to implement change. This is especially important when a new contract or agreement is likely to affect areas well outside the power and influence of your partner.

Individual v. organization power

A more in-depth analysis is impossible here, but influencers will benefit from comparing the following five characteristics:

1 **Charismatic:** generally born of intellect, personality and self-presentation. This can be a power for good but overuse can lead to intimidation, which could be destructive.
2 **Individual:** a person's career may be significantly affected by the outcomes of a case (both positively and negatively).
3 **Manipulative:** for example, learned by children by the way they handle the comparative power of their parents. (Some employees use similar methods with their managers.)
4 **Destructive:** especially when negotiations or the implementation of a deal fail.
5 **Organizational:** indicated by the job holder's power to inflict sanctions or provide 'bonuses' for good behaviour.

A case analysed

A sales opportunity could have a very different value if a company's market is found to be in decline. This shows that the value of partnering can also be affected by factors well outside the partner's control. The following table provides a distinct comparison between the three organization phases that we have discussed:

Review and focus in the case: How partnering is different

	Pioneers	Specialization	Integrated
New proposals	Focus on quick returns	Demonstrate how a new idea helps expansion and reinforces 'difference'	Help achieve individuality and competitive advantage
Hiccups/ complaints	Speedy reaction; quick acceptance of ownership and corrective action	Corrective action and causes examined	Consequences of upset considered and factors affecting image addressed
Investment	Time for feedback	Specialist ideas – developing service/ product/functions	Reorganization of functions, e.g. vertical integration
Management information support	Reduce admin-istration time; help focus on support, how to overcome obstacles and barriers	Share own specialization and/ or knowledge to support one another in a non-competitive way	Focus effort on achieving the results that contribute to the 'big picture'
Promises	Always readily fulfilled and action communicated	Shown importance by actions and words	Delegated but followed up and communicated

In the end, the successful negotiator seeks to build, develop, and maintain a trusting relationship with long-term business partners. This is easily stated but all too easily destroyed with just one careless decision in the organization. For example, if the main point of contact in an organization moves into a new role and their replacement fails to provide the same level of care, then previous organizational influence will begin to wane.

Seniority: effectiveness v. trust

You might think that the best practices listed in the above panel are the normal mark of most senior executives in any organization and that more junior negotiators need to be sharper in order to meet short-term objectives. Wrong!

If we were to substitute 'more economical with the truth' for 'sharper', some negotiators might decide that partnering is too expensive and that 'influential presentation' is all that is really necessary: 'Tell them what they want to hear, back it up with early action and the next events will take care of themselves!'

Wrong again! It is the actions that matter; talking a good game is not enough. Surely there is little point in occupying an influential position unless it provides the opportunity to create change and ensure that it is fulfilled as originally envisaged. Here lies the origin of the expression 'My word is my bond'. Sadly, there have been infamous incidences on the public stage where this expression has definitely not applied to either the outcome or the operational methods involved. Would we want to build a business relationship over years with such a person who has broken trust and clearly not worried about it?

Continuity and behaviour

What if all these expectations seem to be unrealistic? Behaving politely to someone who demonstrates little concern for politeness or manners themselves can be difficult. A lack of manners may be a sign of a lack of interest in the other party's needs, although it may not necessarily indicate that the negotiator is engaging in 'sharp practice' or is being economical with the truth. In this case, you may need to bring a slower pace to a negotiation and take care not to make speedy deals, since trust has not yet been established.

Care should be taken with assumptions made about new 'opponents'; a little prior research could prove invaluable.

Thorough ice-breaking in early meetings helps to build new relationships; there is a vital difference between making a quick sale or purchase and building a longer-term, more trusting relationship.

Resisting the misuse of power

How easy is it to cope with uncomfortable situations that may arise from the misuse of power? In the short term, it may be necessary for a negotiator to grin and bear it on the basis that the concluded negotiations and results delivered are what will earn respect from the other person or organization. However, this does not mean giving in to unreasonable requests or acquiescing to unwarranted bullying tactics. Clear boundaries need to be drawn and defended. Consider the following dialogue:

Client: I would not be able to do business on these terms. Everyone else we work with is offering us 60 days' free credit and accepting full responsibility for advertising us as a stockist. If you cannot match that, I'm afraid we would find it extremely difficult to do business at this time.

Possible response: I understand your point. We too could offer similar terms, but they would be entirely dependent upon the level of business that we are able to do together. The more business you place, the better the terms could be.

This kind of response is really saying: 'We want to do business with you and I understand that you would prefer better terms than quoted. If you are able to clarify what you'd like to buy, then I promise to give you a better insight into how we could help you.' A more explicit response could have led to bargaining over discount rates and declaring a position when there was actually no clear or firm indication that the client wanted to do business at all.

TIP *Negotiation is about uncovering knowledge and information before trading something for something. Giving away information – and gaining little or nothing in return – leads to poor deals and encourages bullying tactics from opponents.*

Summary

Whether they recognize it or not, all organizations need help and support. Negotiators often have opportunities for providing ideas and independent feedback that can be very valuable to their opponents, especially when their track record has shown that they can be fully trusted (and that their suggestions are not just recommendations of self-interest). Senior negotiators must have a good understanding about authority and power and how decisions can be influenced with proven ideas gained from experiences elsewhere. Such relationships underpin long-term partnering that can have a huge impact on business results for both organizations.

Fact-check (answers at the back)

1. As well as achieving measurable results, negotiators should always try to be in control of:
   a) Meeting all objectives that satisfy their own organization ❏
   b) The location of the meeting ❏
   c) Their opponents' strategies ❏
   d) Their own destiny ❏

2. 'Qualifying' your opponent means:
   a) Checking that your opponent has the right qualifications for the job in hand ❏
   b) Being a Completer/Finisher ❏
   c) Ensuring that you are negotiating with someone at the right level for the deal to be implemented successfully ❏
   d) Building a strong relationship with the most senior person available ❏

3. 'Partnering' means:
   a) Exerting power over your contact and their organization ❏
   b) Meeting all the expectations of your boss and the seniors on the other side ❏
   c) Building and maintaining a sharing relationship with your partner organization ❏
   d) Ensuring frequent meetings – even social ones over a coffee ❏

4. Understanding the stage of development of your partner's organization is:
   a) Helpful as it helps achieve much higher results ❏
   b) About understanding the history of the organization and how it achieved its current state ❏
   c) Useful for gaining a better opportunity to maintain influence as a trusted supplier ❏
   d) Helpful for reaching a better understanding of how power is used ❏

5. Playing politics inside the client organization by taking sides and/or promoting one person's interests is:
   a) Understandable, as senior executives often need impartial advice ❏
   b) A matter of how authority is delegated in the organization ❏
   c) Dangerous and should be avoided at all costs ❏
   d) A matter of maintaining a balance between common sense and looking after your own organization's interests ❏

6. When bringing a project team together it is best to:
a) Maintain its membership within the user department to ensure credibility with users ❏
b) Bring together representatives with expertise from a wide range of interests in the organization ❏
c) Ensure that adequate time is made available – both as lead time and as a resource ❏
d) Leave political grandstanding outside the door ❏

7. Power in a project team needs to be carefully balanced if creative as well as practical ideas are to be developed. This is the task of:
a) The project leader who needs authority and leadership skills to manage the team ❏
b) Each member, although they should not overstep their role ❏
c) The person who established the team in the first place ❏
d) The organization's management team ❏

8. Depending on how a pioneer organization is developing, partnering by negotiators provides opportunities for the organization to benefit from:
a) Quick results from proposals (with minimal time investment) ❏
b) Upsets, which need to be handled sensitively ❏
c) Complaints, especially those whose origins cannot be easily identified ❏
d) Delegation ❏

9. Ensuring that agreements are implemented is best achieved by the most senior person available. This means:
a) Negotiators should ignore the efforts of more junior people in a client organization ❏
b) Negotiators should try to match their own seniority in their own organization with their normal contact with their partnered organizations ❏
c) Trust is built up by implementation and actions, not words (or rank!) ❏
d) We can believe what we want to believe when being briefed by the project's senior executive ❏

10. The achievement of longer-term partnerships for all negotiators in all situations is:
a) A luxury that most negotiators have insufficient time to implement ❏
b) Dependent entirely upon the situation and importance to the negotiator's organization ❏
c) A good starting point, enabling negotiators to develop their partnering skills ❏
d) A worthy ideal that would be unnecessary in many day-to-day situations ❏

CHAPTER 10

Effective influence in negotiation

So far we have looked at negotiating during the early stages of building a relationship. Obviously, the longer negotiators have worked together the more likely it is that they have an understanding about each other's style, methods and preferred ways of working. Also, crucially, past arrangements that were agreed will have been opened up to scrutiny and all parties will have a view on how successful they proved to be in reality. At its simplest, this means that negotiators will know who did what to whom, how it worked out, and whether they want to do it again if the opportunity arose.

It is entirely reasonable for past experiences to resurface in later meetings, which is a good reason for ensuring that any disputes are resolved whenever they occur. If ill-feeling is allowed to persist, it could have a negative effect on the next deal and make it much harder to maintain a constructive atmosphere.

The next topic – effective influence – can be defined as how easily we can persuade other people to accept our proposals. We will also introduce an overall framework for meetings – as used by high-performing negotiators – which helps ensure a businesslike approach and that our goals are addressed much more efficiently.

PROD-ProSC – a development framework

Negotiating skills can be more readily developed if a systematic approach is applied. This is not to say that meetings cannot be unstructured or conducted in a very informal way. However, the risk with this style is that one party – or even both – forgets to raise issues or close them off; once the meeting is over, any attempt to reopen the negotiation can feel like a potential trick. In any case, there is no point setting up a meeting and then having to call another one a few days later to renegotiate something that it was thought had been agreed in the first place. Hardly the mark of a well-managed process! And the key aim is to ensure that both sides can arrive at an agreement that they both *want* to implement.

Consider the following framework for effective negotiations:

P - Preparation
R - Research (when needed)
O - Open the meeting
D - Discussion
Pro - Proposals
S - Summarize
C - Close

Creating influential impressions

This book assumes that you already have considerable experience in building a good rapport with other negotiators. Suffice to say that an open relationship based on good manners (and a little charm) will help to keep the wheels of the negotiation oiled. All the relevant points about showing respect for one another through self-presentation are important – this is especially true of the way we dress, speak and display general courtesy and manners.

However, the best starting point is being able to reflect on past deals that have been successfully implemented and, where they have not, being able to agree a suitable action plan to put matters right. New business can now be developed, with lessons learned, so that any past errors will not recur.

All this assumes that, in continuing relationships, the negotiators concerned have already communicated past performance problems so that appropriate action can be taken. Unfortunately, some people (who see life as one long power game) may be tempted to use such events as an opportunity for an unexpected and sudden attack (with the aim of putting their opponent on the back foot), in the expectation that this will wring more generous compensation or allowances. Playing such games rarely creates positive relationships and can easily generate sufficient ill-feeling for opponents to adopt similar tactics. Such an approach, then, may well prove counter-productive.

The starting point

The perfect impression to make is one where the host has managed the environment so that there:

● are no unexpected interruptions
● is a confidential atmosphere
● are witnesses/assistants who are properly briefed and introduced
● are technological samples or displays that work perfectly
● is ready access to past records or paperwork that may be needed.

Clearly, in such a meeting there will also be the expectation that all participants are up to date with all the necessary reading and understand what is involved. This especially applies to the agenda if this has been drafted and shared in advance.

Subtle ways of leading the meeting

High-performing negotiators use specific behavioural techniques that, while they can be used by both sides to good effect, do not, on their own, normally lead to a negative reaction from the opposition. What most negotiators seek is an outcome that meets their aims and objectives – and this also applies to our opponents. Achieving a win/win situation is not about gaining the upper hand but arriving at the point where both sides want to be committed to the deal.

Influence and personality

Can you think of someone you know – perhaps someone you have worked with – whom you find yourself almost always agreeing with? This could be something to do with that person's charismatic personality. Or perhaps they display all the qualities that you think should be found in an ideal manager, contractor, counsellor, teacher or client.

Do you find that you look forward to discussions with them because, whatever the subject, you know that you will not find it difficult to find common ground and reach an agreement? Some of the traits that contribute to an agreeable personality are innate, but good conversation skills can also be developed.

The negative effects of poor conversation skills cannot be underestimated. A negotiator may be self-centred, almost boasting about past or current deals achieved and demonstrating that they are 'top dog'. This might have a distinctly off-putting effect on some people. Equally irritating can be the person who quizzes you about all that you have done, are doing, or hope to achieve while never revealing their own experiences. Both can be conversational tactics designed to gain an upper hand in the relationship.

Good conversationalists and negotiators balance the give-and-take as it takes time to reach an understanding of how a good relationship can be formed (unless, of course the deal is a one-off arrangement and the two parties will never meet again). Take greater care in this situation as many win/lose tricks may be used. We do not have space to cover these in this book, which concentrates on the collaborative bargaining that is normally a feature of long-term relationships.

Behaviours used by highly effective negotiators

Here are some key elements that are worth polishing for future meetings:

Leadership and control in discussion

This does not mean doing all the talking or ensuring that your ideas dominate the discussion and in the final record of the negotiation. Leadership and control come from ensuring that concepts and opinions are shared and this is less likely to happen if one party is too forceful, dogmatic or domineering, effectively monopolizing the discussion. Natural-born leaders with magnetic personalities are, however, the exception to this rule. Although they are not common, if you think you might fall into this category you are very lucky and you may be able to short-cut many negotiations simply by using your natural charisma!

Persuasive outcomes are more likely to be achieved by adopting the following behaviours:

- **Seeking information:** especially by the use of open questions – that is, those that begin with *who?*, *what?*, *when?*, *where? why?* or *how?* These draw information from the opponent and help ensure that all vital details are covered before a deal is decided.
- **Proposing:** this is a vital behaviour as proposals are really the only way of moving a negotiation forward. Ideas are usually too vague to achieve much on their own. However, introducing a trial proposal, phrased something like 'Suppose we were able to...' gives the impression that this is just an idea that could be firmed up into a formal proposal if both sides agree.
- **Testing understanding:** use phrases such as 'Can I just clarify a point here?' or 'Let's just make sure we all understand your idea', followed by a restatement by either

party, or a direct question such as 'What exactly did you mean by...?' or 'How would you see that arrangement working in practice?'

- **Supporting:** this is valuable because offering support for another party's ideas encourages them to listen better to the ways in which you feel the proposal can be enhanced. Nothing is guaranteed to demotivate people more than the rubbishing of their ideas, and there may be serious negative outcomes if you give the impression that your ideas are the only ones that count and any others are worthless. A good way of showing support for others' ideas might be: 'I like the approach you have suggested and would like to discuss it in more detail, especially the costs and how to make it work in practice.' Note that expressing support for an idea does not mean that you have committed to act upon it, only that you would be happy to see it feature in the overall agreement, if possible.
- **Building:** this is another way of expressing support, but this time the other party's ideas are added to by offering an additional/linked idea or proposal that enhances the original idea and makes it even more attractive (either to you or, preferably, to both sides). This approach also provides an alternative to direct and explicit disagreement or using a potentially provocative counter-proposal.
- **Summarizing:** this is a very useful tactic as it gives all parties a second chance to ensure that they have heard any proposals and that they understand these proposals and (preferably) agree with them. Summaries are often signalled with the word 'So...'.
- **Reflecting feelings:** sharing inner thoughts, while not always a feature of negotiators' chosen style of communication, can be a very powerful way of gaining movement or advantage in discussion. The reasoning behind this is that no one can claim that you do *not* feel unsure, uneasy or unhappy (or even excited, pleased or confident) and these feelings are either an encouraging sign or a potential barrier to agreement. An example could be: 'I am feeling a little unsure about this approach to our problem and would like to take some advice about it before proceeding.'

These approaches may seem familiar to you – what might be new is that they are being presented as powerful conversational tactics that can apply in many different circumstances. However, their use can make achieving positive results in a negotiation much easier and they can bring a lasting benefit in that opponents feel more comfortable about the persuasion and influence that have been applied.

Negative behaviours

If this all sounds like an idealized situation where negotiators are always on their best behaviour, the following list will provide behaviours that are best kept under control, since they tend to work against achieving an agreement:

- **Counter-proposals:** if haggling goes on for too long in a meeting, it can become tiresome. It can inject a feeling of competition into the meeting and is best avoided in serious business negotiations where the intention is to arrive at a win/win collaborative agreement.
- **Shutting out:** this is a very frustrating behaviour in which one person endeavours to talk over another with the aim of gaining their submission to the ideas or information presented. In the Western world this borders on bad manners and is therefore best avoided, since it may generate another barrier to reaching agreement. In other parts of the world it may be culturally acceptable but still should not be resorted to as a frequent tactic.
- **Disagreeing:** negotiations do often include disagreements but skilled negotiators are more likely to provide a reasoned statement rather than a plain 'I disagree with you there', which is unlikely to help move the discussion along. A good negotiator will also label the disagreement before it is stated, which encourages the listener to concentrate on the reasons behind the disagreement before reacting.
- **Blocking:** this tactic places an obstacle in the way of the discussion and is designed to prevent progress. A typical statement might be 'We could never agree with that!', with no reason provided, or 'That's not even as good as the

offers currently available from your competitors!' Frequent blocking creates frustration, and frustration can lead to a walkout.

- **Defence/attack:** when all else fails, negotiators have been known to attack their opponents verbally. This might provide a useful means of exhausting their frustration or anger but it is also likely to have unwanted consequences and may well lead to a loss of control on either side. Conflicts are best resolved through reasoned argument. Some people, however, believe that this will come about only after the conflict has been exhausted. An example of this is the peace talks that may follow bitter industrial disputes between management and trade unions.
- **Argument dilution:** this means presenting every single argument in support of your own proposal, only some of which are strong ones. When these have been listed, your opponent only has to wait for you to stop speaking and then they can reverse the process by destroying each argument in turn, from the weakest to the strongest. By the time the strongest argument has been reached you may not be quite so convinced as you were that you have a sound case. This is an example of where quantity is less powerful than quality when it comes to making your argument.

TIP

Remember that skilled negotiators work hard to avoid using these behaviours – even to the point of taking a low-key, placid role in the meeting: 'If I cannot find something positive to say, then I'd prefer not to say anything that might make matters worse.'

Of course, by their very nature meetings tend to feature a considerable amount of conversation, which may or may not have a distinct bearing on the case being discussed. Any meeting will be made easier if there is a little small talk before the parties get down to business. This should give some invaluable clues as to the prevailing mood of the parties present. From the perspective of the case under discussion, however, the small talk used in any meeting are most likely to have a neutral effect on the negotiation, unless one party is tempted to use a conversational red herring and introduce a topic that is really a distraction or a piece of misinformation. Once again, this form of gamesmanship can easily backfire and is best avoided.

Neutral behaviours

Not everything that is shared in the meeting will be readily categorized into having 'good' or 'bad' effects. Consider the following behaviours, some of which you may have witnessed in the course of negotiations:

- **Giving information:** it might be surprising that this behaviour is labelled as 'neutral'. It is defined as such because too much information can overcomplicate or cause confusion. You may have encountered someone whose excessive readiness to chat and share in-depth detail can be extremely wearing. As a consequence, the listener may become less willing to reach a ready agreement, unless it is out of desperation to close the meeting! If the presenter's style is also to bring an excess of obscure technical language to the discussion, the meeting may end up in a 'fog' from which it will become impossible to reach a clear agreement.
- **Talking:** it is highly possible to talk a lot and actually not say a great deal. Equally, if you are a 'low reactor' – or prefer not to talk very much – your opponent may struggle to know how to handle the meeting. They might:
  - babble, that is talk for the sake of filling the silence
  - make lots of proposals, each one better than the last
  - create a 'sob story', seeking your sympathy in order to agree a deal
  - reveal information that actually gives you reasons why you should *not* do business together.

If you have found yourself doing any of these things, then try instead to focus on listening. Using the open questions previously discussed will help you to become a better conversationalist and, hence, negotiator. When we are proposing to do business together, the resulting deal may be intended to be a long-term one; it would be far better to make sure that that relationship is based on shared facts and open information that will help to develop trust between the parties.

Strategy and team building

On our side

Negotiation is important in many everyday relations between people who are interdependent. This may be seen in families, between neighbours, and when we are engaged in everyday interactions such as shopping. These provide good opportunities for team building so that home-based discussions can serve as a model for negotiating agreements outside the home. It can be very difficult to reach agreement with a group of people when there are no constraints in place on the methods to be used (for example, one member may much prefer to attack when another much prefers logical argument), but the most important tool is to be prepared to compromise. Cynics claim that a compromise means that no one achieves what they really want, but a worse outcome would be to end up with no positive result whatsoever after hours of discussion.

Across the divide

Teamworking skills across the supplier/client divide are discussed rather less frequently; this might be because convention dictates that confidences need to be maintained, for example regarding vital elements such as operational costs and profit margins. Much damage to team relationships can result when employees are tempted to share more information with suppliers or customers than they should. It may be tempting to divulge information to opponents if you feel that you have developed a more personal relationship with them, especially if they seem to be more friendly than employees in your own organization.

Why team negotiation?

Some people think that a stronger case can be made by preparing a large team to support the main negotiator at crucial meetings. Certainly, a well-chosen team – who have been thoroughly briefed on their individual and team roles – can be a valuable source of influence in a meeting. However, the reverse is also true and an overly large team with little understanding of order and strategy may risk bringing the meeting to a chaotic end. Hand-picking the delegates needed for a team is important, but so too is ensuring that they are briefed in detail, including guidelines on desirable forms of behaviour to be practised.

Behaviour in negotiating teams

Ideally, a team should comprise no more than three or four people. Sometimes, however, circumstances dictate that it has to be larger, perhaps because of the expertise needed or the representational roles of those attending. The most powerful use of team members lies in casting them into specific roles, which might include:

- leader (and deputy)
- secretary/note-taker
- specialists, such as a finance specialist, a planning officer or an HR adviser
- observers of the opposing team.

For such a team, a plan is needed to manage intra-team communications, for example by passing notes during negotiating sessions (and during recesses if and when they are called). Authority for implementing all of this should rest with the team leader whose task is to consult team members, allocate roles, and orchestrate team presenters as seems appropriate during each session.

A team manifesto

It is easy to prepare such a list in the peace of a quiet office, but the value of an overall plan (albeit a flexible one) will be seen as it should guide discussion and action in the meeting itself. There is always the risk, of course, that if both sides prepare a fixed plan the first negotiation is likely to be about whose plan will be adopted! Leading a team includes ensuring that all members pull together and this may require a thorough briefing: a team manifesto is a good place to start.

Sample team manifesto

Here is our checklist of 12 key points: We aim to:

1 apply a give-and-take approach, that is, seek to exchange something for something

2 use the truth in our descriptions, avoiding claims when we know that they are in dispute or positively untrue

3 take care over arranging the meeting; if we are hosting, we should book a quiet room, ensure that there will be no interruptions, and make sure that visitors and hosts alike are comfortable

4 agree a strategy within our team, including rules regarding who talks and when (avoiding 'multi-speak' and shutting others out by talking over them)

5 agree how the team will be led and by whom – and actively defend that role

6 support the leader's control over the processes involved

7 try to be open-minded to new ideas, which may achieve our desired results but by a different route

8 listen courteously and always speak politely

9 be sensitive to time and timing and encourage the other side to believe that any agreement is their own free commitment, regardless of any power issues

> **10** provide the opportunity for intra-team confidential consultation in a secure place, as no intra-team disagreements should be voiced in the meeting
> **11** accept any deficiencies in performance, apologizing as necessary but stopping short of offering compensation unless this is part of a wider agreement to remove any threat of possible legal action
> **12** resist all temptation to engage in defence/attack spirals, unless the leader gives specific approval.

Rules of engagement

Leaders should also establish rules of engagement. These might include:

- No unplanned inputs are to be made (by anyone!) without the leader's request and approval.
- All discussion on strategy and progress is to take place in recesses which the leader will call if and when necessary.
- During negotiating sessions, communication within the team should be carried out by passing notes.
- The hosting team will ensure that both teams have access to a private and confidential side room to be used for preparation and recesses. (It goes without saying that these need to be secure or the credibility and trust of either party may be compromised.)

Recesses provide valuable opportunities to:

- consider what progress has been made to date against the original objectives
- revise objectives if necessary, especially taking account of proposals received from the other team
- reconsider planned concessions and how they might be exchanged to achieve movement from the opposing team
- regroup the team if necessary (for example, if anyone's attention is wandering)
- obtain feedback from team observers and specialists (particularly on the non-verbal signals being used in the

opposing team, such as eye contact, and also any hints about intra-team communication).

It should always be remembered that the larger the meeting, the greater the risk of discussions descending into chaos, through which all involved can lose credibility. This is an argument for keeping away from team negotiations wherever and whenever possible. The method is certainly not a panacea for all problems.

TIP

Given the potential for things to go wrong, all who are likely to be involved in a team negotiation should attend specialized practical training in order to avoid outcomes becoming chaotic. Especially to be avoided are insufficient listening and thinking before speaking. A lack of self-discipline can have a terminal effect on anything constructive being achieved.

Summary

Two main advantages can be gained from the systematic approach to negotiating meetings described in this chapter:

1 The framework helps ensure that the meeting is complete and that neither party feels it necessary to reopen the discussion days after the meeting because something was missed out.

2 Once the behaviour analysis method described becomes second nature, greater clarity and control over progress towards a mutually acceptable agreement will result.

These benefits will mean that any tension in meetings is reduced and mutual respect is enhanced. Further, the approach can be applied by everyone involved (especially in team negotiations) and thus emotional or unstructured behaviours – which can provide major distractions – reduced or eliminated.

Fact-check (answers at the back)

1. The PROD-ProSC framework is:
a) Only a guide and should not be used as a 'straitjacket' for each and every negotiation ❑
b) Useful for keeping the meeting on track ❑
c) Useful for new negotiators when considering their preparations ❑
d) A valuable planning aid, especially for high-profile or high-risk negotiations ❑

2. A major obstacle to reaching a new agreement is:
a) One of the participants behaving in a provocative manner ❑
b) Being late for the meeting or appointment ❑
c) Either side failing to agree on a suitable course of action ❑
d) Having outstanding issues or failures from earlier negotiations still on the table ❑

3. Oiling the wheels of a negotiation is best achieved by:
a) Ensuring that regular supplies of drinks and other refreshments are available ❑
b) Having an additional room available for confidential recesses ❑
c) Good manners... and maybe a little charm ❑
d) Clarity in communication – both written and verbal ❑

4. 'Neutral' behaviour in a negotiation is:
a) A criticism of the other side ❑
b) Behaviour that achieves very little in terms of progressing the negotiation ❑
c) A compliment ❑
d) A proposal ❑

5. Negotiating in a team requires:
a) Self-control and discipline, thereby minimizing the risk of 'multi-speak' ❑
b) A sense of mission and self-belief ❑
c) Defence/attack if and when necessary ❑
d) Maintaining loyalty to the team and its objectives ❑

6. Seeking advice in a negotiation should invite
a) An attack for wasting time ❑
b) A summary of progress to date ❑
c) The suggestion of a recess ❑
d) The offer of clarification from your opponents ❑

7. You can never provide too many summaries in a negotiation because:
a) Summaries help to clarify all that has been said or agreed so far ❑
b) They give everyone the opportunity to concentrate on what to say next ❑
c) They take the heat off the lead negotiator ❑
d) They help to use up the time ❑

8. A lot of counter-proposing is:
a) A sign of a win/lose culture between negotiators ❑
b) A risk that could lead to defence/attack cycles ❑
c) A hint that agreement will be impossible ❑
d) An indicator of a very competitive negotiator ❑

9. Giving multiple reasons for an argument or proposal:
a) Weakens the proposal as it gives opponents more grounds on which to attack ❑
b) Encourages critics to think that the team is over-eager ❑
c) Strengthens the case because of the increased number of supporting reasons provided ❑
d) Distracts the team from the key behaviours that are needed ❑

10. A team manifesto is designed to:
a) Bring team members together so that they are committed to their strategy ❑
b) Show opponents that the team means business ❑
c) Enable team members to work towards a common goal ❑
d) Avoid misunderstandings occurring in the negotiation meeting ❑

CHAPTER 11

Making proposals and trading concessions

For all the benefits gained from our earlier discussions, you will quickly recognize that productive negotiating will not happen unless the strategic preparation and self-presentation are matched by the ability to manage the potential cut-and-thrust of the actual conversation.

In this chapter we will learn how to make forward progress in the conversation – that is, how best to:

- use proposals
- deal with counter-proposals
- avoid stalemate
- maintain influence
- negotiate in teams and avoid common mistakes, especially when emotions are running high!

Proposals

There are two types of proposal: process proposals and content proposals. Recognizing and consciously using the different applications provides additional practice for both parties (i.e. in talking and listening).

Process proposals

At its simplest, the sentence 'Let's make a start' represents a proposal that begins the process of getting the task started. Even though this is presumably what the parties have come together to do, most of us would prefer to break the ice with some small talk, which has several purposes:

● to weigh up the opposition and find out more about their style and attitudes
● to give the participants a chance to relax, as they may be in a strange place
● to ensure a seamless process from previous correspondence and/or telephone contact, and thus avoid any possible misunderstandings from those starting points.

Content proposals

In a negotiation, the only type of behaviour that will make forward progress is a content proposal. Many negotiators are reluctant to make proposals too early in a meeting as they are worried about pitching too high or too low. If a written specification has already been submitted – together with a quotation – this has to be the best starting point and should be defended – otherwise, why was it submitted at this value in the first place?

From either side, there may be some factors that could help in simplifying the complications and costing of the assignment, which could in turn bring about some changes. Alternatively, it may be that the contractor has a timetable where a new contract could fit into a precise calendar period when there would otherwise be a downturn in work schedules.

Therefore, it is most likely that both sides will have included some wriggle room over the specification and this will provide scope for change in the proposal. This might be expressed in the form of enhanced supply (higher value at the quoted price, or a concessionary price at the same specification, or something at a lower specification).

So, the well-recognized formula 'If you can do *this* for us, then we could do *that* for you' can lead to a series of exchanges until the two sides feel that they are in balance and ready to close. This simplified approach should help to remove some of the mystique and pressure. We shall now explore some of the related skills involved.

Seeking movement: proposals revisited

As we have seen, many people have a dilemma: they don't want to demand the earth but equally don't want to be offered very little. The risk is that a proposal that is too low (or too generous) will be immediately accepted by the opposition who see a quick and cheap way of overcoming a small problem before it becomes widely known – and therefore more costly!

Success from enhanced concepts

Successful negotiations require some action by two people or organizations. For example, 'If you'll agree to take up the old flooring and dispose of it, then we'll agree to fit the new carpet for nothing' – in other words, action on one side is dependent on action on the other. An important improvement point would be to work on improving the balance of cost or value between concessions granted versus those gained. Are you over-generous with concessions granted, perhaps because of a fear that no agreement will be reached? If this is the case, what further research could you undertake to clarify current market values?

The pressure to agree

What are the consequences of a failure to agree? One party feels that the cost/benefit debated is not commensurate with the facilities, services or actions that are offered. It may also mean that both sides are unhappy, in which case the result could be an outright failure to agree. We would consider this situation to be a stalemate or, in simpler language, a lose/lose.

In reality, the loss might be minimal – perhaps only the investment of time – although, if one party had travelled on a plane to a different continent, then the loss would feel real and potentially very costly! Such time investment can also become a pressure point to force concessions to reach an agreement. In one case I know of, the supplier was in Cambodia and, quite unmercifully, used this remote location to put pressure on a visiting client to raise his offer or go home empty-handed. It worked, of course.

The only problem with this kind of strategy is that the client might never want to do business with that company again. However, if your company is confident that it has the best product, guaranteed to be available on time and in full, and clients are queuing up to purchase, then perhaps it is a chance worth taking. Are you faint-hearted when it comes to rejecting others' proposals? Would you like to say, 'Where did that idea come from? There's no way I could ever agree to that!', but are afraid that their response might be 'Goodbye, then!'? Could you practise expressing disagreement more positively without closing the door on discussions?

Draft a positive version – one that still gives you control of the outcome.

Trial proposals can help

In less pressurized climates, negotiators may not feel like making positive proposals too early, instead preferring to pause and tease out reactions to a possible proposal. In such a situation, trial proposals are a useful way to make progress without risking a win/lose outcome.

Try the following examples:

- 'I suppose we might be able to improve the offer... How could you help?'
- 'How about we cancel this account and start afresh?'

In each case there is a clear signal: here is an idea that might move things along and, if it is acceptable, we could make it part of our overall agreement. Clearly, like any proposal, this idea has the potential to be extended or improved.

The way in which a proposal is received usually signals whether further discussion is likely to be fruitful, totally rejected, or somewhere in between.

Counter-proposals

A distinguishing mark of highly competitive negotiators lies in their use of counter-proposals. A simple example would be where one negotiator proposes £10 as the preferred price in a contract and the opponent (with barely a pause) responds that £8 is better. So the bidding continues until agreement – or a sticking point – is reached.

Why is all this significant? Culturally, in Europe (especially the UK) the preference is for negotiators to use a collaborative style rather than a more aggressive, competitive style. This is borne out by extensive research and contrasts markedly with the convention in other parts of the world. For example, a more competitive style can be witnessed in the USA. However, it should be remembered that we are contrasting different cultural conventions, not just those of nationality. This means that a European who works for – or has been trained by – a US-based organization is more likely to favour, and use, the more explicit and sharper competitive style.

Counter-proposals tend to be much less used by collaborative negotiators than by competitive negotiators. In a typical one-hour meeting a collaborative negotiator is likely to use only one or two counter-proposals. Habitual competitive negotiators would find this figure very low.

This difference in negotiating styles extends even further: if the thrust and counter-thrust is not resolved quickly, then exchanges can migrate very quickly into defence/attack. Once that happens, everything has the potential to spiral out of control. All this may occur with little warning – especially if the subject matter for the negotiation is already emotive – and there may be a need to exhaust these emotions before serious bargaining can take place. It may be helpful to engage the services of a conciliator, whose contribution would be to clarify the issues before encouraging the adversaries to move towards each other. Clarification may also involve exposing the inner feelings that have built up through a frustrating period of proposing and counter-proposing.

Exposing inner feelings is a very powerful tactic even in a collaborative meeting; this is mainly because no one can disagree with the existence of another person's inner feelings.

Highly skilled negotiators are able to bring both competitive and collaborative negotiators to agreement by adjusting their style to meet the challenge.

Avoiding stalemate: be creative to avoid a lose/lose situation

When both sides have moved but are still not in a concluding position, we might describe this as a potential stalemate. Here are some alternative actions:

- Trade off movement on this deal with an allowance or concession made regarding another current deal between the same parties.
- Adjust the issues with a very small concession (after a token debate) that accepts the principle but at very low real cost.
- Try to change the timing of the deal, bringing implementation forward and/or improving small payment terms (fast payment in cash, for example, may 'win' an early settlement discount).

Making a large or generous concession is not always the best solution to winning a difficult argument.

Avoid at all costs the thought that a concession made now will be remembered by the other party in your next deal. In such cases, people usually have short memories. In any case, the parties involved may not even be in the same roles when the time comes for future negotiations.

A stalemate position (for example over a complaint or dispute) could lead to legal action. This could bring further consequences – for example:

- fast-growing legal fees
- uncertainty over whether the case will influence current and future business activity
- risk of negative publicity
- loss of business confidence in the organization
- possibility of public humiliation.

How personality can influence the status quo

An important element of persuasion and influence is personality, a factor that is easily overlooked when considering the strength or weakness of a case. It can also help to explain how some people seem able to achieve acceptable results from unpromising situations.

So how is *your* charisma? Do you have a warm, mostly happy, outlook on life and, in general discussions, are you positive, optimistic and charming? People who are naturally inclined to be this way start out with something of an advantage, especially if they are able to rise above the irritating factors that drag many people down.

It is sometimes argued that such elements are a matter of birth and heritage – and reinforced by our early upbringing. A warm extrovert will generally achieve much better overall results with other people than those who are pessimistic and depressive.

Can we change?

Yes, simply by becoming more people-centred and exercising more self-control. What is, perhaps, less fair is that above-average performers may also have been endowed with the gift of charisma; this special quality in their personality seems to lead everyone to want to agree with them and they are, generally, highly valued by their organizations.

Of all the basic personality factors that are essential to negotiators the following are the most relevant:

Authority and persistence

We all recognize that authority inside an organization has to be under some control: the Sales Representative is responsible to the Sales Manager and then to the appropriate functional Director; the Board of Directors is responsible to the Chairman, who is answerable to the shareholders.

A consequence of this structure is that we also know that our level in the hierarchy determines our freedom to exercise authority, to make commitments to delivery dates, to agree advantageous prices and so on. Without such controls, there could never be a coherent strategy inside the business. However, we also appreciate that, if there was no element of discretion present, senior managers and directors would never be able to manage, as they would be engaged in the very negotiations that are delegated to their professional staff.

High achievers in negotiation tend to be people who do not easily accept 'no' for an answer. They persist in seeking to change a 'no' into 'not just now', with the expectation that situations change and an agreement will come in time.

Task-centred or people-centred influence

Negotiators need to have sufficient technical knowledge of the case in hand or to be accompanied by an expert to enable discussion and the weight of argument to be understood and valued appropriately.

It is sometimes a matter of intense frustration among task negotiators that people-centred influence breaks down barriers and leads the way to agreement. In some of the most intractable disputes, the protagonists become so entrenched that the only way to reach agreement is by replacing the negotiators themselves.

In the search for a balanced team, another strategy would be for the negotiation to be undertaken by two participants: a technical person along with someone more people-centred. There may be additional costs involved in this, as well as the need for trust and 'technique experience' to be built up between the team members so that they do not find themselves in disagreement in front of their opponents.

Advance notice should always be given to opponents that there will be a team of negotiators rather than an individual, so that they do not feel this is a rather pressurizing tactic.

Open-minded or close-minded

One of the consequences of preparing a negotiating strategy is that the key players can become entrenched in their positions. If you suffer from this tendency, ask yourself how you could become more open-minded and what stands in the way. Is it one or more of the following factors?

- politics
- money
- attitudes
- prejudices
- emotions
- money
- greed.

The costs incurred could be totally out of proportion to the cost of resolving the problem and, even if blame might be shared, could a solution simply be an unconditional apology or concession?

Tactics

Some negotiators like to prepare a game plan, complete with a set of tactics whose aim is to manipulate their opponents into acceptance. Highly skilled negotiators avoid such approaches since manipulation implies a win/lose strategy that could easily rebound.

There are some basics that, if ignored, can easily generate a negative (or even destructive) atmosphere for meetings. It might be thought that there are some psychological advantages to 'home games', but these can work against you if things go wrong – for example, if distractions or interruptions put the home team at a disadvantage and give additional confidence to the visitors.

Similar results can occur if one team tries to plan a strategy based on a scripted response. (For example, 'When they say "price increase" we will not respond, but will merely nod and immediately walk out for a recess.'] This is a plan that could easily go wrong.

TIP *Straightforward, natural, businesslike behaviour is best – and much less likely to generate problems.*

Stalemate

Stalemate can often happen in a negotiation: the two sides fail to reach agreement, they retire (free to fight again) but the lack of a deal indicates a lose/lose outcome. A supplier fails to win the contract while the client fails to achieve the improved service or facility that had been sought. Of course, failure to agree could have serious results in another few months when the whole contract is up for renewal and the reluctant party discovers that the other side is now looking to change partners.

Such an outcome can be common for salespeople who, by the very nature of their roles, need to be optimistic. As a consequence, they may fail to qualify prospects thoroughly, leading to time and energy invested in a negotiation that later falls apart.

Team-building

Negotiating in teams (even of two people) requires full commitment to achieving a win/win result – before, during, and after the meeting. Any hint of weakness (even a non-verbal signal from one individual in a team meeting) may invite a negative reaction from the opposing team.

The leader must create team motivation by:

● briefing team members thoroughly, so that they are fully committed to the 'party line'
● taking care to listen to any objections or worries and addressing these sensitively
● casting the team so that even junior members have a positive role.

Behaviour in public should ideally be neutral. In session, however, it should be outwardly positive and always showing support of team leaders and their stance.

Negotiating in teams: casting

How large should a team be? The ideal size depends upon the nature of the project and the extent to which specialists might be needed in the team.

Roles that may be needed in a sizeable team include:

- **Leader**, responsible for:
  - opening the meeting
  - setting and promoting the agenda
  - managing and co-ordinating the team (directing who speaks and when)
  - orchestrating specialist input as necessary
  - summarizing (as and when necessary) and closing the meeting
- **Deputy leader**, responsible for:
  - supporting the leader, with notes and prompts if and when needed
  - monitoring the time, especially to help trigger recesses
  - standing in for the leader if necessary
- **Secretary/note-taker**, responsible for:
  - taking notes of the key points made by both parties (particularly important later when it comes to checking who said what and when)
  - ensuring that proposals and agreements accepted are not diluted or lost in later discussion
- **Specialist(s)**, responsible for:
  - supporting the team's case with technical inputs as and when required by the leader
- **Observer(s)**, responsible for:
  - studying selected members of the opposing team, in order to note facial expressions, body language and so on, for discussion in the team during formal recesses.

These team roles may be concentrated into fewer hands, especially if facilities and time resources are in short supply. The size of the team in more dramatic scenarios, such as a labour dispute or a legal dispute between a board of directors and a plaintiff team, could be rather larger.

A vital feature of team negotiations is that team members follow a prescribed code of behaviour:

● The team leader must be respected at all times.
● Team members must speak only when directed or invited to do so and with the leader's agreement.
● Each member must stick strictly to the team's agreed strategy.

Time – the limited resource

Remember that the more people there are involved in meetings the less likely it is that time will be used wisely. If each of the five roles mentioned above are mirrored in the other team and each person spends, say, three minutes asking a question and three minutes receiving a detailed reply, this would take over an hour and would probably see very little progress made.

Furthermore, if emotions are running high, the necessary disciplines of one person speaking at a time and everyone else listening can easily disappear, leading to 'multi-speak chaos' and nobody listening!

Should this occur the best response is to call a recess.

The recess

Calling a recess can be valuable for:

● consulting the team about current progress or suitability of offers
● checking progress against the team's agenda
● gaining feedback from observations of the opposing team
● checking on so-called facts quoted by the opposition
● restoring order in the team.

The timing of recesses can be critical – if they come too soon and are too frequent, it can make the leader look lacking in self-confidence; if they are infrequent (or non-existent), it can leave other team members feeling overlooked and undervalued.

Summary

Proposals and concessions lie at the heart of negotiations and the best results come from being able to balance objectives and concessions on both sides. Such exchanges can be interpreted as both 'wins' and 'concessions', depending upon the starting points, but the most important outcome is that the final agreement is accepted as a close match to the objectives prepared by either side. This can be described as a win/win result. Keeping a clear head is vital as any explicit excitement could lead to serious mistakes and exceptions, which may lead to further negotiation later.

Fact-check (answers at the back)

1. A process proposal is one that:
   a) Sets a value on the subject currently under discussion ❏
   b) The leading party can choose to make to start the meeting ❏
   c) Will be instantly adopted by both parties ❏
   d) Either party can make about the processes in the meeting ❏

2. In a complex negotiating situation that results in a stalemate, the most important quality for the negotiator to apply is:
   a) Persistence ❏
   b) A sense of humour ❏
   c) His/her power to impose an agreement ❏
   d) Patience ❏

3. A concession is:
   a) Something already built into a proposal at the quoted price or value ❏
   b) A special change to the proposal that represents a reduction in the quoted price ❏
   c) An allowance that has the appearance of increasing the cost of an item ❏
   d) A reduction imposed on both sides by an external authority ❏

4. A prepared game-plan runs the risk of chaos if it goes wrong. It is far better to aim to:
   a) Build up trust between the parties through a sense of humour ❏
   b) Reduce the tension by providing a regular supply of refreshments ❏
   c) Be better at gamesmanship ❏
   d) Project the image of being a trusted and experienced businessperson ❏

5. A counter-proposal is:
   a) A statement that differs from an opponent's proposal and follows on immediately from it ❏
   b) Any proposal that is stated in an apologetic way, seeking to avoid a major disagreement with your opponent ❏
   c) A contradictory statement that will lead into a defence/attack spiral ❏
   d) A way to express the inner feelings of either negotiator ❏

6. An above-average negotiator is someone who:
   a) Has persistence and a sense of humour ❏
   b) Is completely task-centred ❏
   c) Is authoritative, people-centred and open-minded ❏
   d) Has a grasp of winning tactics ❏

7. The number of participants in a negotiating team is best limited to:

a) A maximum of two on each side ❏

b) The leader and any specialists who may need to be present ❏

c) The leader plus four others ❏

d) Any number providing all present stick closely to a pre-agreed strategy ❏

8. It is important to avoid a stalemate position in a negotiation because:

a) It will reflect badly on the two negotiators involved ❏

b) Each negotiator will be accused of being inflexible ❏

c) Changing the negotiators would be the alternative ❏

d) A subsequent negative outcome could result in a serious loss of face ❏

9. The best way of enhancing negotiating skills is through:

a) Understanding the theories and practising them in a learning simulation ❏

b) Learning on the job ❏

c) Testing out the theories by talking to experienced negotiators ❏

d) Being committed to continuous improvement ❏

10. 'Let's aim to agree and sign the contract by 5 p.m.' is:

a) An enhanced concept ❏

b) A disagreement ❏

c) An improvement point ❏

d) A process proposal ❏

CHAPTER 12

Problem-solving through consulting and listening skills

General guidelines can easily overlook challenges posed by real human beings. To dismiss such difficulties as just the normal challenges created by people can mean failing to seek practical solutions. Individuals are usually at the heart of disputes and, if filled with the deep conviction that they are right, they can provide a real and powerful obstacle to organizational change and improvement.

The theme in this chapter is all about creating change through discussion and debate, which can be crucial when a negotiation is taking place to achieve measurable and lasting change.

We will cover techniques that are highly desirable – as well as those that, if used, may poison the atmosphere for years to come! The aim should always be to achieve a collaborative atmosphere, discarding those techniques that may deliver quick wins but also leave opponents seeking to fight back on another day.

It is very important that obstacles are not allowed to become hostages to fortune; careless or unpleasant treatment of individuals can generate ill-feeling and a lack of trust that can take a generation to overcome. This is especially true when a workforce has trade union representation, although this does at least provide a route for problems to be represented and debated. Where no such official route exists, complaints can create general resentment, demotivation and even an increase in labour turnover. This, however, is an argument for better, and timely, listening, not for giving in to every demand or request.

Often, the instigator of a dispute starts by being loud, demanding and even offensive because they believe that it is the only way to have their case heard. An uninterrupted hearing, accompanied by patience and a lack of defensiveness, will remove some of the sharp emotion; calm discussion can then lead to a realistic response to the problem.

A greater difficulty arises when human need confronts the organization's system. In such cases, making an exception can work only as a very last resort, because it is possible that everyone else in the organization will demand equal rights. Such difficulties will test the patience of most managers, especially those who have a strong commitment to maintaining output, production, sales and so on. So mediation may be needed in the search for creative solutions to intransigent problems.

Resolving problems through consulting and listening

While it might not be your official role to intercede or counsel colleagues, such opportunities obviously offer the chance to practise interpersonal skills that are also useful in negotiation sessions, especially when the negotiation turns out to revolve around problems relating to systems, failed service or interpersonal relations.

In Chapter 8 we described ten priority roles and invited you to use the self-rating scale. We shall now revisit the same tool with a view to identifying colleagues' or friends' profiles. It is always possible to try to emulate their preferred style, though you might find that this only reinforces their prejudices or attitudes, which may not be helpful in your negotiations in the future.

Go back now to the the series of tasks set in Chapter 8 but this time nominate the individual whose attitudes are typified by each particular topic. Write in their name and then, on the scale, circle your interpretation of their score. This exercise could equally apply to any other individuals whom you know well, perhaps within your family or circle of friends.

The purpose of this exercise is to increase sensitivity to each characteristic and consider how we might be able to influence opinions and ideas through the use of one of the other styles. The aim is to change attitudes and encourage the adoption of a more constructive view.

Seeking movement

Wherever and whenever we negotiate, the chances that we will collide with the attitudes and ideas of others are high – that is, after all, the basis of the need to negotiate in the first place. At its simplest level, it may be that tabled proposals are not acceptable to the other party (although sometimes the rejection is as much to do with the person who is promoting the idea). So, let us now consider some of the barriers to agreement, and explore alternative tactics that may produce constructive movement and ultimate agreement.

Removing listening barriers

Ask yourself the following questions:

- Am I communicating in commonly understood language?
- Could it have been 'corrupted' by double meanings or prejudice?
- Is the way I speak (for example, my choice of words and/or my voice) appealing, or is it provocative?

- Did I correctly identify the best selling points (features and benefits)?
- Was my communication punchy and persuasive, or was it wordy and confusing?
- Did I eradicate irritators (words, phrases and gestures)?
- Did my body language aid listeners' concentration, or did it distract them?
- Were there distractions such as external events and noise?
- Did I make change seem natural rather than competitive, irrational or threatening?
- Did we attract (influential) individuals on to our side?
- Did we spell out the (costly/dangerous/unacceptable) results of not adopting the proposed changes?

TIP *In real-life bargaining sessions, could you be unwittingly creating or reinforcing prejudices and objections simply by the way you talk to your people?*

Improving the atmosphere in bargaining sessions

The overall climate in our organization may be hindering change, and consideration may need to be given to some steps that could help to change that. The following is a checklist of questions to ask yourself that may uncover additional points for change:

- Are we meeting proposals sharply with counter-proposals rather than presenting them as new ideas?
- Are we labelling our disagreement (e.g. regularly stating 'I disagree with you there'), which serves only to underline conflict in our positions?
- Can we remove physical and human barriers (e.g. table blocks, ranking, perks that underline hierarchy and so on)?
- Have we fallen into the trap of defence/attack spirals (where one statement is immediately followed by a riposte

that puts forward the opposite, for example pay increase – pay cut)?

- Do we regularly use 'why' questions, which can suggest aggression? The softer question construction would be 'How did you come to that decision?', and not 'Why do you think that?'
- How are we able to demonstrate differences between fact and opinion? Facts may be unpleasant but they can be handled and managed without conflict; opinions vary and can be formed from opposite forces, providing raw fuel for conflict.
- Do we invite an attack on our proposals by diluting our own case through listing a number of weak arguments in the mistaken belief that more is best? This incurs the risk of our opponent climbing up the list, successfully attacking each one in turn, with the possible outcome being that the top (and best) argument is eclipsed and even destroyed once all the others have been easily rebutted.

Skilled negotiators regularly review their methods to focus on those that are most appropriate to the needs, people and outcomes achieved.

Creative solutions for problem situations

Managers have to manage change, and the success of this is likely to depend on the willingness and enthusiasm of those who have to implement it. For this reason, it is worth investing time in preparing and strengthening your case. Consider the following questions:

- Will the change help us through short-, medium- or long-term situations? If so, how?
- How can we separate the various interests involved in the change – for example clients, suppliers, operators, services and so on – and emphasize the benefits to each of them?

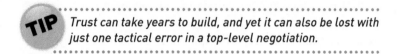

Behaviours to exploit

Here is a reminder of the key negotiating behaviours and techniques used by top negotiators:

Trial proposals

An example is: 'Suppose we were able to build into the agreement a condition that all management and staff will be guaranteed job security for six months after the takeover? Would that help to allay everyone's fears?' A positive response could then lead to a more formal or definite version which could be recorded in an 'If... then...' format.

Timing

Once again, timing can be crucial to success – offering too little, too late is one criticism often applied in industrial disputes. The worry is that any offer may be used as an excuse for the opposing team to increase their own demands even further, as the interpretation may be that 'as management feels obliged to make an offer, we can exploit their weak position by seeking even more benefits'. This is not a helpful response, of course, and could result in the earlier proposition being hastily withdrawn – especially if it threatens the very scheme, transaction or reputation that the organization has been developing.

Motivators of conflict

There is often a feeling that a good argument would be entertaining – a break from the everyday routine. What is not always understood is that, once out of the box, conflict can be both destructive and difficult to resolve and can lead to a game of brinkmanship. Let us examine the motivators of conflict more closely:

Levers

A lever can be used by either side in a dispute to obtain resolution of a long-standing problem (even if it is actually unrelated). To motivate an agreement on the larger stage, in a more important deal, a long-sought demand is conceded. Clearly, lack of progress on either front might not lead to a stoppage but could certainly be classed as a lose/lose position.

Defeat or humiliation

Sometimes a dispute arises simply because the issue involved has become the last straw. Perhaps concessions have already been made by both sides – almost as a gesture of goodwill – but now the aggrieved party feels obliged to fight simply because they feel boxed in, with little alternative but to give in yet again. This could be the ultimate humiliation.

Retaliation

This may seem the most childish motivator of all and is based on the tit-for-tat behaviour we all probably witnessed in our early years. Some adults still think in this way and, although they may not reach an all-out dispute, the consequences can be extremely irritating, such as a voluntary ban on overtime working or the strict application of safety procedures that have become more flexible in everyday operation.

Thin end of the wedge

This strategy may bring stronger resistance if one side feels that relatively minor demands or changes – if accepted – may result in much greater demands next time. This may sound typical of industrial relations but can just as easily apply to terms and conditions of a contract (such as minimum order quantities, pack sizes and so on).

Deterrent

The very risk of one party withdrawing support from another – and the consequential loss of a high-profile image or technical reputation – may cause the main contractor to take a flexible approach on such issues as visiting staff using the car park, the use of the director's box at the football club and so on. No one wants to upset this much-prized client or joint-project company. Such pressure points may be unspoken – but they are very real.

Guerrilla warfare

Again, this potentially destructive strategy is probably more suspected of taking place in today's world rather than actually doing so. However, it might occur when one party, such as a staff association or trade union, has such a strong hatred of the current system that they will sponsor almost any breach of the organization's system. The aim can be expressed as 'Everyone knows it's already broken – so let's get it fixed once and for all.' The management team will be very reluctant to change the system because they know that it will trigger a significant increase in costs. The situation could feel like a guerrilla war – enacted sporadically.

You may well recognize some, if not all, of the above examples, which can become major distractions from meaningful work and productivity. The main aim should be to avoid lose/lose outcomes by addressing the fundamental issues and negotiating them out.

Conflict – the result of competing objectives

From the viewpoint of positive influence, conflict is clearly a dilution of energy that would be better dedicated to the achievement of the ultimate objectives of the organization. However, problems do occur from time to time and there is a risk that, without professional support, matters can get worse and even end up in legal sanctions. Conflicts, without support or intervention, can follow a progressive sequence and cause very unfortunate results: initially anxiety, progressing to loss of self-esteem, then depression, a persecution complex, the loss of any sense of reality, and finally withdrawal and burnout.

Psychological games

We have seen how groups can, effectively, hold an organization hostage. This section covers a similar theme but is concerned with the one-on-one relationship between two individuals, for example a sales representative and a buyer. In each case, there is a potential misuse of power or discomfort, led by the person who thinks that the behaviour provides a motivator for the opponent to make additional concessions.

- **High seat/low seat:** you may recall this method being used in the school headmaster's study: 'I am in control here in my high seat. You have little or none, so you are in a low seat.' A rather obvious act of resistance to this tactic is to plead a bad back and reverse the tactic by standing up!
- **Irritators:** a well-respected retail buyer, renowned for his professionalism, impeccable hygiene and appearance, reviewed a new product range to be stocked in the supplier's prestigious showroom while sniffing loudly all the way round, a behaviour which would be recognized as impolite. Why did he do this? Maybe the irritator motivated the sales manager to help him make some rapid choices, with a generous trade discount, and then make a hasty exit?
- **Defence/attack:** these pair of behaviours can quickly descend into playground politics, with the same risk that the name-calling could get out of hand! What might start out as a fun distraction could end up in a defence/attack spiral that has all the intensity of an arm-wrestling match.
- **Blocking:** habitual blockers are very difficult to deal with; they engage in very little interaction and block discussion with just a few words: 'Can't do that!'; 'There's no point!' Discussion is thus at a dead end. The situation is all the more annoying if this is the only person you can deal with. The solution is to find a new contact and an irrefutable reason for a discussion.

- **Argument dilution:** the user of this behaviour openly lists all the reasons (both good and bad) to support a proposal, which allows the opponent to destroy all the weak arguments and begin to weaken even the stronger ones. This is not a recommended strategy for either player.
- **Unrealistic timescales:** *Buyer:* 'I'd agree to this proposal if you could get the delivery here tomorrow!' *Seller:* 'I can't promise that – our deliveries aren't due to arrive until next month!' *Buyer:* 'Well, that's out then!'
- **Shut-outs:** a shut-out is similar to 'blocking'; the strategy is designed to close down discussion and probably bring the meeting to an end. It is very difficult to react positively to this behaviour except by approaching someone else in the organization. The speaker is almost saying 'See my boss'. If you do, you may not make any better progress, but it is worth trying.

Continuous improvement

A major gain from practical negotiation training programmes is that debate and argument can be tested in a simulation. The strength of a case can be tested through a role-playing exercise, and with professional facilitation and support, as well as with the addition of video-recording, tactical debating skills can be polished.

A key advantage of this form of development is that teamwork can be orchestrated constructively and the ways in which proposals are made can be reviewed for their credibility and potential for improvement. The final learning power lies in being able to obtain honest feedback from opposing teams – and to be able to compare results against the plans made.

This is not rocket science: most top negotiators have benefited from this kind of experience before taking on top management assignments that involve takeovers, mergers and acquisitions as well as major contracting, purchasing or marketing projects.

Summary

In this chapter we have reviewed one of the most difficult aspects of negotiation, which luckily occurs only infrequently. The main aim of all high-profile negotiators is a trouble-free negotiation that leads to profitable repeat business on that contract on a continuous basis. Those who find themselves having to keep renegotiating existing agreements may well be doing something wrong.

Normally, negotiators should be encouraged to follow these sequential steps:

1 observation
2 analysis and diagnosis
3 test negotiation
4 analysis of problem/opportunity
5 application
6 results
7 review.

Following these should ensure that negotiators learn from their negotiating experience – and avoid repeating any behavioural mistakes.

Fact-check (answers at the back)

1. Problems in organizations are a natural consequence of bringing together a rich mix of people. Managers need to:
   a) Confront the causes of problems and any mischievous or disruptive people ❑
   b) Consult any representative body for accurate information ❑
   c) Provide a briefing session for line managers ❑
   d) Listen for feedback from trusted spokespersons ❑

2. Individuals' preferred roles lead to ways in which listening and consulting could:
   a) Help persuade them to be more adaptable to new situations ❑
   b) Provide challenges to their usual way of thinking ❑
   c) Help them analyse and promote new ways of handling problems ❑
   d) Resolve difficulties and regain control ❑

3. Interpersonal skills that are valuable in negotiation situations are:
   a) Listening to the case that is presented ❑
   b) Analysing the case ❑
   c) Absorbing the emotions that have been used ❑
   d) All of the above ❑

4. An extrovert will respond best to a:
   a) Good listener ❑
   b) Controller ❑
   c) Politician ❑
   d) Completer/Finisher ❑

5. The mix that is most likely to result in a noisy disagreement is:
   a) Expert/Teacher and Pessimist ❑
   b) Safety First and Completer/ Finisher ❑
   c) Opportunist and Controller ❑
   d) Naive and Politician ❑

6. An example of a listening barrier is a:
   a) Foreign language ❑
   b) Corrupted meaning ❑
   c) Defence/attack expression ❑
   d) Counter-proposal ❑

7. Obtaining a constructive hearing is enabled by:
   a) Making change seem natural and easy ❑
   b) Not being prepared to discuss the objections ❑
   c) Holding the discussion when there are many distractions ❑
   d) Using known irritators ❑

8. Psychological games in negotiation:
a) Provide valuable additional pressure to achieve acceptance of your proposals ❑
b) Include a risk that the games could backfire on the negotiator ❑
c) Are a poor persuasion method that risks total rejection of the case and the opponent ❑
d) Can involve permissible put-downs of the opponent's case ❑

9. Top negotiators work towards:
a) Building up their personal reputation as sharp negotiators ❑
b) Beating opponents by destroying their case ❑
c) Winning every case and building up a personal 100-per-cent track record of implementation ❑
d) Coping with the renegotiation of existing agreements when demanded by opponents ❑

10. Skilled negotiators build up their reputation as trusted operators by
a) Resisting the temptation of building an extreme personal reputation as a 'guru' ❑
b) Concentrating efforts on building a track record of continuing success ❑
c) Avoiding having to reopen cases once they have been agreed and settled ❑
d) Ensuring that they are never caught out as a two-faced negotiator ❑

What if? – closing skills

Most negotiators experience self-doubt at some time, which can lead to two possible consequences:

1 a slow-down in the pace of the discussion (almost expressing a reluctance to close the agreement in case the deal is deficient in some way)
2 a complete disengagement through a fear of some hidden trap that would lose all benefits from an agreement.

These anxieties are entirely normal, and now we will examine approaches that should help bring closure:

● The power of personality
● How to handle remaining differences
● Using probing skills, for example 'What if...?'
● Managing negative behaviours at the close
● Using creative solutions to bring about a successful close
● Avoiding common tricks.

Now we have moved to the critical end game. Closing the deal should entail arriving at a logical result, a predictable outcome. You may have a sense of anticipation, and perhaps even excitement, but it is best to keep these emotions out of your mind as over-confidence may generate client concern and worry that a legal contract might involve something of a 'catch'. If you find closing off a negotiation difficult or embarrassing, ask yourself:

- What if I am unable to close this deal? What might happen?
- Who else might be involved (for example, a competitor)?
- What if I had allowed more/less time and/or given more/fewer concessions?

If you are asking yourself these questions now, be aware that these factors should have been discovered much earlier in the relationship by simply asking a question such as 'Who else might be in the frame for this contract? ... We appreciate that our clients have a choice about who they may choose as their suppliers – it would be very interesting to know who else they might be talking to about this project.'

Power of personality

Your personality should be your best tool in helping close the meeting successfully. How you present yourself is an important expression of your personality and can provide a signal of what to expect in conversation. The way in which we greet other people is important: our manners are on show and this is especially important if the meeting involves cross-cultural issues. Cultural sensitivities may be vital, so some specialist advice might be required.

Tact and courtesy are essential, especially in any 'warm-up' conversation. Your opponents – like you – may appear to be entirely relaxed and self-controlled, but changes occur as the deal is finally constructed and agreed. Smiles all round are normal, but pressure might have created nervous tension. This is a good opportunity to relax over a cup of coffee or a drink. Once relaxed, your opponents may tell you what those tensions were about and you can address them.

Be prepared to handle some potentially tricky issues – especially if your organization has an 'awkward' track record.

Avoiding failure and embarrassment

All closing methods are perfectly workable, but some professionals still do not use them. Why? Because of a simple fear of rejection. If you are unsure if the deal is heading towards a green light, then be prepared to keep talking, but be careful that you don't talk yourself out of a deal altogether.

If you are sure that the deal is good, ask the closing question: 'So, are we ready to close and sign off this agreement?' One 'yes!' and the deal is done. Be careful, however, that the question does not sound either too relaxed, too assertive or, worst of all, wheedling or scared. Your timing is vital – premature closure could still lose you the deal.

Remaining differences

At this stage, your opponents may still not be explicitly declaring complete support for this deal – which can be quite unnerving – and your own conversational style could create more difficulties. For example, a high reactor may be tempted into a lengthy dose of cross-check questioning:

Question	Response
How do you feel about all this?	OK! (*Not much of an answer!*)
It must feel good to have it almost over?	I suppose so. (*Still a minimal response!*)
Now is the time to say if you have any concerns!	Well, there's not much to say. (*Still little response!*)

(Continued)

Question	Response
So, do you think this is a fair result? I know that *we* are happy.	Of course you are; you've got everything you wanted, I'm sure! Now we see how your business makes so much profit in a recession. I doubt we'll ever be back for another deal like this — or any other, come to that!

Such an attack might seem to be over-aggressive – especially after the minimal involvement of the person during the earlier discussion. If the leader of the meeting is really a very democratic person who strongly believes in the win/win style, the outburst could feel like a sudden shower of icy water. It could also lead to the person inviting the opponent to state their preferred outcome (which could then bring about a very different result).

Question	Response
Is this really likely to happen?	Yes, it could!
Would a win/win outcome be better?	Definitely!

The question that the example raises is whether the approach illustrated is genuine or whether the speaker saw the opportunity to lead the discussion into a win/lose situation, with the tactical aim of coming out on top right at the finishing line.

Probing skills: Who? What? How? When? Where? Why?

Top negotiators find probing skills very valuable. This umbrella term describes the use of a series of open questions. The six question words themselves are non-threatening and generally bring detailed responses from low reactors, which is very helpful in describing needs and wants.

TIP *The 'why?' question is rather more assertive (and can even border on the aggressive), and may need to be rephrased if a collaborative atmosphere is valued.*

If there are still some outstanding issues, the following summary should help:

1 Isolate the issues by asking the other party to summarize them – and listen carefully!
2 Check this list against your own understanding of the objectives, any notes taken, and any concessions agreed from earlier conversations.
3 Work through the items, checking first that there is no misunderstanding that needs addressing.
4 Once this is done, the scale of any difference between the two sides will be clear and a final gesture may be all that is needed to close (it would be best if this can still be phrased as a conditional offer, i.e. 'If... then...').

If a minor concession at the close of the deal maintains a valuable long-term relationship, then it will have been a worthwhile gesture.

Negative behaviours at the close

Top negotiators try to avoid negative thinking and behaviour (both in preparation and in final meetings). This does not mean that they seek to make forward progress regardless of the weight of opinion, preferring to offer a plan B and try to keep options open. When a goal – and a route – have been chosen, positive energy should arise and fast progress will make plans a reality. Any doubts expressed by the manager, colleagues and even team members may be heard but now rejected as 'negative thinking'. When approaching closing sequences, negotiators need to be alert to any hint of negative signals, which may reinforce the need for caution.

Here is a reminder of those influences:

● **Argument dilution:** the tendency to give multiple reasons for an action when only the best may be needed to make the point. Mixing weak arguments encourages opponents to attack the weakest ones and, by inference, arranging all the negative points suggests that it might be better to wait until a better option comes along ('Maybe my critics were right' is the winning thought). In short, the energy has gone out of the positive argument and the deal may be lost.

- **Defence/attack:** extraordinary though it might seem, there are some negotiators who, even at the threshold of a new agreement, cannot resist the opportunity to attack a past behaviour of the other side. This might be related to a complaint, a failed initiative, or having been let down by a team member. Such approaches run the risk of diluting enthusiasm for the current deal and can be seen as a form of 'one-upmanship'.

- **Blocking:** close to agreement an opponent may still seem to block further progress in the debate. This may be a conversational habit that they are unaware of. Either way, comments such as 'It won't work', 'It's not worth it', or 'We'll probably be back round the table in a few months still trying to fix it' may be partly said in jest but, again, can dilute vital energy for the intended deal and are therefore best avoided.

- **Shutting out:** this is impolite behaviour involving one person talking over another before they have completed a sentence or idea. This might be because they find their delivery slow, predictable or weak. Try to be more disciplined and let the other party finish before speaking. If you fear that a long-winded partner will cause you to forget the point you wanted to make, write a brief note so that you can pick up your thread when the moment comes. (Being lectured at for 30 minutes is a sure-fire way of creating a determination not to close the deal today.)

- **Irritators:** at a lower scale, irritators can also create negative reactions and, in combination with any of the items above, can contribute to failure.

- **Exaggeration:** it is probably inevitable that those who are most in favour of a deal feel the need to impress their opponent with their experience, importance (to their own organization), past deals set up and negotiated, high-profile people they have met, and glamorous places they have been. Such behaviour is likely to be viewed as boastful and, again, can be very wearing. On its own, however, it might not be a reason for ditching a deal, unless some of the boasting is known to be totally untrue.

Creative solutions to difficult problems

Whatever the tension, try to relax and focus on the professional need to close this deal with all the *i*s dotted and *t*s crossed, and remember that not all negotiations are fresh, positive and potentially profitable. Some have to deal with less pleasant topics, such as complaints, failures or upsets, and so there may be a very stark choice: reach some kind of agreement that is acceptable to both sides or go to law!

Resolving disputes using a third party can be far better – and considerably less expensive – provided that both sides are prepared to invest effort in reaching a compromise. An unhealthy determination to win and 'punish' the other side might prove counter-productive.

Top negotiators can find themselves in weak positions when a negative news story concerning their company breaks right in the middle of a vital negotiation. After the fuss has died down, the fact is that both sides still have needs that must be satisfied and one can argue that no organization is likely to be right in all that it does 100 per cent of the time.

Closing – the natural resolution

We have explored the effect of irritators and how they can wind opponents up, sometimes unconsciously. When it comes to closing, there is a possibility that an opponent might deliberately create pressure to soften up the opponent with the objective of prising more concessions from them. There is obviously the danger that such behaviour could lead the negotiator into the decision to break off all relations – that is, the result is lose/lose.

Many negotiators concentrate on just one or two easily identifiable closing approaches. Although many sales and marketing professionals are taught eight different ways in which to close a deal, most focus on just the one or two ways that they are most comfortable with.

Meetings can stall because of the following:

- things becoming too long-winded
- resistance created from a mistimed attempt to close, which leads to more objections or queries indicating that the other party is feeling less confident that this deal is right for them
- a time-out has occurred and one party has to leave the meeting.

However, good conversationalists can quickly disperse discomfort or embarrassment and, more often than not, still reach a positive result. Top negotiators are able to gain an insight into how close they might be to the finishing line by asking the question: 'How are you feeling about the progress we have made so far?'

The best approaches

Part 1 of this book provided detailed advice on five methods of closing a deal:

1 Close any gaps.
2 Time and timing: this needs sensitivity. Too long is boring; too short can feel pushy and may be thought to be offensive.
3 Either/or choice: a softer option ('no deal' is not on offer).
4 Last concession: a riskier approach – who says it is the last concession?
5 Recess: time to think it over may be helpful. If you offer this, stay close by so that you can handle other queries and watch that your opponent doesn't gradually lose momentum and interest.

Now we focus instead on simplicity in closing. However, there remains one vital element that must apply in all circumstances: both sides must fully understand and be committed to the detailed deal before parting. This is where trouble can arise: there may be a demand or promise made that actually lies outside the negotiator's authority to trade. The professional way of handling this would be to call a recess, check it out and then conclude.

 It is vital that these additional processes do not siphon off all the good energy and enthusiasm that has brought the parties to the point of agreement.

But what if the vital authority is unavailable to confirm and authorize the issue? You might have to agree here and now on the condition that approval is confirmed in writing after the meeting. In other words, a Memorandum of Understanding must be prepared and acknowledged rather than a full contractual agreement. The disadvantage of this kind of process is that, once the negotiators have parted, the door is open for another round of potential negotiation to be undertaken by the specialists, who may have to handle non-implementation matters in the case of a dispute.

Take care with some common tricks

Closing is the ultimate indicator of commitment and it provides a real test of everyone's integrity. Unfortunately, there are those who may see this step as an opportunity to use fast-talking tactics, leading to confusion and acceptance where rejection would have been a more conservative decision. Here are five of the more common sharp tactics that should be avoided:

1 **The mis-summary:** here, the 'pushy' party deliberately gives a verbal summary that is accepted and turns out to have better terms than given in the formal written contract that the other party will sign. Always check the paperwork thoroughly and reject it if it does not say what you have agreed.
2 **Bullying/blocking/shutting out:** these are not good behaviours but are sometimes used by desperate people.

No matter how attractive the offer is, if you are uncomfortable with these tactics, refuse the deal. This is where having an alternative potential supplier, customer and so on gives you hidden power.

3 **Promoting false deadlines:** as a means of pushing the deal through, the opponent might link bad news about an extended delivery or implementation time to a promotional price (this might be 'special' but how could you check it?).

4 **Misuse of recesses:** what is the purpose of a recess? We would expect that the recess gives both parties the opportunity to make a final check: 'Shall we go ahead, or can anyone think of a reason why going ahead might lead to trouble?' Additional pressure can be put on a nervous opponent by seeming to be a reluctant client or supplier, and calling an additional recess may be an indicator of more uncertainty or reluctance. The response of some anxious opponents might be to make yet another concession in order to clinch the deal.

5 **Building trust with success stories from other businesses or industries:** sharing successful project experiences as a means of promoting the next deal is a common approach used by negotiators. However, such self-promotion should probably be listened to politely but with some scepticism.

Who is the best survivor now?

After all this effort, which negotiator profile is most likely to be successful at the close of the negotiation? In Chapter 8 you read descriptions of ten types of role. Before completing the study, re-examine the ten profiles in that chapter and answer the following question: Who is likely to be the best at applying the advice given in this book?

In the next chapter we will revisit this with a view to setting out some further developments from the overall process. Before you complete the Part, think about which of the ten profiles are most likely to achieve a win/win outcome and which are more likely to end a negotiation in stalemate.

Summary

It is often said that the devil is in the detail, which may mean that a negotiated settlement is useful only if it can actually be implemented. We have seen how important it is that both parties are committed to a clear action plan for implementing the agreement, which may be summarized as 'Who is going to do what, to whom? And at what cost?'

Any misunderstandings at this stage may cause entire issues to have to be reopened at yet another negotiation, or – in the worst-case scenario – a complete breakdown in relations, which in turn can lead to the involvement of intermediaries or conciliators, and perhaps even the additional expense of lawyers.

The underlying aim of this Part is to create unanimity and business growth through strong partnering and the enhancement of trust through mutually supportive behaviours. Any action or thinking that endangers progress towards that end should be carefully avoided.

Fact-check (answers at the back)

1. Closing techniques provide:
   a) A way of checking to see whether the other party is really interested in the deal in hand ❑
   b) A way of helping to narrow down the options on offer ❑
   c) A fast track to finalizing the deal ❑
   d) The opportunity to obtain feedback from the other party ❑

2. How we present ourselves is an important element in:
   a) Impressing the other party ❑
   b) Personal projection ❑
   c) Impressing the boss ❑
   d) Creating an influential presence for all at the meeting ❑

3. The best emotion to experience as the closing phase of a negotiation is reached is:
   a) Excitement ❑
   b) Caution ❑
   c) Regret ❑
   d) Embarrassment ❑

4. Talking your way through the closing phase of the negotiation could vary because of:
   a) Your opponent's reactor profile ❑
   b) The level of comfort there has been during the meeting ❑
   c) How relaxed and thoughtful your partner feels ❑
   d) Your opponent's reaction on closure ❑

5. Taking into account any cultural sensitivities in your meeting means:
   a) Using non-discriminatory language in the meeting ❑
   b) Offering any refreshments as normal ❑
   c) Using greetings and farewells to all those present as normal ❑
   d) Expecting formal dress from all for a formal meeting ❑

6. Closure means that:
   a) You and your opponents have agreed on 90 per cent of the negotiated deal so that it can be implemented ❑
   b) All parties intend to sign up to the deal as an outcome to the meeting ❑
   c) Thinking space should be claimed before further progress ❑
   d) There would be value in having a final recess before signing up to the deal ❑

7. In a negotiation about payment terms for a supply of services, the consideration of choice of currency for use in payment could be recognized as an outstanding issue and should be:

a) Summarized as an item to be discussed in a special meeting agenda ❏

b) Checked carefully against your original tender document and any misunderstanding clarified ❏

c) Re-summarized by your opponent and compared with your original proposal ❏

d) Identified as a stumbling block that is best overcome by making a concession ❏

8. As the time for closure approaches, stumbling blocks may create a rise in the 'temperature' of the meeting. This could cause intemperate behaviour such as:

a) Making more proposals ❏
b) Summarizing ❏
c) Shutting out the speech of the opposition ❏
d) Reiterating objections to the meeting ❏

9. The vital element that brings a greater chance of reaching that final agreement from the meeting is:

a) Clarifying the gaps ❏
b) Inching towards each other by making minor concessions ❏
c) Trying out new ways to achieve agreement ❏
d) Threatening to pull out if agreement cannot be reached within an imposed deadline ❏

10. A final concession may be:
a) A costly way of luring opponents to agreement ❏
b) An irritation, as the term was not available earlier ❏
c) A new baseline from which the next round of negotiating will start ❏
d) A helpful initiative – but only if emphasized as being available only on this deal and only today! ❏

CHAPTER 14

Celebrating the successful outcome

Together, we have analysed how to improve our results in a field that never fails to intrigue regular negotiators. This is mainly because it is negotiators who link businesses together and contribute in a major way to bottom-line results. This process came to a pinnacle in the last chapter as we closed the deal, so what is left?

This chapter carries an important message for everyone who enjoys the thrill of deal-making – namely, setting up the most difficult challenge of all: celebrating the new agreement and then ensuring that its implementation is carried through in a thoughtful, professional manner.

You will be focusing on:

- the pitfalls that can open up in concluding and implementing the deal
- constraints that can hinder that implementation
- how to support the relationship with supportive monitoring
- maintaining high aspirations while developing partnering skills
- focusing on those behavioural skills that help to create and maintain long-lasting business relationships.

Conclude and implement the deal

Now we should have closed our current deal – with all that that meant: excitement, perhaps concern, relief and, deep down, great satisfaction. However, an 'agreement in principle' might have been made with the final pressure of some vital details left over to the eleventh hour. Pressure of this kind (against, say, a press conference deadline) could lead to a demand for extra concessions that could change the value of the deal considerably. For all the earlier effort in striking a bargain, negotiators might still find themselves having to split the difference to avoid threats of a walkout.

Your priorities will no doubt have moved on to the next deal. However, the current project will not be successfully completed until the last phase has been carried out in accordance with the specification – and payment has been cleared. It is this stage that will determine the full success of the project.

It can be very difficult for new suppliers to win significant government contracts without a track record. In one case, a supplier offered a very attractive price for innovative software development for a small industry training centre. This puzzled the client, who questioned whether the project could be delivered at the price quoted. However, the contract was delivered successfully and, unbeknown to the first client, the supplier then clinched a much more lucrative contract with a UK government ministry on the strength of that success. The industry training centre had been a 'door-opener'.

A deal is a deal except...

Negotiation meetings are important – they provide opportunities for the parties to test out their arguments, look for common ground, and reach agreement with all the factors needed for the deal to be complete. But this presumes that the deal is enforceable – a factor that may be beyond the negotiator's capacity to assess. Lawyers are highly skilled at exploring such issues, especially ensuring that, in the case of some subsequent dispute, there is an agreement on the chosen jurisdiction of law that will apply.

In commercial agreements involving goods or services, there will normally be a clear statement which defines comprehensive terms and conditions (T&Cs) of the purchase or sale. These are important because, in the case of a dispute, a vital test could be applied to the issue of whose conditions turn out to be superior – and therefore will apply to the agreement.

Returning to practical issues, supposing a verbal agreement has been struck: what if your opponent contacts you to say that something vital has been missed out of the agreement and the case needs to be reopened? Could this be an attempt to try to obtain a better position for them rather than you? Or could it be an opportunity to avoid major embarrassment with a deal that, in truth, is deficient in some way? What action should you take?

In principle, the deal was presumably agreed without any pressure. If so, you might feel that this situation of 'one more discussion' is likely to lead to another and another until your opponent achieves a major improvement in the outcome of the agreement. If there is any evidence of this happening, a meeting could be politely refused. On the other hand, an outright refusal to hear the case – or, at least, to understand what is being queried – might seem high-handed. Any subsequent problem could easily have negative repercussions. A careful telephone conversation, in which the 'plaintiff' presents the case, should enable the right decision to be made. If a win/win deal is your ultimate aim, clearly any mistake could poison that collaborative atmosphere.

The situation might be very different if contracts have been signed and exchanged. The legal department would probably need to get involved, and clearly your own credibility will be at stake for not spotting an error before the contract was signed.

Celebrate your success

Most of the work we have discussed has assumed that a final agreement or contract will be the final goal. Such a document can be quite complex and, although there will be working papers used to support discussions, it is best practice for the final agreement to be fully detailed – in print – and with all the supporting documents.

TIP *It is essential that the contract matches the verbal agreement – and it must be rigorously checked to ensure that this is the case.*

This is where the documented notes from negotiating meetings are essential. They must reflect the discussions that have occurred and, if they don't, another round of negotiations will certainly be needed.

When a sizeable contract has been agreed, there is sometimes a strong desire among the public-relations community to publicize the good news to the world in general (with a public figure present) – and the markets in particular. This is a natural corollary to all the effort invested in agreeing the contract but it can also create a further 'obstacle course'.

Such an occasion could also cause the client to become a hostage to fortune, as further concessions may be demanded at the eleventh hour before signature is possible. With the clock ticking, and no one wishing to look incompetent in front of the honoured guest and the national or international press, this could provide an opportunistic negotiator with the chance to gain yet more concessions, even after everyone has agreed the final deal.

Monitor progress of implementation

The complex long-term contract you have spent so much time agreeing could marry your and the other party's interests together for some years ahead, so it is important that the agreement includes details on how the progress of implementation will be monitored. This might be achieved by written reports, audits, visits and/or third-party involvement. The commissioning company will almost certainly be expecting to see visible evidence of progress – and such monitoring will most usually be linked to stage payments. More importantly, if visits and reports indicate that progress is slow – or off-course – then corrective action is going to be needed and this must also be negotiated. The implication of this is that it needs to be carried out without conflict or personal unpleasantness. However, it would be worse to allow the deviation to continue only to have to account for an accumulated problem much later on.

It is to be hoped that the contract itself will include provision for the management of any eventual stage failures and how payment will be affected. Failure to include such information in the contract would probably result in another round of negotiation and possibly legal action if agreement could not be reached. This thought concentrates the mind when the parties are concerned with maintaining the original win/win atmosphere that existed when the contract was signed. Now there may be a risk of relations subsiding into blame and counter-blame.

Develop your partnering opportunities and skills

A productive approach for all aspirational negotiators lies in adopting the partnering stance, thereby seeking to grow the business on either side (supplier and client). The rewards will be significant – to both parties. In some instances, this could be a medium- or long-term development of technology that could lead to not inconsiderable wealth. Or it might help ensure that both parties stay in business.

Who is the real client in such a situation? As a supplier, the normal contact person will be the day-to-day client but above this person there will be corporate representatives with whom a supplier may also have infrequent contact. Their loyalty may still, however, be tested in that forum. The temptation to provide uncontrolled (or even critical) feedback needs to be avoided. Trust is everything!

Equally, offering constructive support and suggestions are likely to be increasingly welcomed – especially if these ideas are recycled from current experiences with partners elsewhere. Ultimately, the decision about implementation has to lie with the partner.

An obvious activity where these relationships can become significant occurs when a merger or acquisition is taking place, but such periods can also throw up accusations of partisan and illegal behaviour if the partner's involvement brings intense positive or negative financial effects.

Another partnering opportunity arises when advisers and specialists work together in a consortium (e.g. in an export market); again, care needs to be taken to negotiate the needs of one's own organization with those of other members of the consortium.

Maintain high aspirations

The quality of output is often largely dependent on the personal standards of the individuals involved. These standards have probably been adopted as a result of a wide range of experiences – both good and less successful. It is also a matter of cause and effect – sloppy work can result in poor outcomes.

What is surprising is that so many projects suffer indifferent results, and these must have been foreseen by at least some of those involved, if not the most senior negotiators responsible for setting up the arrangements.

To exploit high aspirations, some organizations benefit from an open management and communication culture so that everyone involved in a project is free to raise critical issues internally if and when the actual performance looks as though it will fall short of the contracted level.

This requires great patience and the ability to provide a listening ear, even for people who might seem unlikeable. Good listening is a rarely taught skill that can be improved. Actually, unlikeable people pose a particular challenge but they can prove remarkably informative if they are approached sensitively.

It is not just sales representatives and buyers who find themselves chasing higher targets year on year; this is a feature of all businesses. So a mark of all negotiators needs to be an understanding of how they can help clients and contacts with the search for continued growth and development. The quid pro quo lies with the return on the investment of time and advice, manifested in increased sales, higher proportional stocks and so on. The point is that business relationships do not stand still – they are subject to the ebb and flow of politics and economics as well as personal credibility. Top negotiators appreciate this. However, it is important that true partners demonstrate continuing care long after a top result on a particular project is achieved.

Monitor and develop your business lifestyle

At the start we introduced the profiling concept and here is an opportunity to revisit those styles. Which did you recognize in yourself? Hopefully, more of your styles belonged to Class A than to Class B.

Class A	Class B
Role 1: Safety First	Role 6: Escapologist
Role 2: Completer/Finisher	Role 7: Politician
Role 3: Expert/Teacher	Role 8: Extrovert
Role 4: Controller	Role 9: Pessimist
Role 5: Opportunist	Role 10: Naive

Plan your future 1

How might you start to change your habitual style? First, we need to identify it – and this may require the support of a colleague or manager who can observe a typical meeting and provide some objective feedback. Evidence that points towards any of the Class B categories may need to be addressed; this could benefit from the support of coaching. Another valuable method would be working through a role-play exercise – preferably with the addition of video recording, which will enable further self-analysis.

It should also be remembered that any improvements in style and technique will be noticed by regular opponents, especially if they have benefited from the less effective influencing styles adopted in the past. However, there is an obvious advantage to both participants if negotiations are more effective – and when win/win results occur more naturally.

If you have enjoyed being a fixer of problems that ought to have been predicted from past negotiations, then you are probably leaning towards becoming an Escapologist. You should ask yourself the following questions:

- Do I prefer this way of life? If so, maybe I should be doing something more suited to my limitations.
- Does sorting out crises make me feel good? If they should never have occurred – or you find that the same type of crisis occurs frequently – you should feel disappointed rather than self-satisfied.
- Is your 'busy-ness' secretly criticized by your team, leaving them feeling cynical – or overly casual – as they know that you like to pick up any mistakes.
- What changes to the organization would help tighten up decision-making in negotiations? If rearguard negotiating is common in the organization, could this be avoided in the future? Who are the worst offenders and how could they be persuaded and trained to change?
- Does your organization suffer from the phenomenon known as Murphy's Law ('If it can go wrong, it will')? How could the risks of non-compliance be recognized at an earlier stage and avoiding action taken much earlier?
- Does greed figure much in your market or in typical deals?
- Is power misused, causing others to cast around for cost savings that are motivated by the need to survive? How could a more partnering stance be adopted?
- Is the level of detail in research and debate, commitment and delivery consistent and adequate?

- Who applies the 'What if?' questions to your market position? For example: 'What if our current partners went out of business within six months?'; 'What if transportation costs were to double within three months?' and so on. Engaging in blue-sky thinking and contingency planning is very rarely a waste of time.

Knowing something is very different from practising it. Take the opportunity to re-examine your normal behaviour. Don't ask yourself 'Is this a new idea?'; ask yourself 'Do I do this? And, if not, how could I adopt this method with sufficient confidence to succeed? Have I prepared a personal action plan (including some personal feedback) to underwrite change and achieve the personal improvements I know are desirable/essential?'

Plan your future 2

If you are trying to improve your involvement in more advanced negotiations, the following checklists of self-development skills will help:

Tips for listening

Try not to:

- **make hasty judgements,** such as tuning out because you believe the speaker has nothing interesting to say; condemning a subject as uninteresting without giving it a fair hearing; or jumping the gun on what you think is about to come in conversation
- **let your attention wander** – avoid getting easily distracted by other sights and sounds around you and try not to show any unwitting signs of impatience or irritation
- **listen selectively,** by turning a deaf ear to certain topics; only listening to certain people; wanting to hear only about the good things and not the bad; letting someone's delivery put you off listening to what they have to say.

Tips for improving your assertiveness

Do you:

- think before speaking, thus improving confidence by eliminating ums and ers?
- maintain a firm, confident tone of voice in meetings?
- say what you mean without waffling?
- show positive body language to support a businesslike image?
- avoid apologetic behaviour?

Plan your future 3

Extroverts with huge amounts of self-confidence tend to rise to the top of the sales profession and often transfer across into buying/purchasing and line management roles. However, they may also continue to use the habitual talk/listen ratios that have helped them to be successful in the past. This may not be the most effective style to use and, if only one resolution is likely to help anyone in this position, it is this: *ask more questions*.

It would be simplistic to say that questions merely bring answers; they also buy thinking/planning time and allow the questioner to gain control (as the opponent loses thinking time because they are busy deciding how to answer the questions that have been fired at them).

Extroverts are notable for talking too much; they may unwittingly give away vital bargaining information without obtaining anything in return. So, asking more questions, designed to tie the conversation down to the case in hand and the vital factors, is extremely important.

In the longer term, your reputation will have been considerably enhanced and you should be actively considering how to build on your success. There is probably no better way to improve one's future prospects than by being attached to a large and successful project – and so it should not come as any surprise if a job offer or two starts to arrive.

The biggest trap for experienced negotiators is complacency – it is easy to draw out the successful projects but what about the rest? It is a challenging but exciting role that can bring great satisfaction – but only if negotiators avoid those tempting shortcuts. Once you have polished your skills in current roles and projects, you may feel that it is important to maintain the sense of personal challenge by applying them in new sectors. After a number of projects have completed successfully, larger schemes will probably open up. However, successful completion is most likely to be the determining success factor when it comes to new appointments. It would be wrong to prejudge here the attraction of such approaches, regardless of how attractive they may appear to be. The right time to be thinking of moving on (if at all) is when the current project is successfully completed.

Good negotiators are always in demand. Keep growing – and try to ensure that you share your experience with younger, less experienced negotiators around you!

If you are inclined to give something back, experienced negotiators are needed all around the planet, often in areas where the necessary level of investment may be impossible to achieve. In such situations monetary benefit may be poor, but the opportunities for great personal satisfaction from seeing good charitable works succeed could bring an even higher level of satisfaction.

Summary

It would be a strange but perfect world if every negotiator were able to claim that all their negotiation outcomes were perfect and all implementation occurred exactly as agreed. However, unfortunately the world is not perfect and it is vital that experienced negotiators continue to learn and grow from each project they undertake. Making mistakes is human – but repeating the same mistakes and *not* learning from them is inexcusable.

This Part should have pinpointed best practices and prompted you to identify keys to enhanced negotiation that simply require your motivation and determination to implement – which is why we have included a framework of a Personal Action Plan at the end. By now, this should feature at least seven action points that you should be able to implement.

If you have found any more improvement points, try to prioritize them and introduce them steadily, monitoring their success as you go. And remember that you might well negotiate with others who are trying to implement their own action plans. Collaborative negotiation, as this Part will have shown you, is all about achieving win/win.

Fact-check (answers at the back)

1. Major stand-alone contracts should be negotiated hard in order to:
   a) Ensure the very best benefits are gained, together with punitive compensation (just in case) ❏
   b) Enable the two organizations to grow together ❏
   c) Ensure that the parties can prove competence should the details become public ❏
   d) Prove that the deal has been struck by competent negotiators ❏

2. The final negotiation phase will benefit from:
   a) Scrutiny by a third party not previously involved in the discussions ❏
   b) An escape clause in case of undisclosed matters ❏
   c) Legal protection against fraud or exaggerated claims ❏
   d) Confidential advisers to ensure the deal can be fully implemented ❏

3. A pre-booked press event brings:
   a) Potential image problems should agreement be delayed ❏
   b) Guaranteed column inches for an agreed deal ❏
   c) The risk that one party will hold the other hostage ❏
   d) The best target for closure of the negotiation ❏

4. Legal advice for a negotiation team approaching closure is:
   a) Vital, to ensure any agreement is enforceable ❏
   b) An item that should be included in the final budget ❏
   c) A service that should be available to both sides ❏
   d) An essential feature of a win/win deal ❏

5. Negotiating in a team requires:
   a) Self-control and discipline against the risk of multi-speak ❏
   b) A sense of mission and self-belief ❏
   c) Defence/attack if and when necessary ❏
   d) Maintaining loyalty to the team and its objectives ❏

6. The best profile for a negotiator to adopt for high-value contracts in the long term would be:
   a) Opportunist ❏
   b) Expert/Teacher ❏
   c) Completer/Finisher ❏
   d) Pessimist ❏

7. The best action to take when there is overt disagreement within your negotiating team is to:
   a) Provide a distraction by changing the subject ❏
   b) Call a recess ❏
   c) Pass a note to the 'guilty' party ❏
   d) Invoke the team manifesto ❏

8. A lot of counter-proposing is:
a) A sign of a win/lose culture between negotiators ❑
b) A risk that could lead to defence/attack cycles ❑
c) A hint that agreement will be impossible ❑
d) An indicator of a very competitive negotiator ❑

9. The biggest trap for experienced negotiators is:
a) Talking in an uncontrolled way ❑
b) Over-confidence and complacency ❑
c) Making assumptions ❑
d) Failure to do one's homework ❑

10. Negotiating skills should be seen as:
a) Vital skills to help survive and grow in everyday life ❑
b) Showing opponents that you mean business ❑
c) A way of avoiding win/lose outcomes ❑
d) Solely the province of commerce and industry ❑

7 × 7

1 Seven key ideas

- Develop (or reinforce) your self-confidence to negotiate – especially when working in an environment that does not seem to be conducive to negotiating.
- Relax your style! If you have prepared thoroughly, discussion, proposing and agreeing should be possible without tension, embarrassment or aggression.
- Fix your negotiation 'zones'. Least and most favourable boundaries should be set before a meeting... by both sides!
- Use 'small-talk' but avoid 'loose talk' (which may give away vital information that strengthens your opponent's position).
- Praise opponents' flexibility and reward it with small concessions that should help to build the feeling of 'win/win'.
- Impress opponents with your command of your subject – but don't let this turn into a competition about who knows most.
- Don't make 'cast-iron claims' about exaggerated points – this risks your credibility (even if you later accept that you have made a mistake and back down).

2 Seven key resources for the negotiator

- Numeracy!
- Computer skills
- Research
- Determination
- Self-belief/confidence
- Building the 'winning' team
- Finishing (realism)

3 Seven best personal resources

- *Confidence: How winning streaks and losing streaks begin and end* by Rosabeth Moss Kanter (Three Rivers Press, 2006)
- *Eyes Wide Open: How to make smart decisions in a confusing world* by Noreena Hertz (William Collins, 2013)
- *Emotional Intelligence Workbook: Take practical steps to improve* by Jill and Derek Dann (Hodder & Stoughton, 2012)
- *Manipulating Meetings: How to get what you want, when you want it* by David Martin (3rd edn, Prentice Hall, 1999)
- *Conflicts: A better way to resolve them* by Edward de Bono (Penguin, 1991)
- *The Trusted Leader* by Robert Galford and Anne Seibold Drapeau (The Free Press, 2011). Trust supports negotiations. This book explains how to gain trust and assess better when to trust others.
- *NLP: The new technology of achievement* by Steve Andreas and Charles Faulkner (Nicholas Brealey, 1996)

4 Seven things to do today

- Review your current practices and build a new action plan.
- Invest time in relation to potential pay-off in terms of technique and results.
- Build your team by sharing insights and skills and being prepared to delegate the progressive projects to trusted people.
- Involve others in difficult cases to maintain open-mindedness about alternative solutions and provide learning opportunities for the team.
  Check it all out! Especially those complex schemes...
- Will it work? Does it meet all the promises you/they are making?
- How does it feel to do 'business' with your 'opponent'? And how might it feel for them to do business with you?
- Is that consistent with other departments/functions/levels of authority? If not, what can be done about it?

5 Seven inspiring negotiation strategies

- 'You are not in a negotiating position – please leave!' A very successful head of a renowned academic institution used this combative approach to buy time – a strong bargaining tactic within his own team that restricted time-wasting debate on poorly thought-out schemes.
- Top lawyers may exploit their 'bargaining positions' by applying an authoritative air that adds weight to all that they say. This can be difficult to break down (in court or in commercial bargaining) because it is based on thorough, and very pointed, questioning!
- 'Negotiation is important because in engaging with someone with a different perspective, you can more easily identify the questions you need to consider in order to improve yourself and your own position.' Alastair Redfern, Bishop of Derby
- Internal negotiations are strongly influenced by political and power relations between competing departments and functions. Top managers quickly form 'unwritten rules' for bargaining, which may include: 'Don't bring me problems – only solutions' or 'No nasty surprises, thank you!'
- The late Lord Mottistone, (first director of the British Industrial Training Board for Distribution) shared his charismatic personality with liberal/public praise for the efforts of all those who deserved it. Praise is a strong motivator and one that can generate further out-of-the-ordinary efforts and results.
- Founder of two pioneering banks, Mike Harris is now a mentor for other pioneers. His mantra is: 'So many leadership conversations are, in fact, a negotiation. You are trying to find the common ground where it is in *their* interest to give you what *you need from them.*'
- 'Negotiating in the Sales and Marketing function often revolves around price ... The consequence of a generous discount can directly affect bottom-line profits whereas quality, value and service build a strong and profitable business.' Ron Coleman, founder of Invicta Training

6 Seven negotiation quotes

- 'You must never try to make all the money that's in a deal. Let the other fellow make some money too, because if you have a reputation for always making all the money, you won't have many deals.' J. Paul Getty
- 'Anger can be an effective negotiating tool, but only as a calculated act, never as a reaction.' Mark McCormack
- 'When a man says that he approves something in principle, it means he hasn't the slightest intention of putting it into practice.' Otto von Bismarck
- 'If you come to a negotiation table saying you have the final truth, that you know nothing but the truth and that is final, you will get nothing.' Harri Holkeri
- 'Diplomacy is the art of letting someone else have your way.' Sir David Frost
- 'The first principle of contract negotiation is don't remind them of what you did in the past; tell them what you're going to do in the future.' Stan Musial
- 'There's no road map on how to raise a family: it's always an enormous negotiation!' Meryl Streep

7 Seven trends for tomorrow

- Continuing greater use of non-personal methods of communicating (i.e. use of media, text exchange, etc.), *leading to...*
- Greater opportunities for exploiting personality and the 'touch and feel' of personal face-to-face communicating.
- More timely communicating – more strictly focused (but 'disguised' as social entertainment?).
- Power and authority more tightly focused in fewer hands (with concentration of business wealth and opportunity), *possibly leading to...*
- Increased opportunities through niche business/organizations with new start-ups by individualistic entrepreneurs, *and ...*
- Greater collaborative business initiatives in unusual sectors, such as lifestyle operations (e.g. fast cars; the rebuilding of

heritage vehicles), stimulating cohorts of traditional and new skills centres.

- Meanwhile, continuing volume business pressure based on price and value for money operations with the emphasis on quantities and inexpensive prices (mainly through energetic agents representing low price/value world economies – dependent on continuing stable political/economic positions). An obvious outcome here will be the requirement for more international negotiators with sensitivity and competence in cross-border and political/cultural negotiations.

Personal Action Plan

Objective	Target Date	Completed
1		
2		
3		
4		
5		
6		
7		
8		

PART 3
Your Persuasion and Influence Masterclass

Introduction

As social animals, we human beings cannot *not* communicate. Even if we are not speaking, our visual appearance and body language will 'speak' for us. It is therefore not surprising that people who have learned to be influential and persuasive communicators enjoy great success in life. This Part will teach you how to master a range of practical and proven techniques for influencing and persuading others, which will work in all aspects of your personal and business life.

This section is more than just a collection of theories on how to persuade and influence others. Spread throughout are real-life examples of people who have been acknowledged globally as highly successful influencers, together with insights into how they achieved this. And if they can do it, you can too!

CHAPTER 15

What is influence?

According to dictionary definitions, 'influence' can mean:

- to affect how others see a certain point or action, and react upon it
- to leave a mark on someone (not literally)
- to have someone or something start acting a bit like you.

Influencing others is one of the prime objectives of communication and is particularly important in the business world. In his 1936 book *How to Win Friends and Influence People*, Dale Carnegie wrote that dealing with people is probably the biggest problem we face, especially in business. He went on to say, 'There is only one way under high heaven to get anybody to do anything and that is by making the other person want to do it. There is no other way.'

In this chapter we will be examining some of the factors that have been proven to be effective and powerful influencers, delivered by personalities as diverse as Sir Winston Churchill and Sir Bob Geldof. We will also explore what influences you – whether you make 'head' or 'heart' decisions, and how you 'sell' yourself when you want to promote yourself to others.

What influences your decisions?

Think about the last time you bought something that was a 'want' rather than a 'need'. Perhaps you were out and about, and you just saw something that caught your eye. You liked the look of it and you decided you wanted it, even though you knew you didn't need it. You might have been aware that, at that point, a voice inside your head went into 'justification mode'. It started generating 'reasons' why you really should have this object of your desire. Before you knew it, you had made your purchasing decision, handed over some money and it was yours.

Perhaps you remained pleased with that purchasing decision, or perhaps, in the cold light of a day or two later, you wondered what on earth possessed you to hand over good money for this 'thing'. Whatever your feelings about that decision, your personality type will have influenced it.

The following is a list of different personality types related to buying decisions. Notice whether you identify with any of them.

The gadget geek

If it's the latest technology, cutting-edge design and it's considered cool to possess one of these, then the gadget geeks want it. They have an image to sustain, after all. If Apple brings out a new iPhone, then they have to be first in the queue to get one. They may even be prepared to pay someone to stand in the queue all night on their behalf so that they get pole position. They don't even need to know what new features this iPhone has: if it's new, it must be a better, improved version of the last model and it's essential for them to be bang up to date.

When the Apple iPhone5 first went on sale in London, among the people in the queue eager to part with £599 was a man who justified his purchase by telling a journalist that he had just bought an Audi A6 and it was 'only compatible with a phone that has a milled aluminium finish'! These people make justified, 'from-the-head' decisions.

The connoisseur collector

These people don't buy; they invest. They seek 'elite purchases', which they refer to as 'investment pieces'. They attend fine-art auctions or – if the item they want has a particular rarity value – they stay away and become a telephone bidder, in case their presence inflates the price. Although they love beautiful things, connoisseur collectors are also prepared to invest in items that are acknowledged as desirable and therefore valuable, even if they are not to their personal taste. These could include fine wines, which they 'put down' in a temperature-controlled wine cellar, never to be consumed.

Admiration is everything and the quality of their possessions reflects their personal aspirations. They want to be seen as discerning buyers with impeccable taste. Although image is important to this group, their purchasing decisions tend to be led by the head rather than the heart because of the investment factor.

The memorabilia collector

These people consider themselves to be similar to the connoisseur collectors but dedicated to a particular theme. The theme might be *Star Wars* merchandise, royal family memorabilia or Barbie dolls through the ages. Because there tends to be no limit to the size of their collections, they are constantly adding to them, sometimes to the extent that their collected 'treasures' take over all the space in their homes. Charity shops, car boot sales, eBay and sci-fi fairs are all happy hunting grounds for these 'from-the-heart' buyers.

The trend follower

Trend followers are celebrity spotters. They avidly read the celebrity gossip magazines and, if they see that someone they admire has just started a new trend – perhaps with a hairstyle, tattoo, beauty/health treatment, fashion accessory or clothes – they have to follow it. Their hope is that, if they emulate their idol, some of their 'stardust' may rub off on them. Plus they will be seen to be 'on trend' with the latest 'in thing'. The higher the profile their adored one has, the more the trend follower will want to replicate them. A prime example of this kind of idol is the Duchess of Cambridge. If she wears an outfit from a high-street retailer, it will instantly sell out, both in store and online.

These people are 'heart buyers', who may not necessarily think through their real reasons for making a purchase. For example, one serious downside of this behaviour has been the fallout from copying the 'handbag dog' accessory trend, i.e. carrying around a small dog in a handbag. First seen in the film *Legally Blonde* and then picked up by celebrities such as Paris Hilton, this treatment of small dogs as fashion accessories rather than as pets often results in the animals developing significant behavioural issues. Battersea Dogs Home has reported that they are increasingly being asked to rehome these disturbed small dogs.

The impulse buyer

Impulse buyers are easily influenced by other people's persuasiveness and by 'bargain' purchases, and they are often great fans of television shopping channels. Their emotional states often drive their spending habits. For example, if they feel sad, they will buy something to cheer themselves up. If they feel happy, they will splash out on a treat of some kind in order to celebrate. If they are out shopping with a friend who is buying, they join in because they tell themselves that it would be unsociable not to and, in any case, they deserve it (whatever 'it' happens to be).

Unfortunately, impulse buys are often not wise buys. The impulse buyer can easily end up with wardrobes full of clothes they never wear. Their 'spend, spend, spend' habit can even take them hurtling towards financial ruin. A famous example of this was the football pools winner Viv Nicholson, who won £152,319 in 1961 (£5 million in today's money), but who became penniless within a few years. These people are definitely 'from-the-heart' buyers.

The self-help junkie

On a permanent quest for personal growth, material success or spiritual enlightenment, the self-help junkie buys a huge number of books, ebooks, training programmes, CD sets and DVD sets on their chosen subject. They are often prepared to travel anywhere in the world to attend their favourite teacher or guru's seminars or retreats, where they hang on their every word. They consider their purchases to be investments, and it has to be said that some of these devotees do indeed utilize what they learn and go on to achieve all they desire in life. However, the majority of followers just accumulate a wealth of books that any library would be proud of, along with an extensive CD/DVD collection.

Until they feel that 'something' in their quest has made a difference to them, the self-help junkie will keep searching and buying because the answer has to be 'out there' somewhere; it's just a matter of time before they find it. They make intuitive, heart-based purchasing decisions in their search for fulfilment and happiness.

In order to influence others, especially in the context of selling them something, we must offer them something to which they will attribute value. This is why it's important to understand their personality type and what drives them to make purchasing decisions.

Personality and perceived value

You may have noticed that only the first two personality types described make 'head' decisions and that only one of those invests in purchases with the potential to increase in value. And yet 'value' is the common denominator for all six types. What converts a 'want' to a 'need' is its perceived value. Every one of the personality types listed has perceived a value of some kind in their potential purchases, and a 'need' has evolved that can only be satisfied by possessing it.

Let's revisit these personality types to understand the different values they attribute to their 'objects of desire'.

- **The gadget geek** is vulnerable to peer pressure and has an innate need to be 'leader of the pack'. This desire is so strong that it is programmed into their mental DNA and thus their purchasing decisions become logical, next-step actions. Possessing the most up-to-date, superior, shiny gadget has the value of fulfilling this non-negotiable need.

- **The connoisseur collector** is always focused on the financial value of a potential purchase and evaluates it in terms of future return on investment. He or she may invest in a Picasso that is not to their personal taste because they know that, whether it is hung on the wall or not, it is an asset that can only appreciate in value.

- **The memorabilia collector** has huge affection for their chosen theme. When they see a new 'desirable', especially if it is something they don't yet have in their collection, their heart starts racing and an 'inner smile' just takes them over. They take great care of their treasured objects and attach much value to their activity because of the happiness they gain from it. They find it hard to part with any of the objects they have collected, even when the size of their collection becomes excessive.

- **The trend follower** is searching for an identity. Lacking the courage to be original, they prefer to emulate others who they perceive to be setting new, desirable trends. Because their idols tend to be well known and publicly admired, the trend follower believes that they, too, will become popular if they dress the same way or do the same things. They have a strong need to feel admired and greatly value anything that might facilitate this.

- **The impulse buyer** readily responds to their emotions. He or she will 'invest' in something that will either change an undesirable emotional state or enhance an enjoyable one to make it last. For example, they are on holiday in Spain, having a marvellous time. On the last day they experience a burning desire to take something home with them that will capture this sense of happiness. They browse the tourist shops and there it is – a straw donkey the size of a small child, wearing a sun hat. They have to have it! It's a challenge carrying it home on the plane but now it sits, in pride of place, in the hallway at home. It's in the way, of course, but every time our impulse buyer pats it on the head, happy memories of that holiday in Spain come flooding back.

- **The self-help junkie**, in search of personal fulfilment and meaning in life, attributes value to anything that appears to aid them in their quest. They see their chosen gurus as having successfully completed a journey upon which they are keen to embark. They are eager to learn and to replicate everything that their chosen one did along the way. If their guru is happy to impart this knowledge in a book, on a CD or DVD, or in person at a seminar, then the self-help junkie is a willing follower, valuing every morsel of advice they can glean.

The role of the champion

Another situation in which people place great value on their needs being met is during a time of crisis. People look for someone to become their 'champion', someone who will take control and lead them forward to happier times. Great value will be attributed to the person who fulfils this role and, in this position, he or she becomes extremely influential. Two examples of such champions are Winston Churchill and Bob Geldof.

The influence of Churchill

During the Second World War, Great Britain's 'champion' was Winston Churchill. An outstanding orator, his inspirational speeches provided a psychological boost to British morale exactly when it was needed. Two of his most memorable speeches – delivered in a tone of voice that resonated with unshakeable confidence and determination – were made during the dark days of 1940.

The first one came on 4 June, just hours after the evacuation of Dunkirk, in which 338,226 British and French soldiers, cut off by the German army, were rescued from the Dunkirk beaches by a hastily assembled fleet of 850 boats. Many of these boats were just small pleasure craft – the smallest was only 14 ft 7 in (4.45 m) long – but they all played an essential role in saving lives. The 'miracle of the little ships' has remained a prominent legend in Britain. Some of the surviving boats took part in the Queen's Diamond Jubilee river pageant in 2012, 72 years on from their finest hour.

The following is an extract from Churchill's post-Dunkirk speech:

> We shall not flag or fail; we shall go on to the end. We shall fight in France; we shall fight on the seas and oceans. We shall fight with growing confidence and growing strength in the air. We shall defend our island whatever the cost may be. We shall fight on the beaches; we shall fight on the landing grounds. We shall fight in the fields and in the streets, we shall fight in the hills; we shall never surrender.

Churchill referred to the outcome of the evacuation as a 'miracle' and the British press termed it a 'disaster turned into triumph'. To this day, the phrase 'Dunkirk spirit' is still used in Britain to describe people who pull together to overcome times of adversity.

Churchill made a second memorable speech on 20 August, when the crisis of the Battle of Britain was imminent. German air attacks were being directed against the RAF airfields in the south of England, and Churchill used the phrase 'so few' to describe the RAF fighter pilots:

> The gratitude of every home in our Island, in our Empire, and indeed throughout the world, except in the abodes of the guilty, goes out to the British airmen who, undaunted by odds, unwearied in their constant challenge and mortal danger, are turning the tide of the world war by their prowess and by their devotion. Never in the field of human conflict was so much owed by so many to so few.

The power of the pause

One technique that Churchill deployed in order to add impact to his speeches was the use of pauses. Read the following extract out loud, exactly as it is written:

'Never in the field of human conflict was so much owed by so many to so few.'

Now read it out loud again, pausing where there are dots, and notice the difference:

'Never ... in the field of human conflict ... was so much ... owed by so many ... to so few.'

Suddenly, it now has a deeper level of meaning, a gravitas that truly 'moved' people emotionally. Churchill knew about the power of the pause and he used it to great effect.

The influence of Bob Geldof

Another, more unlikely, champion emerged in 1984. On the evening of 23 October, rock singer Bob Geldof, like many thousands of others in Britain, was watching the 9 o'clock news on BBC television. Like thousands of others, he was appalled by a graphic report on the human suffering and huge loss of life occurring in Ethiopia as a result of drought, disease and famine.

In his view, '30 million people are dying; meanwhile, in Europe, we're spending tax to grow food we don't need, we spend more tax to store it and we pay further tax, most disgracefully, to destroy it.' He saw this as a crime; it made him angry and this galvanized him into action.

He *needed* to make a difference; the British public *wanted* to make a difference but didn't know how. Geldof had the answer. Within weeks, he had assembled a group of high-profile singers, and composed and recorded with them the Band Aid single, 'Do they know it's Christmas?' with the chorus of 'Feed the World'. It was released on 7 December, became the fastest-selling single ever and raised £8 million.

The following summer, Geldof initiated the satellite-linked UK and USA Live Aid concerts. By now he had support from the highest in the land, with Prince Charles and Princess Diana attending the Wembley concert alongside an audience of 72,000 people. TV pictures were beamed to over 1.5 billion people in 160 countries in the biggest broadcast ever known.

Between music sets, Geldof made frequent passionate appeals to viewers to 'Give us your money – there are people dying right now.' He shouted, he swore, and it worked. Across the UK, 200 phone lines were set up and manned to receive credit-card donations. Geldof personally took the call from the ruling family in Dubai when they made the biggest single donation of £1 million. In the USA, 22,000 pledges of money were received within five minutes of the Beach Boys taking to the stage in the simultaneous concert at JFK Stadium, Philadelphia.

Live Aid eventually raised a total of £40 million; in 1986 Bob Geldof was awarded an honorary knighthood. The success of Live Aid came about because Geldof had shown people a tangible way to make a difference to those who couldn't help themselves. Through our donations we could save lives and at the same time ease any feelings of guilt we may have been experiencing. And we placed *great value* on that.

TIP *You need to convey passion and conviction when you are aiming to influence others, and remember that part of what you are fulfilling is an emotional need.*

Summary

In this chapter we have explored what influence is and how it manifests itself in our lives. We have looked at this in the context of how a 'want' can be transformed into a 'need' if sufficient value is added. This is apparent in our purchasing decisions, for a variety of different reasons, as demonstrated by the six 'buying personality' types.

We are also influenced and even inspired by 'champions' – people who step up into the leadership limelight just when we have an emotional need for someone to fill that role. Winston Churchill and Bob Geldof couldn't be more different and yet they both took on this role to great effect.

Value is thus the essential ingredient if we are thinking about influencing others. In order to influence others, we must offer them something to which they will attribute value. Whether it is a product or a well-reasoned argument that persuades people to do something or feel something, value is what makes the difference.

Fact-check (answers at the back)

1. What is influence?
a) Leaving a visible mark on someone ❏
b) The power someone has to affect other people's thinking or actions ❏
c) Preventing people doing what they want ❏
d) Forcing people to agree with you ❏

2. Which personality types buy 'from the head'?
a) The gadget geek and the connoisseur collector ❏
b) The memorabilia collector and the trend follower ❏
c) The impulse buyer and the self-help junkie ❏
d) The gadget geek and the trend follower ❏

3. How do people justify making a purchase?
a) By being influenced by other people's persuasiveness ❏
b) By copying other people's purchases ❏
c) They need to be bang up to date ❏
d) They convert their 'wants' into needs ❏

4. Which personality type focuses on particular themes?
a) The trend follower ❏
b) The memorabilia collector ❏
c) The gadget geek ❏
d) The impulse buyer ❏

5. What does every personality type need when buying?
a) To perceive a value in their potential purchases ❏
b) To follow their peer group rather than be leaders ❏
c) A potential return on their investment ❏
d) Admiration of their purchases by others ❏

6. Which personality type focuses on the potential return on their investment?
a) The self-help junkie ❏
b) The connoisseur collector ❏
c) The impulse buyer ❏
d) The trend follower ❏

7. Which personality type is in search of personal fulfilment?
a) The self-help junkie ❏
b) The connoisseur collector ❏
c) The impulse buyer ❏
d) The memorabilia collector ❏

8. What was Churchill's value as champion?
a) Supporting RAF fighter pilots ❏
b) Winning the Battle of Britain ❏
c) Inspiring people during a time of crisis ❏
d) Helping people to overcome adversity ❏

9. Prior to Live Aid, what was Bob Geldof famous for?
a) Being a TV chef ❏
b) Being a rock singer ❏
c) Making a difference ❏
d) Raising taxes to relieve suffering ❏

10. What was Bob Geldof's value as champion?

a) Enabling people to help save lives and at the same time ease any feelings of guilt ❏

b) Organizing a great rock concert ❏

c) Allowing credit-card donations ❏

d) Being awarded an honorary knighthood ❏

CHAPTER 16

Conveying the right image

Influencing effectively and powerfully is about more than just being a good speaker. We are most influenced by the type of person who 'walks their talk' – in other words, we look for congruence between the message and the person delivering it.

Even though Bob Geldof seemed initially an unlikely candidate for the role of global fundraiser and humanitarian, in his appearance, behaviour and communication style he remained true to his primary role of 'rock star'. We could label him 'the angry rock star, passionate about a good cause'. The pieces fitted together, we shared his mission and the whole package worked.

In this chapter we shall explore the consequences of being both totally congruent – when image, message and behaviour are all in alignment – and incongruent – where these elements are in conflict with each other. You will learn how and why people stereotype others, and how you can use this phenomenon to your advantage when influencing.

We shall also look at two individuals who have each in their own way been profoundly influential on a global scale. One overturned a stereotyped response and the other 'walked the talk'.

What is stereotyping?

As human beings, we have an innate desire to make sense of things. We need to know what's going on around us and how it affects us so that we can decide how to behave in response. This gives us a sense of comfort and the phrase 'comfort zone' is often used to describe this state of wellbeing. As part of this process, we like to draw rapid conclusions about our environment. For example, within four seconds of seeing someone for the first time, we start to make assumptions and judgements about them.

We may assume that at first glance we can tell the person's:

- age
- occupation
- financial worth
- lifestyle
- level of education
- ethnic origin
- marital status.

In addition, once the person starts to speak, we make further assumptions about their background, where they are from and even their level of intelligence, based on their accent or dialect, the type of vocabulary they use and their style of speech. At this point, our ego gets involved. We start to make comparisons between them and us, to determine how this person 'measures up'. Are they superior or inferior to us in some way? How should we behave towards them?

There is a danger here that we then act out an ego-driven behaviour based on false assumptions. If this happens, we may not be behaving in the most appropriate and best way possible, and in so doing we will not be able to influence effectively.

The positive purpose of stereotyping

However, this instant stereotyping can have a positive purpose, which is that it can protect us from danger. If we detect potential danger, our brain's fight-or-flight response allows us to take action against it. For example, imagine you are walking along a street at night and a figure steps out of the shadows in front of you. Your eyes scan him or her for signs of whether they are a friend or foe and, judging this stranger to have a 'menacing' appearance, your mind concludes that you could be in danger. This instantly triggers your fight-or-flight response, adrenaline is released into your body and you are now equipped either to stand your ground and defend yourself or to run away.

Because you have in your mind your own 'templates' of friend and foe, and you needed to make sense of the situation, you compared the appearance of the stranger before you to these images and found that he or she matched the 'foe template'. At that point, you stereotyped this person as some kind of troublemaker. You allowed yourself to be influenced by appearance and made an assumption that had at least a 50 per cent chance of being correct.

The first impression we form of someone tends to be a lasting one unless we receive some powerful and convincing evidence to the contrary. Moreover, our mind has a 'thinker' and a 'prover'. Whatever the thinker is thinking about, it is the prover's job to provide supporting evidence that says, 'Yes, you're right.' Once the thinker forms a first impression, the prover will only notice corroborative evidence; anything else will be dismissed as incorrect. This will continue until the thinker adopts a different viewpoint, but it usually takes something quite dramatic to bring about this 180° shift.

Overturning the stereotype: Susan Boyle

Susan Boyle is a Scottish singer who attracted worldwide public attention after appearing on the television show *Britain's Got Talent* in April 2009. Born in 1961 with a mild learning difficulty, Susan was bullied as a child and left school with few qualifications. However, her passion was singing and having taken part in, and won, several local amateur singing competitions, her mother urged her to enter the show in order to develop her confidence for singing in front of a large audience. Sadly, Susan's mother died before the audition took place and Susan nearly withdrew her application. However, her voice coach persuaded her to go ahead. Susan's performance on *BGT* was the first time she had sung in public since her mother's death.

When Susan walked out on the stage, a plain, slightly overweight, nearly 48-year-old, and said that her aspiration was to become a professional singer as successful as Elaine Paige, the audience laughed. They had stereotyped her in those first four seconds as delusional and decided that there was no way she could possibly be a talented singer. The judges clearly shared their scepticism, as this unlikely-looking candidate prepared to sing 'I dreamed a dream' from *Les Misérables*.

When Susan's clear, note-perfect mezzo-soprano voice filled the theatre, jaws dropped and eyes widened in astonishment at the clarity and beauty of her voice. The applause started just four seconds after Susan's first note and became a standing ovation that continued long after she'd finished singing, with the judges also on their feet. Judge Amanda Holden remarked on how the initially cynical attitude of the audience (and the judges) had been completely overturned by Susan's performance, calling it the 'biggest wake-up call ever'.

After that edition of *Britain's Got Talent* was televised, Susan appeared on the Oprah Winfrey show in the USA via satellite link. The final of that year's *BGT* commanded a record UK television audience of 17.3 million. Although favourite to win, Susan came second to dance troupe Diversity, but it didn't matter. She became a highly successful, internationally acclaimed professional singer, setting new records in both the UK and the USA for the fastest-selling album of a debut artist in decades.

Susan Boyle's story offers a profound example of how initial stereotyping based on appearance not only can be completely wrong but also *can* be overturned by overwhelming evidence to the contrary. However, she is the exception that proves the rule that 'You only get one chance to make a first impression'. It is far better to make the first impression the one you desire than to have to prove people wrong and force them to change their minds about you.

What is congruence?

An example of someone who very much 'walked her talk', whose appearance and behaviour were 100 per cent congruent with everything that she stood for – enabling her to exert her influence on a worldwide scale – was Anita Roddick, founder of The Body Shop. Although technically an international corporate executive, Anita never presented herself in a way that would have supported such a stereotype, for example dressing in a designer 'power suit' and high heels and carrying a smart leather briefcase. Such an image would have been at odds with The Body Shop 'brand' and seen as inauthentic.

The following case study about Anita Roddick shows the consequences of congruence. Anita believed that businesses have the power to do good in the world and The Body Shop mission statement reflects this sentiment and incorporates her own values, opening with the words, 'To dedicate our business to the pursuit of social and environmental change'. The Body Shop's mission had a global effect: it raised awareness of global issues, promoting third-world trade and discouraging the testing of products on animals. Because she lived her beliefs and values, both personally and in her business life, Anita Roddick will always remain synonymous with The Body Shop.

Walking the talk:
Anita Roddick

Anita Roddick was born in a bomb shelter in 1942 in Littlehampton, Sussex, England, her Italian immigrant family having fled Naples just before the outbreak of the Second World War. Growing up in an English seaside town, Anita always felt she was a natural outsider, drawn to other outsiders and rebels such as her teenage idol James Dean. She also developed a strong sense of moral outrage at the age of ten when she read a book about the Holocaust.

Having trained as a teacher, she worked on a kibbutz in Israel, which led to an extended working trip around the world, during which she spent time in primitive farming and fishing communities, exposed to and learning about the body-care rituals of the women she encountered there. Influenced by her mother's wartime thriftiness of refilling, re-using and recycling, combined with a passion for environmental activism, Anita created a small range of body-care products and opened the first branch of The Body Shop in Brighton in 1976. Within six months, she had opened a second shop and eventually The Body Shop went global through the growth of a franchise network, serving some 77 million customers worldwide.

Anita always retained the appearance and demeanour of a 'wild child', her natural attractiveness the perfect advertisement for her beauty products. The issues she cared passionately about, such as social responsibility, respect for human rights, the environment, animal protection and community trade, became absorbed into The Body Shop's values. The company was at the forefront of using ingredients that had not been tested on animals and of actively trading with developing countries. For example, a moisturizing oil used in some of its products is extracted from Brazil nuts gathered sustainably by Amazonian Indian tribes.

During her lifetime, Anita was awarded many accolades, including the OBE in 1988 and the DBE in 2003, but perhaps one of the most significant and meaningful awards was presented to her in 1999 when she was made the 'Chief Wiper-Away of Ogoni Tears' for her involvement in the movement for the survival of the Ogoni people in Nigeria. Anita died in 2007, having fulfilled her promise to leave her estate to charities on moral grounds.

Presentation: the four-second rule

The way you present yourself sets the scene for how well you can influence others. The following table lists aspects of your appearance that people *will* notice within four seconds of meeting you. Although they might sound like common sense, neglecting any of these can result in the projection of a negative first impression, which can then undermine your ability to influence.

Aspect	Impression
Hair	Messy, unwashed hair or, worse, flakes of dandruff on your shoulders projects an extremely unprofessional image.
Nails	Bitten-down or dirty nails or chipped varnish indicate low personal standards.
Personal hygiene	A strong body odour makes it unpleasant to be around you. Ensure that you wash and use deodorant daily.
Perfume and aftershave	Use sparingly. An overwhelming 'vapour trail' can be almost as offensive as a strong body odour.
Breath	If you have been eating garlic or spicy food such as curry or drinking alcohol within the past 12 hours or so, your breath may still reflect this. Consider carrying mints and/or breath freshener with you at all times.
Dress code	Always dress appropriately for your audience and take cultural norms into account. For men, this could mean a smart suit, collar and tie, and for women a skirt length on or below the knee and tights rather than bare legs. Whatever you are wearing, it must be clean and pressed. If you are a smoker, check for the smell of stale cigarette smoke on your clothes, as this will be particularly noticeable to non-smokers.

Aspect	Impression
Shoes	Footwear must be clean and in good repair. Dirty, scuffed shoes with worn-down heels can let down the smartest outfit.
Tie	You may love the brightly coloured, cartoon-character tie your child gave you and it may reflect your quirky personality, but unless you know your audience really well, err on the side of formality and choose something more sober. Ensure that your tie has no marks or stains on it; because it is immediately below your face, it will always be noticed.
Neckline	Wearing a top with a low neckline is not acceptable in a business environment as it sends out the wrong message. Keep clothes like this for your personal life.
Frayed collars/ hanging threads/loose buttons	All indicate an attitude of neglect. Missing buttons, tears and holes are even worse. Make it a habit to carry out occasional wardrobe checks and repairs so that problems such as these can be avoided.
Jewellery	The principle of 'less is more' works well in the workplace, particularly for men. Wearing an excessive amount of jewellery distracts your audience from you and your message.
Make-up	As with jewellery and perfume, it is important not to wear too much. However, it should be noted that in a corporate environment, a woman wearing no make-up at all may be perceived as not professional enough. Cosmetics need to be well applied with subtlety so as to enhance rather than dramatically change the appearance of the wearer.
Handshake	A firm handshake, but not a bone-crusher, inspires confidence. A limp or damp handshake may be interpreted as a 'weak' personality trait.

TIP *Something as apparently insignificant as a stain on a tie or bitten-down fingernails can make the difference between your ability to be an effective influencer and a mediocre one. The little things really do make a big difference; take them seriously.*

Consulting the professionals

To enhance aspects of your visual and vocal impact, which will in turn improve your ability to persuade and influence, think about consulting the following professionals.

Image consultant

An image consultant will carry out a colour and style analysis for you, enabling you to select clothes and colours that significantly enhance your appearance and improve your confidence levels. The intention is that you 'dress to impress', which will also strengthen your ability to influence others. A reputable image consultant can make all the difference to your 'visual charisma' and I cannot recommend this service highly enough.

Voice coach

If you feel that your voice lets you down in some way, consider consulting a voice coach. Many people in the public eye do this. Margaret Thatcher, in preparation for her bid to become leader of the Conservative Party, worked with such a coach, who enabled her to lower the pitch of her voice and slow down the speed of her vocal delivery. The result was that her voice gained an authority and gravitas that ultimately helped her to become the first female British prime minister.

Summary

In this chapter we discovered that, in order to influence and persuade effectively, it is essential to convey the right image. We explored the phenomenon of stereotyping and how this occurs naturally within the first four seconds of seeing someone for the first time. The example of Susan Boyle demonstrates this well, but it also shows that a negative stereotype *can* be turned around. However, it does require something extraordinary to make this happen.

For most situations it's important to make sure that you and your message are in complete alignment. Failure to do this results in an inauthentic impression of 'Do as I say', rather than 'Do as I do' and reduces your powers of persuasion. You may have noticed that politicians often fall foul of this principle!

To generate the most positive stereotype you can in those crucial first four seconds, you learned the importance of thinking about your personal presentation. The elements to consider may seem obvious, but they are easily overlooked. Consulting professionals can also help you to enhance your impact.

Fact-check (answers at the back)

1. What does 'congruent' mean?
   a) Your image, message and behaviour are out of alignment ❑
   b) You won't be stereotyped ❑
   c) Your image, message and behaviour are in alignment ❑
   d) We like people who look like us ❑

2. How quickly do we make assumptions about others?
   a) Within the first four seconds of seeing them ❑
   b) Within five minutes of seeing them ❑
   c) After we have talked to them at length ❑
   d) As soon as they start to speak ❑

3. What are stereotypes based on?
   a) Assumptions about others' financial worth ❑
   b) The attractiveness of someone ❑
   c) Comparisons with ourselves ❑
   d) What someone looks and sounds like ❑

4. What's the role of the ego when making assumptions?
   a) The ego never makes assumptions ❑
   b) Determining whether someone is superior or inferior to us ❑
   c) Making sure our assumptions are correct ❑
   d) Assumptions play no part in determining our behaviour ❑

5. What is the positive purpose of stereotyping?
   a) To protect us from potential danger ❑
   b) To release fight-or-flight hormones into the body ❑
   c) To make instant assumptions about others ❑
   d) To enhance our powers of persuasion ❑

6. How can we overcome initial stereotyping based on appearance?
   a) Through overwhelming evidence to the contrary ❑
   b) It's impossible ❑
   c) By ignoring our initial view ❑
   d) By forgetting what we first thought ❑

7. How does congruence enhance our ability to influence?
   a) By reflecting and incorporating our values into all our actions ❑
   b) By showing the world we mean business ❑
   c) By giving a good impression in a meeting ❑
   d) By making sure we dress smartly ❑

8. Why is the way you present yourself important?
   a) It helps us relax ❑
   b) It sets the scene for how well we can influence others ❑
   c) It keeps us one step ahead of the competition ❑
   d) It stops us feeling like a 'natural outsider' ❑

9. What's the best way to make a good impression?
a) Telling others to 'do as we say' rather than 'do as we do' ❏
b) Cultivating a 'lived-in' look to show we are 'hands-on' ❏
c) Paying attention to aspects of our appearance that people will notice ❏
d) Splashing out on perfume, aftershave or cologne ❏

10. What's a useful rule of presentation to remember?
a) Dress appropriately for your audience ❏
b) Scuffed shoes don't matter, as nobody will notice them ❏
c) Wear as much gold jewellery as possible, to impress others with your wealth ❏
d) A limp handshake is good, as it demonstrates your sensitive nature ❏

CHAPTER 17

Becoming a voice of authority

So far, we have looked at what influence is, the factors that affect it, both positively and negatively, and the importance of conveying the right image so that, when others construct a stereotype impression of you, it is exactly the one you intended. In this chapter we will explore how and why a voice of authority influences people.

The 'authority research' originally carried out by Stanley Milgram in the 1960s, and successfully replicated on television by Derren Brown in 2006, showed the extent to which people were willing to follow an authoritative voice, even to the point of them obeying that voice without question. Being aware of the conclusions from these experiments will enhance your ability to be authoritative, while remaining approachable and respected.

You'll also discover one of the reasons why Martin Luther King's famous 'I have a dream' speech had such a memorable impact and how you can adopt his tactic for yourself when making a presentation. You will also learn a technique for sounding assertive, reasonable and in control in even the most confrontational situations, as well as some other proven strategies for becoming a confident, effective and influential figure of authority.

Who are your authority figures?

Let's start by examining examples of authority figures. Think back to your childhood and specifically to the people who represented figures of authority to you. These are the people who impressed and inspired you, people you admired and respected. If one of these people asked you to do something, you would have done it willingly and without question. You listened to their advice and took it on board. They may have been your parents or other family members, a teacher, a friend or someone else in your peer group, a neighbour or some other member of your community.

Identify three of these authority figures and write down their names in a table like the one below. Then, for each one, define exactly what characteristic(s) it was about them that generated your respect and prompted you to call them to mind.

Name	Characteristic(s)
1	
2	
3	

Now repeat the exercise, this time identifying the authority figures you feel you have in your life now. Choose three people whom you did not select before, and include any public figures who fulfil the criteria for you, even if you have never met them. The following are typically some of the characteristics that you may have identified:

Good listener
Very understanding
Showed compassion and empathy
Championed my cause
Took a genuine interest in me
Always had time for me, even when busy
Believed in me and my ideas
Led by example

Gave support and encouragement
Brave, courageous
Light-hearted, always positive and smiling
Never made unreasonable or unfair demands
Generous spirit
Decisive
Knowledgeable and competent

Reassuring	Took complete responsibility
Optimistic in the face of	for him/herself and his/her
uncertainty	actions
An achiever, but never	Always embraced a challenge
arrogant about it	Constantly strove to be their
Happy to share their ideas/	'best self' and to make a
solutions with me	difference to others
Prepared to step up and lead	Good problem solver with
when someone was needed	innovative ideas

You may have identified some additional ones. However, the common theme here is that all of these are qualities we tend to admire and respect so, if we attribute any of them to another person, we are more likely to accept them as a figure of authority, deserving our respect and co-operation.

In identifying significant authority figures from your childhood, you were recalling people who were important to you when you were at an impressionable age. You may have found that, when you then identified more recent authority figures, the characteristics you sought in them were different from the childhood ones.

Now take some time to review the list above and the characteristics you identified in this exercise. How many of these attributes do *you* have? The more of these that you possess, the easier it will be for you to become a figure of authority.

Select a characteristic from the list that you feel you don't currently have and set yourself an action plan to develop it.

The Milgram experiments

During the early 1960s the Yale University social psychologist Stanley Milgram conducted some experiments. His intention was to measure the willingness of participants to obey an authority figure – one who would instruct them to perform actions that conflicted with their personal conscience and deepest moral beliefs.

The experiment involved three roles:

- The experimenter – this was an authoritative role of 'experimental scientist'
- The teacher – this role was fulfilled by a volunteer, intended to obey the orders of the experimenter
- The learner – this was a role fulfilled by an actor who pretended to be another volunteer, and who would be the recipient of the actions carried out by the teacher

Although the volunteer and the actor drew slips of paper to determine their roles, both slips would say 'teacher' and the actor would always claim that his slip read 'learner'. They were then separated into different rooms where they could communicate but not see each other. In some instances, the learner would make a point of mentioning to the teacher that he had a heart condition.

The teacher was then told that he/she would be teaching a list of word pairs to the learner. Having read through the entire list to the learner, the teacher would then read the first word of each pair together with a list of four possible answers. The learner would press a button to indicate his response. If the answer was correct, the teacher would read the next word pair. However, if the answer was incorrect, the teacher would administer an electric shock to the learner, with the voltage increasing in 15-volt increments for each wrong answer. Before commencing, the teacher was given a mild electric shock as a sample of the initial shock they would be administering to the learner.

In fact, the learner in the next room received no electric shocks whatsoever. The actor playing this role would deliberately get some answers wrong and then react to the 'shock' administered by the teacher by crying out, apparently in pain. With each increase in voltage, the actor would also ramp up his performance so that it would sound as if he was in significant distress, at times even begging for the exercise to stop.

Meanwhile, the teacher was being instructed by the experimenter – as the voice of authority – to continue administering the increasingly powerful 'shocks' despite the apparent cries of pain from the learner. Throughout the experiment, the volunteer 'teachers' displayed varying degrees of tension and stress. Every one of them at some point paused and questioned the experiment but, nevertheless, more than 60 per cent of them continued up to the point where they were inflicting 'fatal voltages'.

Milgram and obedience to authority

The conclusions drawn from the Milgram experiments were as follows:

1 Somebody who has neither the ability nor the expertise to make decisions, especially in a crisis, will leave decision making to someone they consider to be more authoritative.
2 If a person comes to view themselves as the instrument for carrying out another person's wishes, they will no longer see themselves as responsible for their actions.
3 When experts tell people something is all right, they think it probably is, even if it does not seem to be.

Derren Brown's *The Heist*

In 2006, as part of a UK Channel 4 TV special called *The Heist*, Derren Brown re-enacted the Milgram experiments as part of a selection process to determine which of his volunteers would be prepared to stage an armed robbery, if instructed to do so. The results were almost identical to those of the original experiments, with over 50 per cent of participants continuing to administer 'shocks' up to the fatal voltage of 450V. From his final selection of four candidates, three did in fact carry out an 'armed' robbery of a security van, albeit with toy guns.

After filming, all four participants were 'deprogrammed' of any temporary criminal inclinations, spending time with Brown and an independent psychologist. *The Heist* faced some controversy after it was aired, but the four final participants reported that they were all pleased with the programme and, indeed, they are shown stating that it was a positive experience. A 2011 viewer poll revealed that *The Heist* was the viewers' favourite of all of Derren Brown's specials.

Similarly, 84 per cent of Milgram's participants surveyed after his experiments said that they had been 'glad' or 'very glad' to have taken part. Many of them wrote to Milgram later to express their thanks and some offered further assistance or asked to join his staff.

Authority and leadership

While it is unlikely that you would want to influence people to administer electric shocks to others or carry out an armed robbery, the following learning points are also relevant to a leadership or other influential role in a business environment:

1 If people are in a situation of uncertainty, they not only look to be led but *like* to be led and to be told what to do.
2 The views of someone who appears to be knowledgeable, confident, assured and an expert in their field are unlikely to be challenged.
3 Because of the previous two learning points, it is vital that the person fulfilling the role of authority figure conducts him- or herself with the utmost personal integrity.

Influencing with the 'power of three'

Although this book is not primarily about selling techniques or presentation skills, it is worth examining a principle that works effectively as a 'convincer' and is therefore a good tactic to use in a situation where you need to be influential.

Research has shown that people need repetition in order to feel 'convinced'. Further, it has been found that the 'magic' number of repetitions is three. In a sales context, this is often used as a closing technique where the sales person will ask the potential customer three questions, to which the answers will most likely be yes. The fourth question will then be the 'closing-the-deal' question and, because the customer has just replied positively three times, there is a strong chance that they will say yes again.

The power of three in action

Q1. 'So have I covered everything you need to know about this product?'

A. 'Yes.'

Q2. 'And you're happy with our free delivery service?'

A. 'Yes.'

Q3. 'And it's this particular model that you're interested in, isn't it?'

A. 'Yes.'

Q4. 'Good. So shall we process the paperwork and get it all sorted for you now?'

A. 'Yes.'

The same principle, of the power of three, also works well as a convincer when we are making a presentation. For example, a commonly used presentation structure is:

1 Tell them what you're going to tell them (introduction).
2 Tell them (content).
3 Tell them what you've told them (conclusion).

This structure means that your content is, in fact, delivered three times and thus gains more impact and becomes more memorable. There are many ways of using the power of three in a presentation or speech.

Martin Luther King and the power of three

An American Baptist minister, Martin Luther King Jr was best known for his role as a leader in the African-American civil rights movement. An advocate of non-violent civil disobedience, in 1964 he received the Nobel Peace Prize for combating racial inequality through non-violence and, over the next few years, until his assassination in 1968, he was also an activist in the fight against poverty and the Vietnam War.

In 1963, during a march on Washington, he established a reputation as one of the greatest orators in American history when he delivered his 'I have a dream' speech. Although it was just one of many speeches he delivered during his career, this is the one that people tend to remember him for, and the power of three played a very important part in it.

King not only used the power of three with the phrase 'I have a dream' but he also used it *to* the power of three – in other words, three times three times, in a total of nine iterations. The following is an extract from that speech with the key phrase shown in bold a total of nine times:

*And so even though we face the difficulties of today and tomorrow, I still **have a dream**. It is a dream deeply rooted in the American dream.*

***I have a dream** that one day this nation will rise up and live out the true meaning of its creed, 'We hold these truths to be self-evident, that all men are created equal.'*

***I have a dream** that one day on the red hills of Georgia, the sons of former slaves and the sons of former slave owners will be able to sit down together at the table of brotherhood.*

***I have a dream** that one day even the state of Mississippi, a state sweltering with the heat of injustice, sweltering with the heat of oppression, will be transformed into an oasis of freedom and justice.*

***I have a dream** that my four little children will one day live in a nation where they will not be judged by the colour of their skin but by the content of their character.*

***I have a dream** today!*

***I have a dream** that one day, down in Alabama, with its vicious racists, with its governor having his lips dripping with the words of 'interposition' and 'nullification' – one day right there in Alabama, little black boys and black girls will be able to join hands with little white boys and white girls as sisters and brothers.*

***I have a dream** today!*

***I have a dream** that one day every valley shall be exalted and every hill and mountain shall be made low, the rough places will be made plain, and the crooked places will be made straight; 'and the glory of the Lord shall be revealed and all flesh shall see it together.'*

This is our hope, and this is the faith that I go back to the South with.

After using the phrase for the first time, King repeated it *at the beginning* of each of the next eight statements, which was another good tactic for making it memorable and for positioning himself as a voice of authority.

Authority and tone of voice

In order to project a voice of authority, it is important that you consistently speak with a confident, firm (but not arrogant) tone. As already mentioned, Margaret Thatcher worked with a voice coach to lower her voice pitch and slow down her pace of speaking in order to give gravitas and authority to her voice. King George VI famously worked with Australian speech therapist Lionel Logue in order to overcome a stammer that was proving to be a major vocal impediment for his many public-speaking duties. (The story is captured in the film *The King's Speech*, which won Colin Firth an Oscar for his excellent portrayal of the king.)

Bad habits

When presenting, beware of the following (very common) habits that can undermine your voice of authority:

- Making very little eye contact with your audience
- Saying 'um' or 'err' a lot
- Speaking too quietly for people at the back to be able to hear you
- Rocking on your feet
- Turning your back to your audience to read from the PowerPoint slide displayed behind you
- Repeatedly clicking the top of a ballpoint pen
- Fiddling with cufflinks
- Fiddling with jewellery
- Repeatedly scratching the top of your head
- Clapping your hands together at the end of every sentence
- Hands in pockets

Sounding firm, fair and assertive

Maintaining a voice of authority when faced with an aggressive person or some other confrontational situation can be a challenge. However, the following structure, known as the **assertive sentence**, works extremely well. The results you get will greatly increase your confidence and generate a perception of you as someone who sounds like a voice of authority, to be respected. The assertive sentence is a valuable 'tool' to have in your mental toolbox, to use whenever an opportunity arises.

The assertive sentence has four parts, as follows:

1 **Acknowledge the other person's situation** – this demonstrates that you have listened to them and that you understand their position.
2 **Next, say 'However...'** – never use the word 'but', which will set up a barrier to what you are going to say next.
3 **State your position** – this might be quite different from theirs and needs to be out in the open.
4 **Suggest a mutually acceptable outcome** – you are looking for a workable compromise, a 'win/win' that will accommodate both their needs and yours.

An example of this is:

> *'I appreciate that you currently have a very high workload; however, your input at today's meeting is vital so that important decisions can be made, and therefore I'd be grateful if you could attend for the first 20 minutes to provide us with your data.'*

The end result always sounds very reasonable and, because the other person's situation has been acknowledged right at the beginning of the sentence, it is hard for them to refuse to co-operate. However, if you don't get the desired result the first time, and particularly if the other person says, 'Yes, but...' and puts forward another line of argument, then run through it again, this time using their new situation at the beginning.

Summary

In this chapter we explored how you can become a 'voice of authority' by looking at the characteristics of someone acknowledged as an authority figure.

The research by Stanley Milgram, later replicated by Derren Brown, proves that, in certain circumstances, people will do whatever they are told to do if they believe that the request is initiated by someone who is knowledgeable and in a position of authority. If you relate this to the business environment, you may observe that effective leaders tend to be those who are perceived as having expertise combined with confidence.

The power of three is a 'convincer strategy' that works well in a variety of situations, including that of making an influential presentation. The analysis of Martin Luther King's famous 'I have a dream' speech shows that that key phrase was used three times multiplied by another three times, for maximum effect.

You also learned about the importance of tone of voice, the bad habits to avoid and a technique for sounding firm, fair and assertive.

Fact-check (answers at the back)

1. What's an 'authority figure'?
    a) Someone older than you are ❑
    b) Someone not generally respected ❑
    c) Someone who impresses and inspires others ❑
    d) Someone who, if they asked you to do something, you would refuse ❑

2. What is a key skill of an authority figure?
    a) The ability to listen ❑
    b) Seeming to be too busy to have time for others ❑
    c) The ability to sound like an expert ❑
    d) The ability to enforce obedience ❑

3. What characterizes authority figures?
    a) Arrogance ❑
    b) A habit of making unreasonable demands on others ❑
    c) A willingness to keep secrets ❑
    d) The ability to embrace a challenge ❑

4. What were the Milgram experiments designed to measure?
    a) Obedience to an authority figure ❑
    b) Disobedience to a teacher ❑
    c) How people learn ❑
    d) How people react to electric shocks ❑

5. What roles did participants play in the Milgram experiments?
    a) Experimenter, teacher and learner ❑
    b) Questioner, teacher, onlooker ❑
    c) Interrogator, victim, onlooker ❑
    d) Evaluator, learner, convincer ❑

6. What were the conclusions of the Milgram experiments?
    a) People will let an authority figure make decisions for them ❑
    b) If people see themselves as the instrument for carrying out another person's wishes, they won't feel responsible for their actions ❑
    c) People learn that, when experts tell them something is all right, it probably is, even if it does not seem so ❑
    d) All of the above ❑

7. How many 'teachers' in the Milgram experiment continued to increase the voltage up to fatal levels?
    a) Fewer than 20 per cent ❑
    b) 35 per cent ❑
    c) More than 60 per cent ❑
    d) 100 per cent ❑

8. What was the purpose of *The Heist* TV special?
    a) To stage an armed robbery of a bank ❑
    b) To show that people can be influenced to behave out of character ❑
    c) To show people receiving electric shocks ❑
    d) To show that people like to be told what to do ❑

9. What is an effective method of convincing people of something?

a) Clapping the hands together loudly ❑
b) To use the 'power of three' technique ❑
c) Mentioning it once is enough ❑
d) To speak in a soft tone of voice ❑

10. What's the best way to project a voice of authority during a confrontation?

a) To speak quietly and hesitantly ❑
b) To use the assertive sentence technique ❑
c) To avoid making eye contact in case they turn hostile ❑
d) Keeping your hands in your pockets ❑

CHAPTER 18

Speaking the language of influence

The best influencers are superb communicators – this is the *key* skill that will deliver the best results for you.

Whether you're communicating with others face to face, over the telephone or in writing, you need to be clear, positive and persuasive. Your message does not have to be verbal: even the way you dress delivers a message about you that may enhance or damage your ability to influence others.

In this chapter we will explore how to improve your communication using proven, effective techniques. You will learn about rapport, why it's essential to have it in order to influence others, and how to build it effortlessly and rapidly. You will understand what makes everyone unique, and why it's so important to have a flexible communication style in order to influence the maximum number of people.

You will also learn how to calm down an angry person easily and assertively, without taking on board their emotional state. You will discover the language to use and the actions to take to get people on board with your way of thinking. You will even learn how to 'read' people's eye movements and understand what they *really* mean.

There is only one version of you

Each one of us is as individual as a fingerprint. Although we might be similar to others, there will always be differences that contribute to our uniqueness. The way we make sense of the world around us – and how we think, feel and behave as a result of that – has an effect on how we communicate with others and how we like others to communicate with us. By understanding how this process works, you can start to develop flexibility in your communication style, which will enable you to become far more persuasive.

The following diagram represents the 'core model' of neuro-linguistic programming (NLP) and illustrates how we take in information from around us (external events), pass it through our own individual set of 'filters', make sense of it, react to it emotionally and physically, and finally behave in a way that feels appropriate to us.

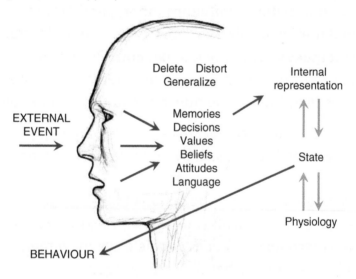

The NLP model of what we do with external information

We take in what is going on around us through our five senses. However, if we tried to process all this information, it would be more than our conscious mind, with its limited capacity, could handle. By contrast, the unconscious mind has a virtually unlimited capacity: it contains thoughts, memories and desires as well as automatic skills that are under the surface of our conscious awareness but which still have a great impact on our behaviour.

Filters and our 'map of the world'

To protect our conscious mind from overload, we all have a set of 'filters', made up of such things as memories, decisions, values, beliefs, attitudes, language and a lot more. We create and amend these filters as we progress through life, based on our ongoing experiences. Because everyone's experiences of life are different, everyone's set of filters is unique to them.

The role of the filters is to delete, distort or generalize information coming in, in order to make sense of it. The information then becomes an 'internal representation' of what is going on outside us – in other words, it becomes a thought. Attached to the thought is a state of mind, or emotion, so the thought could, for example, be happy, sad or angry. Aligned to the emotional state of mind is the physiology, or body language.

As a result of this whole process, we create an internal 'map of the world', which we use to find our way around the 'territory' out there. The output from this core model is our behaviour, which will always make perfect sense to us but may not be perceived in that way by other people.

Given, then, that everyone is unique, it is a challenge to influence other people and gain their co-operation. To achieve this, we need to find a way to 'build a bridge' across to their personal map of the world. We do this by building rapport.

What is rapport?

The word rapport stems from the French verb *rapporter*, which literally means to carry something back. In 'building our bridge' across to someone else, they connect with us and a feeling of mutual understanding flows right back. If you experience resistance or negativity in someone you wish to influence, this may indicate that rapport is missing.

Rapport builds naturally and can often be witnessed when the body language of two people who are getting on well together becomes 'matched' or 'mirrored'. Matching means that their body language is identical – for example, each person has their right leg crossed over their left and is leaning to their left. Mirroring means that one person is the mirror image of the other, so if one of them has their right leg crossed over their left and is leaning to their left, the other person will have their left leg crossed over their right and be leaning to their right. You are more likely to be *matched* with someone you are sitting or standing next to and *mirrored* with someone opposite you. Both are external indicators that rapport has been built.

This natural matching and mirroring process is also referred to as 'entrainment'.

Entrainment

A Dutch scientist named Christian Huygens discovered the phenomenon of entrainment in about 1665. Huygens had a room with a number of pendulum-driven clocks in it, and he observed that, over time, the pendulums of all the clocks fell into synchronization with each other. Even if he deliberately started them swinging at different times, he would inevitably return to find they had all become synchronized. He named this synchronization tendency 'entrainment'.

Building rapport

It is, of course, possible to speed up this process of rapport building through entrainment by deliberately matching or mirroring the other person. If you choose to do this, subtlety is essential because, if what you are doing is too obvious, it may cause offence.

The following pie chart shows the three elements of communication – physiology (body language), tone of voice and words – and their relative proportions. Much research has been conducted on these figures, principally by Albert Mehrabian, Professor Emeritus of Psychology at UCLA.

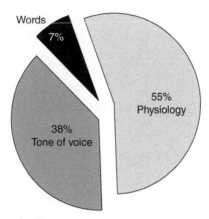

Segments of communication

The largest slice of the pie is physiology, or body language, at 55 per cent. Even if you are not speaking, your body language 'speaks' for you. However, on the telephone, you have lost this element because your body language cannot be seen. However, a smile can be heard: if you change the shape of your mouth into a smile, your voice will sound different. It will sound happier and more positive, so it's always a good idea to answer the phone with a smile on your face.

Let's explore how you can utilize each of these three elements to build rapport.

Physiology – the 55 per cent

Start by matching or mirroring the other person's posture, gestures and movements. Be careful to avoid mimicry. For example, if someone is sitting opposite you and they suddenly cross their legs, lean forward, put one elbow on the table and rest their chin on their hand, do not immediately do the same thing. This would be too obvious and could well cause offence.

Instead, make gradual movements of your own until you have created a similarity to their body language.

Matching another person's breathing rate is a far more subtle and yet powerful way to build rapport. Watch for the slight rise and fall of their shoulders and adjust your breathing into the same rhythm.

The final thing that you can match on body language is your blink rate. Again, don't be obvious, and if the other person has an eye defect such as a squint, don't hurt their feelings by mirroring this. Otherwise this is another very effective way of creating a similarity and building rapport at an unconscious level.

Tone of voice – the 38 per cent

Have you ever spoken with someone who had a strong accent or dialect and become aware that you were unintentionally starting to speak in that same accent or dialect? This is a guaranteed way of offending through mimicry, caused by your unconscious mind's desire to create a similarity and build rapport. Although this can happen when you are speaking face to face, it is more likely to happen during a telephone conversation, when physiology plays very little part and tone of voice becomes approximately 80 per cent of the communication.

Instead, you can safely match the following characteristics of the other person's voice:

- volume
- speed
- tone
- pitch
- energy
- intonation
- phrasing

Imagine for a moment that you have an angry person in front of you. What has happened to their voice? It has probably speeded up, got louder and become higher pitched. Perhaps you've been in this situation and you chose to stay really calm, but the other person, instead of calming down, got even angrier. The reason for this is that rapport was lacking; the gap between you was too wide for you to be able to be a calming influence on them. The other person's unconscious mind was telling him or her that, because you were so different from them, you just didn't understand the gravity of the situation and so they would have to 'ramp up' their own behaviour in order to make their point more clearly.

In this scenario, you can use a technique called *pacing and leading*. If you listen to the vocal characteristics of this angry person and reply using those same characteristics, you are expressing empathy and building a bridge across to their map of the world. This is called *pacing*. After a short time of doing this, start to slow down your voice, turn down the volume and lower the pitch. If sufficient rapport has been built, the other person will now start to follow you and calm down. You are now *leading*. This is a very effective strategy and, because the other person is responding at an unconscious level, it will feel completely natural to them and not manipulative at all.

Words – the 7 per cent

Words form the smallest element of communication. If ever you have spent many hours writing a speech or a presentation, you will be pleased to know that this constituted just 7 per cent of your total message. The other 93 per cent was conveyed in how you stood up and delivered it! Over the telephone, words play a greater part in rapport building, increasing in value to about 20 per cent.

In order to match someone else on their vocabulary, listen for the following:

● **Key words** – these are either individual words or short phrases that we like and use a lot. They vary from individual to individual, depending on their preferences, and may include words such as:
  – basically
  – actually
  – cool
  – like

- you know
- OK
- at the end of the day
- the bottom line is...

If you detect that someone is using a particular word or short phrase repeatedly, then you are hearing their key words. When you respond to them, incorporate those same words into your reply, and you are then 'speaking their language'. A word of caution – do not reflect back their key words in every sentence you speak as it will be too obvious that this is what you are doing.

- **VHF words** – when we speak, we tend to use words that fit into our preferred 'channel' of communication. These can be:
  - **visual**
    'I see what you mean', 'Looks good to me', 'Show me more'
  - **hearing**
    'I hear what you're saying', 'That rings a bell', 'Sounds familiar'
  - **feeling**
    'I want to get a grip on this idea', 'I'm going with my gut feeling', 'That really touched me', etc.

If you can hear someone using vocabulary that falls predominantly into one of these three channels, then adjust your language so that you are using the same type of words. When you do this, you have 'tuned into their wavelength' and can begin to 'speak their language'.

What's your preference?

Because we naturally communicate in the channel that is our predominant one, you may not be aware of whether your preference is visual, hearing or feeling. Complete the following questionnaire by reading each question in turn and circling the answer a, b or c that is most appropriate for you.

Question	Answer
1 What would make you think that someone might be lying to you?	a) The way they look – or avoid looking – at you b) Their tone of voice c) A feeling you get about their sincerity
2 How do you know that you have had a good day at work?	b) A productive meeting or good news over the telephone a) A clear desk or a 'to do' list with everything ticked off c) An inner glow, a smile and a feeling of deep satisfaction
3 What kind of activity do you prefer on holiday?	c) Lazing on a sun-drenched beach, swimming to cool off b) Attending a concert or a lecture on local culture and history a) Seeing the sights and local colour, visiting a museum or art gallery
4 Which of the following groups of hobbies/ interests appeals most to you?	a) Cinema, photography, art, interior design c) Sport, sculpture, cookery, gardening b) Playing a musical instrument, listening to music or an audio book, singing.
5 What types of television programme do you prefer to watch?	c) Wildlife and animals a) An artist at work b) Musical concert
6 Which of the following would you prefer as a 'special' treat?	b) A personal dedication on the radio by a celebrity you admire a) A weekend break away somewhere you have never visited before c) Your favourite meal with good wine and good company
7 Which would be the best way for you to unwind at the end of a hard day?	a) Gazing at something relaxing such as a candle flame c) An aromatherapy massage b) Talking to a friend
8 If you want to thank or reward someone for doing you a favour, what would you do?	b) Telephone them to tell them how grateful you are c) Give them a bottle of their favourite drink/bottle of perfume a) Write them a thank-you note

Question	Answer
9 Which of the following groups of careers most appeals?	a) An artist or designer in television b) Lecturer, telesales or professional speaker c) Gardener, nurse or counsellor
10 Which accessories do you like to have in your home?	b) Wind chimes, background music, ticking clock a) Lots of pictures, accented lighting, a focal point, e.g. a fireplace c) Pot-pourri, soft cushions, comfortable, squashy chairs
11 Which type of magazine would you be most likely to pick up and read?	c) Home decorating, sports or creative crafts b) Music or current affairs a) Art, photography or fashion
12 How would you discipline a naughty child?	a) With a severe look or frown c) With punishment by deprivation, e.g. no pocket money b) By shouting or using a stern tone of voice

Add up your scores by letter and make a note of them.

a) .... (visual)
b) .... (hearing)
c) .... (feeling)

Your preferred 'channel' is the one with your highest score.

The VHF types

The following are descriptions of the three types. Notice whether the description of your preferred 'channel' is a good match for you.

● **Visual**

Typically, people who are in a visual mode stand or sit with their heads erect and their eyes up and will be breathing from the top of their lungs. They often sit forward in their chair or on the edge of the chair. They tend to be quite organized, neat, well groomed and orderly. They are appearance-oriented, and may sometimes be quieter than other people. They are generally good spellers, memorize by seeing pictures and are not easily distracted by noise. They may have trouble remembering verbal instructions and are bored by long verbal explanations because their mind tends to wander. They would rather read than be read to and, ideally, like to have information presented to them using pictures, charts and diagrams.

A visual person will be interested in how someone looks at them, and will notice details of others' appearance such as their dress style. They will tend to use visual imagery in phrases like 'See you later', 'Looking good', 'In my mind's eye', 'I get the picture', etc.

● Hearing

Someone who has a 'hearing' preference will move their eyes sideways and may tilt their head to one side when they are listening. They breathe from the middle of the chest. They often move their lips when they are mentally saying words and may even talk to themselves when thinking something through. They are easily distracted by noise but can generally repeat things back to you easily. They may find spoken language easier than maths and writing. They like music and learn by listening; they memorize by using steps, procedures and sequences.

A 'hearing' person is often interested in being told how they're doing and is more likely to notice tone of voice and other vocal characteristics. They tend to use hearing imagery in words and phrases like 'Tell me more', 'That rings a bell', 'Sounds familiar', etc.

● Feeling

There are two types of 'feeling' people. The first type has a posture that tends to slump over and they may move and talk slowly. They are laid back, with a calm demeanour, and fond of relaxing. The second type is more active and 'talks with their hands', i.e. they gesticulate when speaking and may fidget when sitting still. Both types will typically access their feelings and emotions to 'get a feel' for what they're doing, so they may be naturally intuitive.

Feeling people can be quite tactile and they like to learn by doing – the 'hands-on' approach. These people will really notice a limp handshake and be thoroughly unimpressed by it! They use feeling words and phrases like 'I've got a gut feeling', 'Get in touch', 'I'm going with my instincts', 'Let's make contact', etc.

Eye movements and thinking styles

Imagine that you're having a face-to-face conversation with someone. You're listening for the VHF words but the language seems neutral. There is another way of telling whether someone is thinking in pictures, sounds or feelings and that is by the way their eyes move when they are thinking of what they are going to say next or when they are processing the answer to a question.

Carry out the following exercise with the participation of someone else. You will see that there are a series of questions, five for 'A' and five for 'B'. Take it in turns to ask each other the questions, one of you as 'A' and the other as 'B'. Use a grid for each question like the one shown below and, for each one, position your pen or pencil in the middle of the grid and trace the other person's eye movements on the grid as they mentally process the answer to that question. Draw exactly what you see. If their eyes move upwards and to the right, draw that, even though this would be to their left. The eyes may move to several different places before the answer has been processed and this is fine – just track every movement you observe on to the grid.

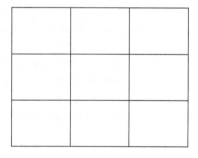

Questions for 'A'

1 What does your favourite actor sound like?
2 What would a pink giraffe look like if it were wearing sunglasses and open-toed sandals?
3 Can you spell your full name backwards?
4 What was the front-page headline in your newspaper yesterday?
5 What would the national anthem sound like if it were sung backwards, under water?

Questions for 'B'

1 What would a whale singing 'Happy birthday to you' sound like?
2 How many doors are there in your home?
3 Who was the first person you spoke to on the telephone yesterday?
4 What clothes were you wearing last Saturday?
5 How much is 1,296 divided by 4?

When we are thinking about what we are going to say next, or we are processing the answer to a question, our eyes move in particular directions, depending on whether we are mentally processing in pictures, sounds or feelings.

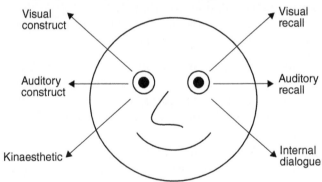

How people think – eye-accessing cues

V: visual thinkers

If the eyes go up, we are visualizing:

● Up and to our right (left if you are observing someone else's eyes) means that we are visually constructing an image of something we haven't seen before.

- Up and to our left (right if you are observing someone else) means that we are visually recalling something that we have seen before.
- We are also visually processing if our eyes are looking straight ahead into the distance, or if they are closed, as if we are getting images on the backs of our eyelids.

H: hearing thinkers

- If our eyes move sideways and to our right (left in someone you are observing), we are imagining what something could sound like that we haven't heard before.
- If our eyes move sideways and to our left (right in someone you are observing), then we are remembering what something sounds like that we have heard before.

F: feeling thinkers

- If our eyes move down and to our right (left in someone you are observing), then we are processing in feelings, or kinaesthetically. These could be emotions or we could be imagining the physical feel of touching something.
- If our eyes move down and to our left (right in someone you are observing), then we are listening to our internal dialogue – that voice inside our head that lets us know what we are thinking and feeling.

You can use this eye movement information as an aid to influencing. Let's say that you are having a discussion with someone and you have made some kind of proposal to them. As they are silently considering it, their eyes look upwards. You now know that they are processing in pictures, so you could match your language to their thought patterns. You could, for example, say, 'I can *see* that you are giving this a lot of thought. Is there anything else I can *show* you that might make it *clearer*?'

You cannot not communicate. Even if you are not speaking, your body language and overall appearance will speak for you. Make sure the message that you're sending out is the one you want to convey.

Rapport in writing

If you are writing to someone and you don't know their preferred VHF channel, or if you are writing something that will be read by many people – so that there will be a mix of all three channels – then balance the number of visual, hearing and feeling words you use. This will ensure that at least a third of your text will be 'speaking their language'. For example, 'We love to keep *in touch* with our customers, to *show* them that we are really interested in *hearing* how they are getting on.'

One author who does this very effectively and successfully is J. K. Rowling. If you open any of her Harry Potter books anywhere, you will see that she has skilfully balanced the visual, hearing and feeling words on every page. If you are an aspiring author, this could be a good technique to emulate.

Summary

In this chapter we explored how to communicate influentially and build rapport with others, at both a conscious and an unconscious level.

The NLP 'core' model illustrates how everyone is unique, constructing their own personal 'map of the world' determined by internal 'filters'. Building rapport with someone creates a bridge to their world which enables a two-way spirit of co-operation to develop. The three elements of communication – body language (physiology), tone of voice and words – provide opportunities for matching and mirroring face to face, over the phone and in writing.

You now know whether you are predominantly a visual, hearing or feeling person and how to detect these different ways of thinking in others by observing their eye movements. By matching your vocabulary to the 'channel' in which the other person is thinking, you'll be able to 'speak their language' and thereby become more influential.

Fact-check (answers at the back)

1. How do we protect our conscious mind from overload?
   a) Through a set of 'filters' that are unique to each of us ❏
   b) By ignoring our memories ❏
   c) By using our unconscious mind with its unlimited capacity ❏
   d) By processing input from three senses only ❏

2. What do our filters do?
   a) Exclude painful thoughts ❏
   b) Separate us from others ❏
   c) Cause the conscious mind to become overloaded ❏
   d) Make sense of incoming information ❏

3. What's the fastest way to change our state of mind?
   a) Change our environment ❏
   b) Talk to someone with a different point of view ❏
   c) Change our physiology, or body language ❏
   d) We can't – our thoughts and emotions are fixed ❏

4. What is our 'map of the world'?
   a) Our unique way of seeing the world ❏
   b) What we make of others' memories ❏
   c) A three-dimensional map of our neighbourhood ❏
   d) How we visualize our thoughts ❏

5. Why is rapport important in communication?
   a) It's not important ❏
   b) People like to see others copying their movements ❏
   c) It makes us more aware of others' eye movements ❏
   d) It enables us to build a bridge to someone else's map of the world ❏

6. What are the three elements of communication?
   a) Physiology, tone of voice, words ❏
   b) Eye contact, handshake, written word ❏
   c) Dress code, smiling, gestures ❏
   d) Telephone, face to face, emails ❏

7. What makes up the smallest element of communication?
   a) Physiology ❏
   b) Words ❏
   c) Tone of voice ❏
   d) Pacing and leading ❏

8. When should you use pacing and leading?
   a) When you want to experiment with a new way of communicating ❏
   b) To mimic the other person's accent ❏
   c) To help calm down an angry person ❏
   d) When you can't match somebody's blink rate ❏

9. What is 'speaking somebody's language'?
   a) Matching their key words ❏
   b) Mimicking the other person's breathing rate ❏
   c) Speaking more loudly if someone is quietly spoken ❏
   d) Using the same tone of voice over the telephone ❏

10. What does VHF stand for?
   a) Virtual, hearing, feeling ❏
   b) Visual, hearsay, feedback loop ❏
   c) Visual, hearing, feeling ❏
   d) Viral, healing, falling ❏

CHAPTER 19

Flexible influencing

You can use several further NLP techniques to enable you to develop more flexibility in your influencing and persuasion methods.

In this chapter we shall look at some of the 'presuppositions' or 'excellence beliefs' upon which NLP has been built and see how operating within these beliefs can improve your success. We'll also explore some of the NLP language techniques that work particularly well when influencing. We will review the importance of having empowering beliefs in place when you are aiming to increase your ability to influence well, and how your own language may be undermining your belief in yourself.

Finally, you will learn how to create a 'future history' through a specific visualization technique. This technique allows you to visualize a future event unfolding in exactly the way you want it to, in order to help you generate a good outcome in reality. You can use the technique in advance of any situation in which you need to be at your influential best.

The power of 'excellence beliefs'

NLP was first developed in the 1970s as a study of excellence, with top achievers such as Walt Disney being researched and 'modelled' so that their tried-and-tested techniques for success could be learned and used by others. It is now accepted globally as one of the most powerful and effective personal development methodologies available. Working within its 'principles of excellence' or presuppositions, listed below, can strengthen your communications and in turn improve your power to persuade and influence others.

'The person with the most flexible behaviour can have the most influence on an outcome.'

This 'excellence belief' means that, if your strategy is to have a number of different approaches planned in advance, then you can easily switch between them to achieve a desired outcome. By contrast, if you have planned only one route to your goal and an obstacle occurs that blocks this route, you will not achieve your goal. This attitude is typical in people who say things like, 'It's my way or the highway.' In other words, if others do not 'buy into' their views, they have no fallback option as an alternative.

'The meaning of communication is the response it elicits.'

In any communication, whether one to one or one to many, the only way you can know how you are doing is by noticing the feedback you are getting. You will probably have experienced this, perhaps if you were explaining something a little complicated to another person and you noticed a puzzled expression on their face. You instinctively realized that they did not understand what you just said, so you might have continued with, 'In other words...' and then explained it again in a different way. When their response changed to one of comprehension, indicated perhaps with a slight smile and nod of the head, this told you that your message was understood.

During any kind of influencing scenario, it is essential that you are continually noticing the feedback you are getting from your audience.

The fastest way to change your state of mind is to change your body language. If you are feeling nervous before a presentation or meeting, choose to adopt upright, open, confident-looking body language and it will have a positive effect on how you feel. You could say that this is 'fake it 'til you make it', but if it works, why not?

'If you always do what you've always done, you will always get what you've always got. So if what you're doing isn't working, do something different.'

Einstein's definition of insanity was 'doing the same thing over and over and expecting to get different results'. If, for example, your presentation that you hoped would influence and persuade didn't work the first time, there is a strong chance that it will fall short next time also. Revisit it, review it, revise it – do whatever it takes, but make sure you do something differently in order to generate a different result.

'There is no such thing as failure; there is only feedback.'

Imagine that you have an important meeting with a senior director in your organization. Your objective is to present your ideas for a radical new product or service that you are passionate about and which you would like your organization to adopt. You think it goes well but the director rejects your proposal. You leave the meeting feeling that you have failed.

You didn't fail. In fact, all that happened was that you got a result that wasn't the one you wanted. Instead, what you actually got was a valuable learning opportunity. Use it well and then do something different next time. When things go the way we expect them to, we learn nothing. When things *don't* go the way we want them to, they present fabulous opportunities to learn and grow. Allow your mind to formulate an answer to this question: 'What would you do if you *knew* you couldn't fail?'

'If one person can do it, others can too.'

This presupposition reflects the fundamental principle of NLP, that of modelling excellence in others. Think of someone you know who has influencing abilities that you admire. What exactly are they doing to be so persuasive, and how could you adopt their techniques for yourself? And then think of others whom you admire, and do the same thing. Model their excellence and you will be able to replicate their success.

Modelling excellence: the four-minute mile

Before 1954, when Roger Bannister became the first person to run a mile in under four minutes, many 'experts', including doctors, had confidently stated that it was impossible for a human being to achieve this feat. They said that their heart would explode, their lungs would collapse and their shinbones would shatter. Perhaps not surprisingly, the previous record of four minutes 1.4 seconds had stood for nine years, because who would want to have all these awful things happen to them? However, Bannister, himself a junior doctor as well as an athlete, decided not only that it was possible but that he was the man to do it.

The record he set, of three minutes 59.4 seconds, stood for just 46 days until it was broken and it has since been broken by many more athletes. In the last 50 years the record has been lowered by almost 17 seconds, and it is now estimated that well in excess of 1,000 athletes have run a mile in under four minutes.

'Resistance in someone you wish to influence is a sign of lack of rapport.'

The better the rapport you have with someone, the more productive the conversation will be and the easier it will be to influence them. If you sense from the feedback you are receiving from the other person that there is some kind of unseen barrier between you, there is a strong chance that rapport is missing. Chapter 18 focused on rapport building using the principles of matching and mirroring body language, tone of voice and words. It might be that, in your keenness to start influencing, you skipped over this important step. Remember that you need to build a bridge across to the other person's 'map of the world'. Without this bridge in place, there is little or no connection.

'The mind and body are part of the same structure and affect each other.'

The power of body language

Here's a short exercise for you: sit up straight in your chair, look up at the ceiling, hold a big smile on your face and, staying like that, try to feel really miserable.

How was that? Did you manage to feel really miserable? Perhaps not, so let's try the opposite to see if that is any easier. This time, slump down in your chair, look down at the floor, hold a really 'long' expression on your face and try to feel really happy.

Was that a success? You probably could not do it. So what is going on? The mind and body are inextricably linked and will always reflect each other's 'states'. In this exercise, you first adopted a body language that reflected happy thoughts and feelings, and then tried to create a state of mind – miserable – in complete opposition to that body language. In that conflict, probably the body language won. Similarly, the body language probably won again when you adopted a 'miserable' body language and tried to feel happy.

The exercise above deliberately asked you to *try* to feel an emotion that was in conflict with your body language. Your mind interpreted this as 'try and fail'. The word 'try' has a get-out clause in it. If this is a word you use in your vocabulary, you are setting yourself up to fail. It is much better to say what you *will* do rather than what you will *try* to do.

In a similar fashion, your mind cannot process a negative command because it doesn't understand what it is not supposed to do. For example, whatever you do now, don't think about a yellow door. Now, what are you thinking about? Perhaps a yellow door? If you use the word 'don't' in your vocabulary, you may well get the opposite result to the one you want. To achieve a better outcome, always say what you *do* want rather than what you *don't* want.

People will stereotype you within four seconds according to your visual appearance so, if your body language is in any way negative or uncertain, this will set the scene for you before you have spoken a single word.

'There is a solution to every problem.'

This inspiring excellence belief tells us that, no matter what the problem is, there is always a solution – we just may not have discovered it yet. While it may not be the 'ideal' solution, nevertheless, it is a solution. For example, in the course of running my business, I have occasionally had clients who didn't pay my invoices and then went bust. The solution I would have liked was to be paid the money they owed me but, because these companies had stopped trading, that just wasn't going to happen. The actual solution was to write off the debts, put those clients behind me and move on with my business. All the time that we hold on to a problem, we are holding on to a potential stressor. We must therefore seek alternatives that will resolve the problem and give us closure with it.

Memory and imagination

'Memory and imagination use the same neurological circuits and can potentially have the same impact on the individual.'

Because memory and imagination use the same neurological circuits, your mind cannot tell the difference between a remembered activity and an imagined one, which means that if you visualize something vividly enough, your mind thinks it is looking at a memory. And your mind believes that if you've already carried out this activity in the past, then you can do it again.

Visualization: Linford Christie

In 1992, British sprinter Linford Christie won the 100m gold medal at the Barcelona Olympic Games, becoming at 32 years of age the oldest athlete to have achieved this feat. As part of his training, he had worked with a visualization of running down an imaginary tunnel on the stimulus of the sound of the starting gun. The purpose of the tunnel in the visualization was to eliminate all other visual distractions such as the other competitors and the crowd. The auditory stimulus was the 'B' of the 'bang' from the gun.

In his mind, Christie had run this race hundreds of times and, of course, he had won it every time, so when he lined up on the starting blocks that day, there was no doubt in his mind that he was about to replicate his imagined, gold-medal-winning performance. And so he did.

This is the reason why so many outstanding performers, whether in sport, business or other arenas, attribute their success to visualization. Roger Bannister visualized himself running the four-minute mile. Boxer Muhammad Ali would create what he called 'future history' by visualizing every round of a forthcoming boxing match in minute detail and then predicting the round in which he would knock out his opponent. He would then take great delight in announcing this to his opponent prior to the fight commencing, along with his affirmation, 'I am the greatest.'

How to create a winning visualization

If you have a meeting or presentation coming up at which you need to be at your influential best, then create a visualization of the event unfolding exactly the way you want it to and keep running through it as a mental rehearsal. For the best results, incorporate the following points:

1 You need to be fully 'associated' with it, so imagine that you are seeing the event through your own eyes, as if it is going on around you.

2 Break the event down into stages and build a checkpoint into each one. For example, when you enter the room where the event is to take place, who is the first person to greet you and what exactly will they say? What would be the next stage and what checkpoint could you create for that? And so on.

3 The more sensory information you can incorporate, the better. What do you see? What does the room look like? What are you wearing? What do you hear? Include specific words that the other people there would say, such as 'impressive' or 'this sounds really good'. How are you feeling? Confident? Relaxed? Include whatever feelings are appropriate. Even include smell and taste if you can – perhaps you would be drinking a cup of coffee or a glass of water. If so, include these.

4 Imagine that the final part is the successful outcome that you want to achieve. Build in exactly how that will feel and imagine how you will congratulate yourself on a job well done.

Influencing through language

When we speak, we are usually conveying a shortened, simplified and generalized version of what we are thinking. In so doing, we often leave out or even distort some of the information, which leads to misunderstandings and to some important facts being withheld.

Much of the language adopted in NLP was modelled from well-known psychiatrist and hypnotherapist Milton Erickson, who was able to facilitate phenomenal changes in his clients conversationally. The NLP 'meta model' uses language to clarify meaning and thus ensure that you gain a clear understanding of the words used by others. The benefit of using the meta model is that it helps you to gain a better understanding of what somebody is *really* saying. Because a person will always be speaking through the filters of their own personal map of the world, we may often be unsure about what they really mean. However, we can clarify what they mean by asking specific questions. This will then enable us to be far more effective as an influencer.

The following are elements of the NLP meta model.

Unspecified nouns

This is where we replace the noun in a sentence with words such as 'they' or 'it', or where the noun is implied rather than specified. To gain a more accurate understanding, ask questions such as 'Who or what, specifically?' For example:

● 'They are making a decision today.' 'Who are?'
● 'It's always been done this way.' 'What, specifically?'

Unspecified verbs

This follows the same principle as unspecified nouns, but here it is the verbs used that fail to convey enough information to get across the full message. In this case, ask, 'How, specifically?' For example:

● 'I was helped to do this.' 'How, specifically?'
● 'Just get on and do it.' 'How, specifically?'

Comparisons

Comparisons are often used in advertisements, for example when a product is described as 'better' without the ad saying what it is being compared with. Clarify by asking, 'Compared with what?' For example:

- 'This one is better.' 'Better than what?'
- 'He was at his worst today.' 'Compared with what?'

Judgements

These are similar to comparisons, in that a view is expressed without specifying whose view it is. Clarify by asking questions to establish whose judgement it is and/or on what basis the judgement has been made. For example:

- 'This is the best one on the market.' 'By what criteria is it the best?'
- 'This does the best job.' 'In whose opinion?'

Nominalizations

Also called abstract nouns, nominalizations are nouns that started off as verbs. As nouns they are vaguer and more intangible than the original active verb. A verb such as 'educate' becomes a static noun ('education'). To clarify its meaning, turn the nominalization back into a verb and ask for qualifying information. For example:

- 'I received a good education at home.' 'Who educated you? How did they do that?'
- 'We had lengthy discussions.' 'What did you discuss?'

Modal operators of possibility

These are words that reflect our beliefs around what is and is not possible for us. They may well reflect limiting beliefs and can be explored by asking, 'What would happen if you did?' or 'What stops you?' For example:

- 'I can't present in public.' 'What would happen if you did?'
- 'I can't speak to him.' 'What stops you?'

Modal operators of necessity

These are similar to the possibility words but they reflect needs rather than beliefs. They can be explored using similar questions as for modal operators of possibility. For example:

- 'I must be the last to leave the office.' 'What would happen if you weren't?'
- 'I ought to learn how to do that.' 'What would happen if you didn't?'

Universal quantifiers

These are sweeping generalizations that allow for no exceptions. They utilize words such as 'all', 'every', 'always' and 'never' and can be challenged by reflecting them back or by asking about any possible exceptions. For example:

- 'I never remember people's names.' 'Never? Has there ever been a time when you did remember a name?'
- 'I always make bad decisions.' 'Always? Have you ever made a decision that wasn't bad?'

Complex equivalence

This is when two statements are linked to imply that they mean the same thing, but they may well be based on an incorrect assumption. Clarify the statements by asking how one statement 'means' the other one. For example:

- 'He doesn't attend our weekly meetings any more ... he must be too busy.' 'How does his lack of attendance necessarily mean that he is too busy?'
- 'She never rings me any more ... I must have offended her.' 'How does her not ringing you mean you've offended her?'

Presuppositions

Presuppositions – a term also used to mean beliefs that underpin NLP – imply, in the context of language, assumptions that may or may not be correct. Clarify such an assumption by asking, 'What leads you to believe that...?' For example:

- 'Would you like the blue one or the red one?' 'What leads you to believe that I wish to purchase either of them?'
- 'When you go to the meeting, what will you say?' 'What makes you think I'm going? How do you know I'm going to speak?'

Cause and effect

Although similar to complex equivalence, in cause and effect one statement is taken to have caused the other one. This can reflect an inappropriate 'blame' being allocated, especially if emotions are involved. For example, 'You make me so angry when you do that' implies that one person has complete control over another person's emotions, whereas the reality is that we all choose our own emotions. Clarify the statement by asking exactly how one element has caused the other one. For example:

- 'I'd like to exercise more but I don't have the time.' 'What would have to happen for you to have the time to exercise?'
- 'I was going to say something but I knew he'd take it the wrong way.' 'How do you know he'd take what you said the wrong way?'

Mind reading

This is where one person presumes that they know what another person is thinking. We often base our presumptions on how we ourselves would be thinking or feeling in the same situation and we project it on to the other person. Alternatively, it could be the result of a misinterpretation of the other person's body language. We can ask for clarification by saying, 'How exactly do you know...?' For example:

- 'I know you don't like my idea.' 'How exactly do you know that?'
- 'She's ignoring me.' 'How can you be sure?'

Summary

In this chapter we have drawn on some of the key principles of NLP in order to incorporate flexibility into your influencing style. The more flexible you can be, the better equipped you will be to 'think on your feet' during any interaction in which you need to influence others.

The quality of your language will determine the quality of your results. You discovered how the elimination of words such as 'try' and 'don't' can make profound positive differences to your outcomes, and you saw how you can filter language not only to influence others but also to influence yourself.

You also discovered how to create and use an effective visualization, a technique used by highly successful people as a mental rehearsal for their achievements.

We also explored the meta model of language, which employs questioning to clarify what others are saying, avoid misunderstandings and open up opportunities for influential conversation.

Fact-check (answers at the back)

1. What does NLP stand for?
   a) Neuro-linguistic procedures ❑
   b) New language perception ❑
   c) Neuro-linguistic
      programming ❑
   d) Neurotic language principles ❑

2. What's the best way to
   ensure that your message is
   understood?
   a) By ignoring the feedback –
      it's unnecessary when you
      are communicating with
      someone ❑
   b) By repeating it more loudly
      until it is understood ❑
   c) By noticing the feedback you
      are getting and adjusting your
      message accordingly ❑
   d) Trying again later by going
      over it again in the same way ❑

3. What is the best way to achieve
   a goal?
   a) By having several possible
      routes to that goal ❑
   b) With one good, well-thought-
      out route ❑
   c) By keeping on with what you
      are doing, even if it doesn't
      work first time ❑
   d) By being content with any
      result, even if it isn't the one
      you wanted ❑

4. What's the best way to think
   about a problem?
   a) Some problems have no
      solution ❑
   b) There is a solution to every
      problem, although it may
      not be the ideal one ❑
   c) Holding on to a problem is a
      stress-free option ❑
   d) Solutions must be ideal, or
      they are no solution at all ❑

5. How did athletes break Roger
   Bannister's four-minute mile
   record?
   a) By modelling excellence ❑
   b) By ignoring the naysayers ❑
   c) By competing with one
      another ❑
   d) By improving their fitness ❑

6. How can you tell whether you
   have achieved rapport with
   someone?
   a) They show resistance to
      your ideas ❑
   b) They start to match and
      mirror your body language ❑
   c) You have made physical
      contact with them ❑
   d) You feel that you can read
      their mind ❑

7. What's the fastest way to change your state of mind?
a) Ask your mind to process a negative command ❏
b) Change your body language ❏
c) Leave the room and do something else for a few minutes ❏
d) Say what you don't want in order to get what you do want ❏

8. Why should you never have the word 'try' in your influencing vocabulary?
a) It makes you look weak ❏
b) The mind can't process it ❏
c) It's too vague ❏
d) The mind interprets 'try' as 'try and fail' ❏

9. What's the NLP meta model?
a) A way of disguising your feelings ❏
b) A method of getting along with people ❏
c) A way of using language to clarify language ❏
d) A modelling technique ❏

10. What is visualization?
a) A mental rehearsal of a future situation ❏
b) Seeing yourself running down a tunnel ❏
c) Sensory overload ❏
d) Daydreaming ❏

CHAPTER 20

Proven persuasion techniques

In this chapter we will explore a range of proven persuasion techniques that will further enhance everything you have learned so far.

Listening is an essential communication skill and a key skill in influencing. A good listener will easily detect all the cues (which could be buying signals) in the other person and then just match their proposal to their needs. You will discover the three levels of listening and which one never to use if you want to influence someone.

You'll also learn about two tried and tested persuasion formulae – FAB and AIDA – and how to incorporate them into marketing and sales activities, including conversations.

Significant research has been conducted on which words are the most influential and are therefore used most often in 'persuasive literature'. Now you'll learn why each of these top 15 words works so well. Some of them will be obvious but others may surprise you.

In Chapter 18 we looked at 'convincers' and the power of three. We will explore some additional convincers and other 'emotional triggers' here that have been proven to work well in situations such as networking events.

The three levels of listening

While hearing is a function (you have ears and they detect sounds), listening is a skill. The more you develop this skill, the better a communicator and an influencer you will become. There are three different levels of listening, as follows:

- **Level 1 – internal listening**
  At this level, the listener is focused on him/herself. They are interpreting whatever is being said in terms of what it means to them. If it brings something to mind, they will interrupt the speaker in order to share that thought. This is a very selfish type of listening; continually interrupting someone else is extremely disrespectful. *Never* use level 1 if you want to influence someone.
- **Level 2 – focused listening**
  This is attentive listening, with the focus on the speaker. The listener may be leaning forward, engrossed in the conversation. They will notice the speaker's body language, tone of voice and words, as well as elements such as energy, expression, what is being not just said but also implied, and so on. This is a good type of listening to use if you are in a one-to-one situation.
- **Level 3 – global listening**
  Also known as 360° listening, the speaker is being listened to as if part of a wider environment. The listener is using their intuition to sense 'signals' and to take in all information available. (The best stand-up comedians use this type of listening to interact with their audience and to know the exact moment to drop in their punchline for the greatest effect.) This is the best level to use if you are making a presentation to a group of people that you want to influence.

 As with any skill, the more you practise effective listening, the more competent – and influential – you will become.

FAB statements

Everyone's favourite radio station is WIIFM, or 'What's in it for me?' This means that, whatever it is that you want to convey in your influencing conversation, the other party must be able to see some benefit, and be able to sense that benefit quite quickly in order to stay interested. One technique that achieves this very effectively is the FAB statement.

FAB stands for Feature, Advantage and Benefit. The statement is structured as follows:

● **Feature** – here you say what a product or service is or focus on a specific aspect of it: 'Because...'
● **Advantage** – this describes what that product/service/aspect does: 'It can/you can...'
● **Benefit** – this explains why the advantage is a really good thing to have: 'which means that...'

An example is: '*Because* this mobile phone has a camera function, *it can* take photographs and even short video clips, *which means that* you will never miss a photo opportunity again.'

FAB statements incorporate the conventional 'features and benefits' format but, with the addition of the 'advantage' element, two levels of benefits are being presented, which makes it even more persuasive. It is always a good idea to have several FAB statements prepared in advance of any situation in which you may need to influence others. Use a table like the one below to create three examples for yourself. For each one, think of a particular aspect of your product or service, ideally one that is unique to you or your organization.

Feature	Advantage	Benefit
1 Because...	it can/you can...	which means that...
2 Because...	it can/you can...	which means that...
3 Because...	it can/you can...	which means that...

Having a variety of FAB statements prepared will give you flexibility. Depending on the cues you pick up from the other person by listening attentively to them, you will be able to choose the appropriate statement to use. It may be that they have outlined a problem they have; if you can phrase your FAB statement so that it sounds exactly like the solution they need, they are likely to be very interested in what you have to offer.

AIDA

Another formula with a proven track record in terms of influencing people to respond to marketing communications is AIDA. (This has nothing to do with Verdi's opera of the same name, although that connection does help to make the acronym more memorable.) The letters stand for Attention, Interest, Desire and Action:

- **Attention**
  Attract the attention of the reader by making a bold statement that is relevant to them and that will generate awareness of your product or service, or of a problem that they may not have realized they have.
- **Interest**
  Raise interest by focusing on and demonstrating advantages and benefits (rather than promoting features, as in traditional advertising).
- **Desire**
  Convince the reader that they really want your product/service and that it will satisfy their needs or solve their problem.
- **Action**
  Tell the reader what to do next; what action must they take now in order to buy your product or take you up on your offer?

For example:

- **Attention**
  Do you have any old mobile phones lying around that you no longer use?
- **Interest**
  Did you know that they could be worth a significant amount of money?
- **Desire**
  We buy old mobiles and will pay you a good price for yours.

● **Action**
Go to our website now and check out how much yours is worth. Then simply post it to us and you will receive a cheque by return.

This formula also works well in letter format, in which case each letter of AIDA would comprise one paragraph, building up to the call to action.

The 15 most influential words in marketing

Research has shown that certain words are extremely effective for influencing people, especially if they communicate at both the conscious and unconscious levels of the mind simultaneously. The following list of words, compiled by Kerry L. Johnson and reproduced here with his kind permission, have been shown to be the most influential. If you look at advertising in magazines and newspapers and on advertising hoardings and billboards, and listen to television and radio adverts, you will see and hear these words being used repeatedly.

Word	Effect
1 Discover	This generates interest, evokes a feeling of opportunity and suggests a better life.
2 Good	This is not a high-powered word, which is the secret of its success; it evokes stability and security. If something is good for your clients, they will want to buy it. If it's good, it's not bad. Everyone wants to be associated with what's good.
3 Money	Few people feel they have enough and everyone wants more.
4 Easy	What everyone wants is more simplicity and the ability to do things more easily. If your product can make something easier for potential purchasers, they will be more likely to buy it.
5 Guaranteed	Most people fear taking a risk. They want to know that, if your product doesn't work out, they can get their money back.
6 Health	'If I've got my health, I've got everything.' If a product promises financial, emotional or physical health, it offers a big plus. To many people, this is more important than money.

Word	Effect
7 Love	Said to 'make the world go round', love is important in everyone's life and is a prime selling enticement.
8 New	If it's new, it must be better, improved and at the 'cutting edge'. Unless a product is specifically targeted to evoke nostalgia, anyone trying to sell something old-fashioned meets with limited success.
9 Proven	Although we like new things, we want reliability as well. We want something that has been tested and proven not to be harmful in any way. We need to know that it will neither break down nor require a lot of servicing. We don't want to doubt that something will work.
10 Results	We want to know exactly what we're getting for spending our money.
11 Safe	This closely parallels health. We all value our lives and if a product is safe, or our assets are safe, we are much more trusting.
12 Save	Saving money is almost as important as making money. If a company can't promise that you will make money with a product, it usually promises to help you save money. Saving is better than spending.
13 Own	We all like to own things. Owning is better than buying because it implies possession rather than more spending. When you present a product, talk about owning it rather than buying it.
14 Free	We love to say that you can't get something for nothing, but we don't believe it! 'Free' is an instant eye-catcher, something that compels you to look or listen further. If you can use the word 'free', pointing out that your customer will get something for nothing, you will get that customer's attention immediately.
15 Best	If you know that a product has been shown to be the best in any way, shape or form, be sure to make your customer aware of it. Something that has been shown to be the best in any context exerts a powerful pull on us to possess it for ourselves.

Because all these words work so well, both in writing and verbally, keep a list of them by your telephone so that you can drop them into a conversation and thus become instantly more influential!

More convincers

In Chapter 18 you discovered that people have preferred channels of communication – visual, hearing or feeling. Not only will they speak in these channels, but they also like to be communicated with, and influenced, in their preferred channel. If you are in a one-to-one situation and you become aware from listening to the other person's language and watching their eye movements which channel they fit into, then you will need to think about the following:

● **Visual people**
What evidence do they need to see in order to be convinced? Can you show them examples, pictures, charts, diagrams, or even a short video clip? Don't use long verbal explanations with visual people, because they will lose interest quickly. They will also notice your appearance in far more detail than hearing or feeling people, so be meticulous about how you present yourself.

● **Hearing people**
What do they need to hear from you to be convinced? Hearing people like to be 'talked through' things in steps, procedures and sequences, so structure your presentation in that way. Also, vary your voice tonality, speed and volume, as this will appeal more to them.

● **Feeling people**
What do they need to feel in order to be convinced? These people will go with their gut feeling and they like to be tactile when evaluating something. If you can give them a sample of your product to touch, they will appreciate that. They are

'hands-on' learners, so if you can demonstrate something to them and then give them the chance to have a go for themselves, this will work well. Feeling people will notice the quality of a handshake, so make sure that yours is firm without being a bone-crusher.

The law of reciprocity

It is human nature that when someone has done us a good turn, we feel a need to reciprocate and do something for them. This is known as the law of reciprocity. In terms of communication, if you show a genuine interest in somebody by asking them questions and listening attentively to their replies, there will more than likely come a point at which they will say something like, 'So what about you? What do you do?' People like to be listened to (this is the 'good turn' you are doing for them), so on no account lapse into level 1 listening.

In his book *7 Habits of Highly Effective People* (1989), Stephen Covey defines habit number 5 as 'Seek first to understand, then to be understood'. He states that most people listen with the intent to reply rather than to understand, and this affects the quality of their listening. He also says that we tend to be keen to put our point across and be understood rather than first wanting to understand the other person. If you find yourself at a networking event, you will see this happening constantly. If you make sure that you are the person who asks questions and really listens to the answers, you will make a very positive impression on the other attendees.

The law of scarcity

If we think something is in short supply, we want it. Even if it is only rumoured that there could be a shortage of a particular commodity, we may feel a need to 'stock up' in case it runs out altogether. You will have seen this happening with, for example, petrol. If it is reported in the media that service stations may run short of fuel for some reason, immediately queues will form. People will sit in their cars in a queue for an hour or two (burning fuel), sometimes just to top up an almost-full tank. As a result, the service station runs out of fuel and the rumoured shortage becomes a reality.

How could you use this 'law'? If you are launching a promotion of some kind, think about imposing some limitations to create scarcity and thereby increase desire. For example:

- 'Only seven places remaining!'
- 'Offer must close at midnight on Friday!'
- 'Discontinued model – only two left at this price!'

Emotional triggers

Just as we tend to buy what we *want* rather than just what we *need,* so emotions play a key part in influencing our behaviour. For instance, Bob Geldof activated our emotions and feelings of guilt with his Live Aid appeal, raising £40 million to help alleviate suffering and starvation in Ethiopia.

Another curious and amusing example of an emotional trigger is the interesting phenomenon of cute cat pictures becoming widespread on the Internet. Several different, corroborative sources now suggest that, if you have a business page on Facebook and you would like to attract more visitors, posting a photo of a cat on there will do the trick! Yes, honestly. I suspect a photo of a cute kitten sitting on your keyboard may be even better, but apparently this works. Do with this as you will!

Summary

In this chapter you have learned some proven practical and effective persuasion techniques.

To be influential, we have to know how to communicate successfully. One of the most important communication skills is the ability to listen well. If you identified yourself as a level 1 listener, you now know that this is a skill you need to practise!

The FAB and AIDA techniques also work well, so familiarize yourself with them so that they will come naturally to you in an influencing conversation. It's also worth learning how and when to use the 15 most influential words.

By presenting information to people via their preferred channel of communication, you can increase your powers of persuasion. The laws of reciprocity and scarcity and emotional triggers also present opportunities to be influential.

Fact-check (answers at the back)

1. What is level 3 listening?
   a) Speaking more than listening ❏
   b) The best one to use in a one-to-one conversation ❏
   c) The best one to use when presenting to a group of people ❏
   d) Being focused on your own internal dialogue ❏

2. What does FAB stand for?
   a) Feature, Advantage, Benefit ❏
   b) Feature, Adaptability, Brightness ❏
   c) Fitness, Advancement, Benevolence ❏
   d) Flexibility, Assistance, Benison ❏

3. What does AIDA stand for?
   a) Administration, Influence, Design, Action ❏
   b) Audience, Interest, Designer, Animation ❏
   c) Attendance, Individuality, Desire, Activity ❏
   d) Attention, Interest, Desire, Action ❏

4. How many words have been identified as the most influential when used in marketing?
   a) 15 ❏
   b) 18 ❏
   c) 25 ❏
   d) 35 ❏

5. How should you influence a visual person?
   a) With visual evidence ❏
   b) By asking them to sing along with you in a duet ❏
   c) By using long verbal instructions ❏
   d) By being tactile with them ❏

6. What is the law of reciprocity?
   a) Seeking first to be understood, before understanding ❏
   b) If you do someone a good turn, they will naturally want to reciprocate ❏
   c) People like to be listened to, so use level 1 listening ❏
   d) Stocking up in case something runs out ❏

7. What is the law of scarcity?
   a) It means that there is plenty for everyone ❏
   b) If we think something is in short supply, we'll decide we don't want it ❏
   c) Scarcity makes a commodity less desirable ❏
   d) If we think something is in short supply, we want it ❏

8. What are emotional triggers?
   a) Small brain pulses that release a stimulus ❏
   b) External signals to stop buying ❏
   c) Appeals to feelings of guilt ❏
   d) Photos of snakes and other reptiles on your Facebook business page ❏

9. Who make the best influencers?
a) Those who talk the most ❑
b) Those who listen well ❑
c) Level 1 listeners ❑
d) Those who avoid words like good, love and new ❑

10. Why should you listen attentively?
a) To find out whether the other person is using influential words ❑
b) To pick up another person's 'cues' and then match to them in order to influence ❑
c) To indicate that you have a strong character and you will not allow the other person to leave until they have agreed to your proposal ❑
d) To avoid having to say anything ❑

7 × 7

1 Seven quotes by influential people

- 'Be the change you wish to see in the world.' Mahatma Gandhi
- 'Keep away from small people who try to belittle your ambitions. Small people always do that, but the really great make you feel that you, too, can become great.' Mark Twain
- 'Logic will get you from A to B. Imagination will take you everywhere.' Albert Einstein
- 'If you look at what you have in life, you'll always have more. If you look at what you don't have in life, you'll never have enough.' Oprah Winfrey
- 'Our greatest weakness lies in giving up. The most certain way to succeed is always to try just one more time.' Thomas Edison
- 'I like things to happen; and if they don't happen, I like to make them happen.' Winston Churchill
- 'You don't learn to walk by following rules. You learn by doing, and by falling over.' Richard Branson

2 Seven key ideas to become more influential

- Become a blogger and share your expertise; position yourself as a trusted resource. Blogs create the perfect environment for an influential, interactive relationship. Think of it as your own public relations forum. An additional benefit is it may generate actual PR. Business bloggers often receive requests for interviews or quotes from journalists who consider them industry experts.
- Develop an influential charisma. How do respected world-class leaders generate a positive impact when making

speeches? Watch their body language, gestures, style of speaking, pauses for effect, etc and experiment with replicating them for yourself.

- Think of your last significant purchase. What exactly influenced your buying decision? Was it how the product/service was marketed? The written word? Maybe the spoken word? Was it a word-of-mouth recommendation from someone you trust? What can you learn and adopt from these sources of influence?

- Carry out a regular 'shoe review'. The smartest outfit can be let down by scuffed, dirty shoes. Invest 20 minutes at the weekend to clean the shoes you will be wearing in the coming week. If they still don't look smart after cleaning, it's time to turn them out.

- Make a list of famous, influential people that you admire and then check your local library for their biographies and autobiographies. For each one you read, jot down five key elements that contributed to their success, e.g. beliefs, values, strategies, decisions, etc. Then create a written plan to adopt as many of these proven traits as possible for yourself.

- Continually review and expand your networks, both informal (friends of friends) and formal (networking groups). The opportunities for being influential are unlimited when you network regularly.

- Social media provides a huge opportunity to be influential. On Facebook, join groups with which you have a shared interest. Start by following discussions and contributing short comments. Then build up to initiating discussions and eventually, starting up groups of your own.

3 Seven tips for making influential presentations

- Remember that feeling nervous is normal – in fact you need adrenaline to make a 'sharp' presentation. Everyone gets butterflies when presenting but it's the professionals who can get them to fly in formation!

- The symptoms associated with nervousness are identical to those associated with excitement, e.g. racing heart, sweaty palms, dry mouth. Instead of telling yourself that you are nervous, substitute the word 'excited' and you will feel quite different.
- If you need to read from a sheet of paper during your presentation, hold it in both hands with your hands pulling away from each other so that the paper is held taut. This prevents it from shaking and gives an impression to your audience (and to you) that you are confident and in control.
- Be a lighthouse. Make eye contact with your audience by looking around in sweeping arc-shape movements. This maintains a connection with them and there are bound to be some friendly faces looking back at you.
- Always have a glass of water to hand. Then if you experience a dry mouth or you need to pause momentarily to recover your composure, taking a sip of water fills the pause and looks completely natural.
- To avoid 'death by PowerPoint', follow the 5 × 5 rule. Use bullet points of no more than five words each, with a maximum of five bullet points per slide. Keep the overall number of slides used to just enough to support the content that you are delivering verbally.
- Practice makes permanent. The surefire way to become a confident, competent, persuasive presenter is to seek out opportunities to present and make the most of them. Toastmasters is a non-profit organization developing public speaking and leadership skills through practice and feedback in local clubs. For further details, check out their website at www.toastmasters.org

4 Seven ways to be a more influential networker

- When you introduce yourself at a networking event, say your first name twice to make it more memorable, e.g. 'My name is Alex, Alex Smith.'

- It is very easy to forget someone's name shortly after being introduced because your mind is busy processing your initial perception of them. When you know you are about to hear a name for the first time, 'prime' your memory by saying to yourself, 'I am about to hear this person's name and I *will* remember it.'
- Always have an 'elevator pitch' prepared. This is a very short statement, one minute long at most, that describes what you do in terms of how you help your clients successfully overcome their business challenges. This generates far more interest than just saying your name, job role and where you work.
- At networking events, it is essential to mingle and then keep moving around and introducing yourself to as many people as possible. Ensure that you maintain a genuine interest in the people you are meeting and always be seeking mutually beneficial collaboration opportunities.
- Collect business cards from everyone you speak to and then follow up with a personalized e-mail within 24 hours. If you jot down a few words on the cards relating to each person, then you can incorporate that into your e-mail and thus generate the personal touch.
- When someone tells you about their business, ask how you could identify their ideal client with a view to brokering a beneficial introduction. This will almost certainly invoke the Law of Reciprocation and they will be thinking about what they can do for you.
- If you identify a collaboration opportunity, ask the other person whether you can schedule a time for a 'coffee on the phone' chat. This assumes that at some time, probably around 11 am, they will pause for a coffee and in those few minutes, there is an opportunity for the two of you to explore mutually beneficial opportunities over the telephone. This is less 'in your face' than asking a busy person for a face to face meeting and they will respect you for that. If the conversation goes well, then they are far more likely to be amenable to a follow-up meeting.

5 Seven things at which the best social media influencers excel

- They persevere and put in the time that is needed. They understand that nobody gets famous overnight and they are prepared to spend countless hours on social media building their brands and their influence.
- They become the 'go-to' source of valuable content. They get to know their followers and share content that will benefit them. Influencers always keep their audience in mind when they post.
- They use social media to help others rather than to promote themselves. And yet in doing this, they have provided value and a service, and have thus indirectly promoted themselves.
- They contribute to the social media community whenever possible. They engage with the people who connect with them, and give back, thereby positioning themselves as a direct source of valuable knowledge and support.
- They only post positive comments. They never use social media to criticize, condemn or complain. This generates a very positive perception and increases followers.
- They consistently post high-quality content and in doing so, build a high quality reputation for themselves. They are seen as experts in their field.
- They recognize that whilst none of these things is difficult, consistency and constant focus are required and they are committed to provide these in bucketfuls.

6 Seven things to avoid

- Being 'needy'. Avoid being so focused on the outcome of a situation that it takes on the drama of a being a life or death scenario – it repels people.
- Being over confident. Even if everything has been going well during a persuasive conversation, never assume that the outcome is a foregone conclusion. People can be very unpredictable.

- Being a quitter. You must be prepared to be patient in order to achieve your outcomes. Many people need to take time to consider their decisions and just because they haven't said 'yes' yet doesn't mean that they won't. Countless goals are abandoned so close to their successful achievement because of impatience with the process.
- Being a 'limpet' – holding on to a situation that you believe you are influencing positively but in reality, is never going to come good. It is far better to recognize that you have done your best but that other influences outside of your control are determining the outcome and it is time to leave.
- Losing control and your temper when things aren't going how you want them to, and in particular, when there is a personality conflict. Even if you are in the right, you will not look good if you have allowed yourself to get drawn into a volatile situation.
- Talking more than listening. You have two ears and one mouth and it is essential you use them in that proportion. When you really listen to others, you gain insights into what is important to them and clues as to how they are most likely to be influenced.
- Making assumptions – there will always be at least a 50 per cent chance that your assumption is incorrect. Never attempt to persuade or influence someone based on an assumption. Check it out first for accuracy.

7 Seven best resources

- Holly Weeks' *Failure to Communicate: How Conversations Go Wrong and What You Can Do To Right Them* (Harvard Business Press, 2010). Difficult conversations cause stress and jangle nerves. This book serves as a reference for leaders from every profession.
- Dr Robert Cialdini's *Influence: The Psychology of Persuasion* explores the six universal principles of persuasion and how to use them to become a skilled persuader.
- Roger Fisher and William Ury's *Getting to Yes: Negotiating an Agreement without Giving In* has been in print for over 30 years and has helped countless people achieve win/win agreements both at work and in their private lives.

- Website http://www.businessballs.com is an invaluable resource for up-to-date thinking on business training and personal development in a business environment.
- http://www.theinvisiblegorilla.com/gorilla_experiment. html is a video clip that demonstrates how easily we can be influenced by our intuition into not seeing something obvious that is right in front of us.
- Daniel Pink's *Drive: The Surprising Truth About What Motivates Us* is an exploration of the secrets of high performance and personal satisfaction at work and at home.
- Sally Hogshead in *Fascinate: Your 7 Triggers to Persuasion and Captivation* promotes the concept that fascination is one of the most powerful ways to attract attention and influence behaviour, and explains how companies can use these concepts to make their products and ideas irresistible to consumers.

PART 4
Your NLP Masterclass

Introduction

Welcome to the world of NLP, or neuro-linguistic programming. This Part will introduce you to the main themes and ideas that constitute NLP. It will give you an outline knowledge and understanding of the key concepts, together with practical and thought-provoking exercises. NLP has its own language and organizing systems, which are fully explained with examples relating to work and personal issues. The theories and practice of NLP will help you discover what makes some people excel in all aspects of their lives, and will enable you to do the same.

The following chapters provide a dynamic collection of tools, techniques and strategies that can facilitate excellence in all aspects of your life. This book will help you communicate more effectively and develop your interactions by studying:

- the way you access and disseminate information through the language you use
- your perceptions and the values you hold.

NLP was developed to answer the following questions:

- How, specifically, do outstanding individuals consistently achieve the results that make them outstanding?
- What is it that makes the difference between somebody who is merely competent at any given skill and somebody who excels in it?

NLP is based on the idea that mind, body and language interact to create our individual perception of what happens around us and that these perceptions, and their accompanying behaviours, can be changed. Developers of NLP believe that happiness and success are the result of specific patterns of thinking that can be learned by anyone.

Neuro-linguistic programming is something you do already, only you may not *know* you are doing it. Through understanding what works for you and for others, you remove the element of chance and can, by design, create your own effective outcomes in any situation. The better we understand ourselves and others, the better we can change what is not working in our lives and increase what is.

CHAPTER 21

What is NLP?

NLP, or neuro-linguistic programming, is the study of how human beings make sense of their world. It is a powerful change management tool that transforms the way people think and act. This can have a beneficial impact on users, both professionally and personally.

NLP has been growing in popularity since the mid-1970s. It has many applications in the fields of communication, commerce, personal development and psychotherapy.

Although its early use was primarily in psychotherapy, it was soon clear that NLP had a part to play in the business and commercial worlds. It can be used to relieve stress, improve confidence and tackle problems that people have in their personal and professional lives.

NLP's practical focus on finding what's useful and converting that to action enables teams and individuals to achieve peak performance in areas as diverse as presentations, coaching, motivation, team building, sales and new product development.

In this chapter we will work through the following:

- How NLP developed and its basic features
- The 'principles of excellence'
- The importance of identifying and establishing outcomes.

NLP: thinking, words and behaviour

The way you think affects the internal and external language you use and the concepts you hold. This, in turn, affects the way you behave. We can change our behaviour by changing our thinking and we can change our emotional state by changing our behaviour. It is a dynamic and synergistic process: the whole is greater than the sum of the parts. Any internal or external change to any of the components will have an impact on the whole.

> Neuro-linguistic programming provides a model that enhances understanding of:
>
> ● **Neuro** – your thinking processes; the way you use your senses of sight, hearing, feeling, taste and smell to understand what is happening around you
>
> ● **Linguistic** – your words; the way you use language and how it influences you and those around you. Do your words and the stories you tell put you down or build you up?
>
> ● **Programming** – your behaviour patterns and emotions; how desired habits and attitudes become ingrained and the way you organize your ideas and actions.
>
> NLP enables you to replace negative behaviours and habits with positive ones.

NLP is sometimes referred to as 'software for the brain'. Just as a computer's software defines the way it operates, so your internal programming affects your emotions and the way you behave. If you don't like a particular piece of software, you can change it, in the computer or in yourself.

The history of NLP

NLP was developed by Richard Bandler and John Grinder in the early 1970s as they set out to identify the patterns used by outstanding therapists who achieved excellent results with clients. They discovered a number of processes which they fitted into an accessible model to enhance effective communication, personal change and personal development. They attempted to 'get under the skin' of Virginia Satir, Fritz Perls and Milton Erickson to understand both how they reached their levels of excellence and how to reproduce their skills. Bandler and Grinder wanted to be able to communicate and work with people as effectively as possible. They used their path to discovery as a way of showing others how to achieve success, too. They began to develop NLP by doing it.

Basic operating principles

One of the key drivers at the core of Bandler and Grinder's work was to discover how people excel, especially when managing change. With this information, they devised processes to teach those methods to others.

Their studies indicated that certain basic operating principles, or presuppositions, needed to be in place to create 'the difference that makes the difference'. At first these may seem untenable, even awkward; however, in time they facilitate positive change and can change the way you behave.

Take a few moments to imagine how you might approach situations if you accepted and worked within the 'principles of excellence' listed below. What would it be like if you presupposed these principles to be true? Be curious, and rather than dismissing ideas that don't fit with yours, notice how these principles could strengthen your communications.

> ## Basic principles of excellence
> - We have all the resources we need.
> - The meaning of any communication is the effect it has.
> - There is no failure, only feedback.
> - The map is not the territory: every person's map is unique.

We have all the resources we need

At various points in our life we have achieved success. The findings of NLP suggest that, if we recall the ways we did so, we can transfer these to any present-day challenges. Imagine reaching that longed-for senior position in your place of work. After the initial euphoria, you may wonder what you have let yourself in for. By remembering how you successfully managed changes in the past and re-accessing those resources, you can continue with confidence and anticipate fulfilment. Whether you need confidence, energy, strength or any other personal resource, be assured that you have used it somewhere in your past and can access it again.

The meaning of any communication is the effect it has

Case study

Colleagues were discussing a fractious decision-making meeting that had just ended. The final decision was made by voting after lengthy discussions to help four 'undecideds' cast their vote and press the 'yes' or 'no' button. 'How did you eventually decide?' Terry asked Sarah. 'I listened to all the arguments and then imagined how they would work in my department.' 'No. *How* did *you* decide?' A confused Sarah answered, speaking slowly: 'I listened to all the arguments and then imagined how they would work in my department.' As Terry was about to ask his question a third time, Ashra translated: 'Which way did you cast your vote?'

What happens when you talk or write to someone and the reply you receive is completely unexpected in content? Sometimes, you will assume that they are being awkward or ignorant in not responding the way you want. As long as you put the onus on them to somehow achieve your interpretation of what is 'right', you cannot change things. However, once you understand your own part in the equation, you can consider doing something different to put across your intended message.

There is no failure, only feedback

How do you react when, in your opinion, things go wrong? Are you a tryer who persists in doing the same thing over and over until, if ever, you get it right? Or do you think it over, and decide what you can do differently for a better result next time?

Think about a time in the past when you know you made a mistake. Imagine calling yourself a failure. What does that look or sound like? How do you feel? Now imagine the same situation and ask yourself 'What could I have done differently to achieve what I wanted? What can I learn?' What does that look or sound like? How do you feel? The notion of learning from feedback means that you are more likely to be flexible than rigid in your dealings with yourself and others.

Remember: if what you're doing isn't working, do something else. Thomas Edison, when called a failure after taking so long to invent the light bulb, responded: 'Every wrong attempt discarded is another step forward.'

The map is not the territory: every person's map is unique

My way of looking at things is unique to me, yours unique to you. If you had chosen to write this Part, you may have read all the same research material and taken the same courses as me, yet the end result would have been very different. That is why there are so many reference books available on any given subject.

Think of the people with whom you are in contact at work: internally, colleagues, staff, senior managers; externally, customers and suppliers. How might their 'maps' differ from yours? If you are able to put all the different perceptions together, you will come much closer to a complete picture than if you each stay within the boundaries of your own view. If you accept this NLP principle, then you respect and rejoice in difference.

Choosing outcomes

Identifying and establishing outcomes is a central and first step in NLP. It's easy to say what you don't want. Focusing on an outcome you *do* want creates a much more engaging concept and gives you a clear indication of your commitment. If you don't make the choice for yourself in any aspect of your life, then, by default, someone else will make it for you.

Creating well-formed outcomes

1 Positive

Every time you focus on what you can't do or don't want, you are creating a negative outcome and reminding yourself of what you want to avoid. How would you react if someone said to you: 'Don't look behind you!'? I know I would immediately turn my head. In order to avoid something, I have to think about it, and then react to it. A much more useful instruction would be: 'Keep looking ahead.'

Case study

Divya, a manager in a busy customer-care office, agreed to reduce poor timekeeping in the office as part of her annual appraisal. This was a negative and restrictive outcome. When she decided to put a positive angle on it, she considered the question: 'What do I really want to happen?' She was then able to think about the real issue. Poor timekeeping meant the office was sometimes empty. An empty office led to the 'hotline' phone ringing continuously without being answered, meaning lost customers. What Divya wanted was to maintain existing customers and increase the number of new ones who joined the 'hotline' service. She was now able to think about changing conditions and creating flexible working patterns that would lead to at least one phone being operated all the time – a more creative and outward-looking outcome. She decided to introduce flexible rostering, particularly at 'twilight' and 'sunset' shifts.

2 Specific

Be specific in describing your positive outcome, and use as many questions as you can to check how specific you are. Moving from general to specific enables you to concentrate on answers and solutions.

> Divya asked herself the following:
>
> **Where?** In the red office.
>
> **Who?** I need at least one member of the team to be available for customer calls.
>
> **When?** From 0800 until 2200 hours.
>
> **What?** I will arrange a change of working hours.
>
> **How?** In individual and team discussions and meetings. We will review after the first three months.

3 Evidence

To enhance the energy and application of your outcome, it is useful to imagine as much sensory-based evidence as you can. This will increase your motivation, too. If you do not know when you have achieved your outcome, you could still be using up resources long after you have actually succeeded.

> For Divya, this meant asking: what will I see, hear and feel, and how will others know this has been achieved?
>
> ● I'll see at least one phone operator in the room at all times.
>
> ● I'll hear only three rings before the phone is answered.
>
> ● I'll feel confident and relaxed about covering the lines.
>
> ● They'll be able to see the roster every week, they'll hear words of encouragement from me and they'll feel acknowledged in their needs.

4 Ownership

Whose outcome is it? Be aware of whether you are dependent on someone else for your success. If you are waiting for others to change, you risk becoming a passive spectator. Consider your own part in, and contribution to, the process.

> Divya's key contribution is to identify what she wants, initiate discussion and, having agreed the procedures, to put these into practice.

5 Fit

How does the outcome fit in with other aspects of your life and your overall plan? Are there other people or factors to take into account? If you were to achieve your outcome, how would you feel about it? The response to this last question will indicate how important the outcome is.

> In terms of Divya's 'fit', knowing that customers' calls would be answered and that staff would be clearer about their responsibilities tied in with her being a constructive and collegiate manager. Other areas of the company would be positively affected by additional orders, and they would need to consider the additional administrative impact.

6 Resources

Sometimes, we forget that our resources are internal as well as external. A well-formed outcome will include consideration of both for initial achievement and then continued maintenance. If you accept that you have all the internal resources you need, the skill is to relate them specifically to your outcome. The acquisition of external resources may need greater planning. If you know what you need, you have a much better chance of designing the means of acquiring the requisite resources.

> Divya remembered the time she was on the receiving end of changes at work. She had felt involved and valued when Toby took the time to ask for her ideas and suggestions. She knew she had used his example to create an atmosphere of trust in her team, and felt confident of her ability to listen to their views.

Outcome checklist

Start with the questions below as you create your outcomes. It may be that, as you go through the process, you find you are not meeting all the criteria. Keep amending them until you are happy. This is the linchpin of NLP and will give you the foundations you need for success.

Positive What do you want? What would you like to happen?

Specific Where, who, when, what and how?

Evidence What will you see, hear and feel when it is happening?

Ownership Whose outcome is it, and what is your part in it?

Fit How much do you want it? How does it fit in with other aspects of your life?

Resources Which have you used before that are transferable? Which external resources do you need?

Summary

This chapter has provided an overview of neuro-linguistic programming. As you go through the rest of the Part, you will be able to devise your own answers to the question, 'What is NLP?'

We have covered the main principles that underpin NLP thinking, giving you the opportunity to consider those basic presuppositions of excellence that can help you start changing your behaviour and the way you react to yourself, your colleagues, your family and your friends. Although they are not absolute truths, they are useful to stimulate thought, which can help avert misunderstandings.

The section on outcomes is designed to help you clarify and focus on what you want in your life. This will lead to you having far greater chances of success. As you follow the outcome checklist, you can imagine what it would be like if you achieved your outcome and experience it as if it had already happened. This will give you the information that will tell you whether or not this is the outcome that you truly want.

Fact-check (answers at the back)

1. What is NLP?
a) Software for the brain ❑
b) A marketing technique ❑
c) The study of excellence ❑
d) A change management tool ❑

2. Who co-founded NLP?
a) Richard Bandler and Paul McKenna ❑
b) Richard Bandler and John Grinder ❑
c) Sigmund Freud and Carl Rogers ❑
d) Carl Jung and Milton Erickson ❑

3. Which therapists inspired the co-founders of NLP?
a) Fritz Perls ❑
b) Milton Erickson ❑
c) Virginia Satir ❑
d) Sigmund Freud ❑

4. Who can use NLP?
a) Doctors ❑
b) Therapists ❑
d) Anyone ❑
e) Managers ❑

5. What does the 'N' in NLP refer to?
a) Neuralgia ❑
b) Neurosis ❑
c) Neuro- ❑
d) Nuclear ❑

6. What does the 'L' refer to?
a) Logical levels ❑
b) Linguistic ❑
c) Language ❑
d) Legislation ❑

7. What does the 'P' refer to?
a) Psychotherapy ❑
b) Principles ❑
c) Problems ❑
d) Programming ❑

8. What are NLP principles also known as?
a) Rules ❑
b) Beliefs ❑
c) Presuppositions ❑
d) Mission statements ❑

9. What do well-formed outcomes need to be?
a) Realistic ❑
b) Achievable ❑
c) Specific ❑
d) Positive ❑

10. What does NLP offer?
a) Techniques for change ❑
b) Strategies for success ❑
c) Solutions ❑
d) All of the above ❑

CHAPTER 22

Identify empowering and limiting beliefs

Have you ever encountered someone who keeps telling you that no one can help them? No matter what you do or say, they will always have a reason why something is not right for them. In the end, you probably give up and thereby successfully reinforce their belief. They are not being deliberately obstructive, even though it may seem that way. They have held their belief for many years and would have to face many challenges in order to let it go.

Such beliefs are so familiar that we often don't know they are there until someone starts to ask questions such as 'Who says so?', 'What would happen if someone *could* help you?' and 'What needs to change for you to be helped?'

In this chapter we will consider the origin of your beliefs, how they influence you and how they can be changed if necessary. We will also think about some additional beliefs that can enhance your communications and behaviour and an NLP technique named 'perceptual positions', which gives you valuable information in understanding another person's perspective.

In NLP it is paramount to start with yourself and understand what drives you to be the way you are before considering other people's styles and preferences.

From beliefs to action

What exactly do we mean when we talk about beliefs? In NLP terms, beliefs represent the assumptions we make about ourselves, about others in the world and about how we expect things to be. These assumptions determine the way we behave and shape our decision-making processes. They are often based on emotions rather than facts. We tend to notice 'facts' that reinforce the beliefs. For example, if you believe that 'everyone is easy to get along with', you will only notice how well you interact with people. If, however, your belief is that 'you can't trust anyone', you will be suspicious and expect to be duped, and the chances are that others will sense this and be wary of you. It's a 'self-fulfilling prophecy': what you believe about yourself is often what happens to you.

Case study

Samir's greatest challenge as a graduate manager was conducting performance reviews with older, more experienced staff. He had been brought up to believe that he should respect his elders and that they knew best. The young Samir took that to mean that he should not contradict or correct older (wiser) people. Stuck with that belief, how could he possibly discuss their underachievement? He knew all about preparation and setting objectives; it was just that every time he thought about one particular staff member, Riannon, he felt increasingly anxious. To make matters worse, she had once mentioned she was old enough to be his mother.

He described what he did at her review: 'I decided to get straight to the point, and indicate where Riannon could make some improvements. Only I seemed to open my mouth and no words came out. She sat there smiling benignly and I told her everything was fine. I couldn't wait for it to be over.'

Samir's underlying belief was limiting his ability to do his job effectively.

Begin to notice which beliefs drive your thoughts, feelings and actions. If your behaviour is not what you want and you think you can't change it, you have probably identified a limiting belief. If your beliefs are supportive and empowering, keep them. If they're restrictive, discard them.

Choices and changes

How do you know what to believe? You don't have to dwell too much on the origin of your beliefs, but knowing from whom or where they came can help you understand what they mean to you. It can also lead you to a way to change. We are generally given injunctions with the best will in the world and for a very good reason at the time. Trace back and identify the roots of what you believe about yourself – notice where your beliefs originate. Can you hear someone telling you to have that belief? Can you picture being told, maybe more than once, or did you just *sense* what was expected of you?

It may well be that you have beliefs that you no longer need, and their purpose is obsolete. If that is so, then change them. Depending on their source, this may seem quite challenging.

Samir decided to revisit his original belief and work out its meaning and relevance for him now. At school he had always been a quick learner and could outwit his parents in an argument. They felt intimidated, and concerned that his teachers would consider him cheeky. Therefore they wanted him to accept the wisdom of their experience without question – as a protective measure. They also wanted him to progress at school with the teachers on his side.

As you can imagine, this was not the way the young Samir perceived it. Having realized this, now he could start to think it through and consider his choices: either to keep the limiting belief and not question his older staff members, or to find a more suitable and facilitating belief.

> Samir decided that it was important for him to respect other people and himself as equal and different human beings. This was a present-day belief that he knew to be important in all aspects of his life. His feelings about the next review had changed to excited (and a little apprehensive), and he thought about what he would say and how he would say it. He reminded himself that 'There is no failure, only feedback', and he went in search of Riannon to rearrange the meeting, prepared to learn and develop.

Take your time to work through and understand the origin and intention of your beliefs. You can choose whatever you want to believe. Sometimes we choose, or have imposed on us, beliefs that are restrictive in nature. We bring them with us into all kinds of situations. Once we recognize them, we can choose to replace them or discard them completely.

If you approach the question from the other side, you may be following the belief 'I have learned many things in my life. Now is the time to update my repertoire.'

Whether you believe that 'NLP will work for me' or whether you believe 'it won't work for me', the chances are you will be proven right until you investigate the origin of the belief further. Your beliefs can work either with you and for you or despite you and against you. Which would you prefer?

NLP will work for me

- 'I enjoy new ideas.'
- 'I know I can change.'
- 'I've learned so much before – here's another opportunity.'
- 'I've an open mind.'

NLP won't work for me

- 'You can't teach an old dog new tricks.'
- 'I never pick up new ideas.'
- 'I've tried things like this before – they never work.'
- 'Nothing will make me change.'

Which of your beliefs help or hinder you? Compulsive language – which includes the words 'should', 'ought' or 'must' – leads to patterns of behaviour that can become compulsive. If you have a belief that you want to change, you could ask:

● Is this an empowering belief?
● Is this a limiting belief?
● Where has it come from?
● What was the positive intention behind it?
● How do I want to change it?

Which of your beliefs would you like to change? Here's an example:

Belief	Empowering?	Restricting?	Source	Intention	Change
I must not make mistakes	No	Yes	School	Best performance	I can learn from my mistakes

Working beliefs

In Chapter 21, you considered the basic principles of NLP and imagined how it would be if they were yours. These were related to excellence and how it could be achieved. Now we look at the following additional principles, or beliefs, that relate to the workplace.

We come to work to do our best

It is in everybody's interest that their work is as enjoyable and fulfilling as possible. Most people do the best they can, given the system they are in. If you or your company can create conditions in which individuals can take responsibility and feel valued in their role, they will put their best into their job. If someone appears to come to work intent on sabotage, it may be that their needs are not being considered or that their beliefs are contrary to those of the company. They may well be trying to do their best in what is for them a challenging environment.

Our decisions are right at the time we make them

If this is your starting point, you are likely to be calmer and more understanding when you are reviewing performance with your staff. You do not have to accept their decision; just that it was right for them with the knowledge they had at the time. In fact, if you don't accept their decision, then take time to assess whether you have different or additional information that could help them reach another conclusion.

There may even be a chance that, in the light of the ensuing discussion, you reconsider your position. If their decision has resulted in an error from you, remember to think in terms of feedback and learning.

Behind every action is a positive intention

Imagine how it might be if you had this among your working beliefs. It is not always clear why we continue with behaviours that are not apparently beneficial or make no sense to us. What makes us act in a way that sabotages our development? And, if we do so, how does this belief make sense? We need to understand the intention and personal belief behind the action to understand it.

Case study

Ros was a manager who regularly complained of overwork and stayed late most nights to sort out her filing, even though she had clerical assistants in her team. What was her positive intention behind this behaviour?

Ros felt somewhat out of her depth in her existing role. She had always enjoyed general administration and knew this to be an area in which she was highly competent. Her intention, therefore, was to boost her confidence through familiar routine. The effect, though, was to alienate her staff and give herself unnecessary extra work.

There are a number of answers to every question

This is the belief about flexibility and creativity that is central to NLP thinking. If you close your mind to allow in only your own personal beliefs, then you close off many opportunities. If you are working as part of a team and are prepared to listen to all the ideas available, a more satisfactory outcome is likely.

Notice when you switch out of listening to other people's ideas. Does this happen with particular people, subject areas, times or places? Now imagine that these are useful ideas and that you want to incorporate them. This can open up a new way of behaving, thinking and believing.

Imagine that these working beliefs were your own working beliefs, and try them on for a period of time. Notice how they work for you. Write down their effect on you and your colleagues, and where you would like to apply them – for example, in an appraisal, discipline session, selection and recruitment, team meetings or negotiations.

Your colleagues may be surprised if your behaviour changes significantly. Stick with it, and over time you will reap the rewards.

Perceptual positions

One powerful way to increase your effectiveness in relating to others is to extend your information about the way they behave and how they make their choices. The NLP technique called *perceptual positions* provides a practical way to do this. On those occasions when you seem stuck in your communication, it can be very valuable to change your position (literally and figuratively) and take different views of the situation. This is sometimes called *second-guessing*. If you can understand other people's thinking and work out their positive intentions, then you have added knowledge to take you forward.

Within companies, you can become so involved in production or service delivery (first position – *your* map) that you may not know whether your efforts are being channelled in the most productive way. Your many customers will have their own views about your service, and you may find it useful to gain insight into *their* map through the second perceptual position. Ask yourself: 'What would I think about delivery times and quality if I were one of my customers?' The third, observer's, position enables you to assess the interactions between first and second without the emotional interference. You imagine you are *outside* the situation. You could then ask: 'What does the relationship between Shmikes Ltd and its frontline customers seem like?'

From **2nd position,** she studied the other views and beliefs that might be around. She concluded that both the top team and the shop stewards came to her because she was able to communicate equally and fairly. From their positions, Hannah was an objective onlooker who listened to their opinions with no vested interest. The more she considered their positions, the more she was able to see her role as constructive.

In **3rd position,** Hannah noticed that her sense of frustration was blocking her effectiveness and that it would be beneficial if she valued the trust they had in her and could maintain neutrality to help their cause.

Using the three perceptual positions, 'piggy in the middle' became a skilled mediator.

Practise perceptual positions for yourself and notice how they help the situation you choose.

Exercise

● Think of an unsatisfactory situation between you and someone else.

● Put three sheets of paper on the floor, labelled 'self', 'other' and 'observer'.

● Stand on the 'self' sheet, facing the 'other', and recognize how you experience the situation you have chosen. Know how you feel and what you would like to say to the other person. Then move away and turn around.

● Stand on the 'other' sheet and imagine you are that person looking at the 'self'. Recognize how you, as the other person, might experience the interaction. What would you like to say to 'self'? Then move away and turn around.

● Step on to the 'observer' sheet and look at 'self' and 'other'. From this neutral position, notice what is happening. What is or is not being achieved? Remember that you do not take sides: this is the place for objective assessment. If you notice any emotions as you stand on 'observer', check whether they belong to 'self' or 'other' and go back to that sheet. 'Observer' is a neutral position. Then move away and turn around.

- Move back to 'self' and repeat the stages as many times as you need to gain full information and insight.
- Decide what you will do as a result of your new understanding.

Perceptual positioning is also useful when you are considering launching a new product, have a proposal to make or are checking the 'fit' of an outcome. By thinking in the following terms, you will be able to broaden your approach and increase your flexibility:

- How might other staff feel about this approach?
- How will this look from the customers', suppliers', manufacturers' and employees' points of view?
- What would this sound like to the sales team?

Create some of your own questions to help you collect as many explanations as possible for any situation.

'When you already have a belief there's no room for a new one unless you weaken the old belief first.'

Richard Bandler and John Grinder

Summary

Now you have been able to clarify those beliefs that are empowering and have started to change or discard those that are limiting. Some of your beliefs, of course, will be easier to change and release than others.

Some of your beliefs are not fully your own, but rather blindly taken on from others. Once a belief is formed, you work overtime to prove it right, even if the belief is something negative such as 'Nobody likes me,' or 'I am a failure'. Consider the following: do you have to let your beliefs govern you, even if they are harmful to others and yourself? Can you consciously make changes to what you believe?

Some of the beliefs you hold give great strength. Studies show that, on average, people who believe they are healthy live seven years longer than those who think they are unhealthy, regardless of their actual health condition at the time of the survey.

Fact-check (answers at the back)

1. What are beliefs?
   a) Assumptions we make about ourselves ❏
   b) Always limiting ❏
   c) Always empowering ❏
   d) Self-fulfilling ❏

2. From where do beliefs emanate?
   a) We are born with them ❏
   b) From our parents and family ❏
   c) From religion ❏
   d) From peer groups ❏

3. Which of these words are associated with NLP beliefs?
   a) Should ❏
   b) Perhaps ❏
   c) Must ❏
   d) Might ❏

4. What characterizes limiting beliefs?
   a) They are unchangeable ❏
   b) They hold you back ❏
   c) They are inconvenient ❏
   d) They have a positive intention ❏

5. What characterizes empowering beliefs?
   a) They make life easy ❏
   b) They can prolong your life ❏
   c) They are good to focus on ❏
   d) They are a gift ❏

6. Which are examples of NLP work-related beliefs?
   a) 'We come to work to do our best.' ❏
   b) 'Our decisions are right at the time we make them.' ❏

   c) 'Our pay is directly related to our skill.' ❏
   d) 'Attitude is more important than qualifications.' ❏

7. How many perceptual positions are there?
   a) Two ❏
   b) Five ❏
   c) Three ❏
   d) One ❏

8. What happens in the third perceptual position?
   a) You incorporate everyone's feelings ❏
   b) You are a neutral observer ❏
   c) You don't take sides ❏
   d) You decide who's right and who's wrong ❏

9. What is the purpose of the perceptual positions exercise?
   a) To test a new product ❏
   b) To understand people better ❏
   c) To change people's mindset ❏
   d) To analyse behaviour ❏

10. What happens in perceptual positions?
    a) You change position literally ❏
    b) You consider your position from different vantage points ❏
    c) You imagine you are someone else ❏
    d) You change position figuratively ❏

CHAPTER 23

Recognize how we and others represent the information around us

The *neuro-* in NLP refers to the way we use our senses to acquire, process, store and recall information. We use our senses outwardly to perceive the world and inwardly to 're-present' experiences to ourselves. In NLP, the ways we take in, store and code information in our minds are known as *representational systems*.

Memories, for instance, use all the senses. To take one example, a musical trigger might activate memories that lead us to:

- feel the sand
- see the azure sea
- hear the laughter
- taste the food
- smell the spices.

Notice which of your senses are activated when you look at your favourite photos.

Now we will concentrate on the clues and cues that help you recognize your own and other people's preferred thinking and communication styles. In NLP, these are called *accessing cues* because they help you access the way someone is processing whatever is happening around them.

Accessing cues

Eye-accessing cues are probably the part of NLP with which people are most familiar. You may think that all you need to do is watch someone's eyes and then you have all the information you need about them. This is only one part of the story. The knowledge you can gain from observing someone's eye movements relates to their preferred way of thinking about issues. People also give you information through the words they use, the gestures they make and the way they breathe. When you know how someone is processing information, you can work out the best ways to communicate with them.

Representational systems

When someone poses a question or says something to you in a conversation, you may need anything from a fraction of a second to a couple of minutes to process your thoughts and then respond. The way you do this has an important effect on the way you communicate – or miscommunicate – with others. *Representational systems* describe this processing of information.

We represent information internally through our basic senses, i.e. in pictures (*visual*), sounds (*auditory*), feelings (*kinaesthetic*), tastes (*gustatory*) and smells (*olfactory*). The words in brackets are the NLP terminology used to refer to the senses. In general, we all have the capacity to see, hear, feel, smell and taste, unless we have some neurological damage.

> As you **look** at this page in the book, the ringing of the telephone may distract you. As you **hear** your HR manager's voice on the line, you **feel** nervous and slightly apprehensive, wondering about your recent promotion interview. You tell yourself that if you are successful you will go out for a meal at your favourite restaurant. You may remember the last time you ate there, the **smell** of the herbs and spices and the **taste** of the... as you took your first mouthful...

Be aware of how many of your senses you used to follow the above passage. You may have found it easier to picture people or places as you read. You may have been more comfortable recreating sounds or noticing sensations and feelings. The senses of smell and taste may have made you salivate, distracting you even more. What you were doing was using your internal senses to *represent* the external experiences described through the words.

Different people will have different responses. None is right or wrong; they just are. It is important to remember that these comprise information and are not a way of stereotyping or labelling people. The skill is to recognize, without judging, the systems being used and to work with them. Excellent communicators do this instinctively. They move around the *representational systems* to include and reach each member of their audience. In any communication they will use all the three main representational systems (visual, auditory and kinaesthetic) to be sure that everyone can see, hear or make sense of the points they are making. In the same way as our map of the world represents only part of the territory, so our preferred representational system is only part of the picture, or is only one soundbite, or feels incomplete.

Predicates

Predicates are the words we use to distinguish and differentiate between representational systems.

> In visual mode, Sasha would like to **see** the minutes of a meeting written down for her to read. In auditory, Denise would prefer to **hear** what happened or **talk** it over with someone else, particularly the section that wasn't on her **wavelength**. If Phil wanted to **touch** base after the meeting to weigh up his and others' **sense** of the meeting, he would be in kinaesthetic mode. These three could have a frustrating post-meeting discussion if they became stuck in their own preferred system.

Over time, we develop a preference for one of the representational systems, and will tend to use that more often. Although, in different contexts, we will use the other systems, we may often be more comfortable and practised in one of the three. In any discussion where each person is using a different system exclusively, an interpreter may be needed.

Which is your preferred system? Think back to your last meeting or team briefing and record the words to describe it, or draw a diagram. What were the first words that came into your head? Now consider a recent customer meeting, with internal or external customers, and repeat the process. Finally, think about your most recent experience of moving house, and record the words. Did you find your preferred system?

There was probably a strong secondary system and a weaker third. Now listen to and note your colleague's words. When you recognize their preferred systems, you may understand them better. Are you speaking the same language? You may well find that these systems change depending on the context. Notice what happens and extend your knowledge of yourself and others.

Predicate identifier examples

Visual	Auditory	Kinaesthetic	Olfactory/ gustatory
Looks good to me	Sounds right	Feels good	Fresh as a daisy
Outside my picture	Can't hear myself think	Heated debate	Smell a rat
Seeing eye to eye	Singing our tune	On common ground	A sweet person
Shed some light on...	Clear explanation	Hands on	Get the flavour...
Colourful show	Rings bells	Smooth operator	Whiff of success

Eye movements

You can find out more about representational systems via the eye-accessing cues, which concentrate on eye movements. You may wish to refer back to Chapter 18 for more information. Research in NLP suggests that, in general, people using the visual representational system tend to look upwards or ahead, while those using auditory look sideways and those using kinaesthetic look downwards.

Further refinement indicates that, in general, a right-handed person looks up to their left when they are recalling past experiences and up to their right when they are creating an image, sound or feeling for the first time. For some left-handed people, the patterns are reversed. As this is a generalized model, check your observations in as many ways as you can, using *calibration* as a way of observing each person's unique cues.

As you go through the following exercises, you may find that you respond differently from the suggested eye movements. This does not mean that you are wrong or strangely built; work out your individual patterns.

Visual

A person using visual accessing cues will answer the questions below after locating a picture in their mind. Invite someone to ask you these questions and to note where your eyes go. Then swap with them and note their eye movements. You don't need to speak the answers. What matters is *how* you arrive at them. Analysing eye movements takes practice, and over time you will notice patterns with ease.

> **What did your first workspace look like?**
> (*Your eyes up and to your left.*)
>
> **Imagine your MD with pink hair and wearing a bright orange suit.**
> (*Your eyes up and to your right.*)

A person with a preferred visual representational system will want to see diagrams and charts and be more likely to use flip charts or PowerPoint. They may need to see things in writing and prefer email to telephone calls.

Auditory

When people are thinking in sounds, their eyes move across to their left for remembered sounds and to their right for imagined sounds.

Those with a preferred auditory representational system will want to discuss issues. They like to talk things over and often 'think out loud' as they gather their thoughts. They tend to prefer the phone to email.

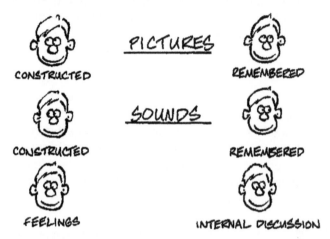

Typical eye-accessing cues for right-handed people as you look at them

Kinaesthetic

If someone's eyes look down and to their right, they are processing in kinaesthetic mode, and this puts them in touch with either their internal emotions or an external tactile feeling. They may also be in olfactory or gustatory mode.

Kinaesthetics will start with their 'gut feelings' in the way they react to different situations. They will want to work out how they feel about an issue – they will often say that they 'just have a sense' about things. They pick up underlying and unspoken feelings.

Internal dialogue

When people are in conversation with themselves – having an 'internal dialogue' – their eyes will tend to look down and to their left. This is another system of thinking, and people can take some time to process their thoughts before they respond. It is often associated with people being 'deep in thought'. The key to communicating with a person using this mode is to give them plenty of time. They can become confused or frustrated if you keep asking supplementary questions through your impatience.

In quiet times, what do you find yourself thinking about?
Repeat silently: 'I am who I am and I am fine.'

(Your eyes down and to your left.)

QUICK, HIGH PITCH

CLEAR, RESONANT

DEEP, SLOW

VISUAL   AUDITORY   KINAESTHETIC

Please note that these are generalizations. Not everyone fits neatly into them. What you may notice is that, although someone's eyes move in an unexpected direction, they are likely to be consistent so you can learn to recognize their system. Remember to notice their *predicates* (words they use), too, for confirmation.

Body language

The gestures we make, the qualities in our voice and the way we breathe are further indicators of the representational system being used at any time. These may be the first aspects you notice or the final check after you have heard the predicates and detected the eye movements.

Body language and representational systems

	Visual	Auditory	Kinaesthetic
Voice	Speak quickly and in a higher pitch than A or K	Clear, expressive, rich and resonant	Deeper, slower, with pauses
Head	Head up, shoulder muscles tense	Well-balanced or leaning to one side	Angled downwards
Breath	Centred high in chest area and shallow	Evenly over whole chest area	Deep and low in abdomen
Gestures	Exaggerated; sit/stand erect; gestures upwards	Move rhythmically; touching ears or near ears; lips move	Relaxed posture, with rounded shoulders

Calibration

Where eye movements and body language give you a general view of representational systems, calibration involves recognizing and applying the different information that is unique to each person. How is this useful at work? As you become increasingly aware of the individual and minimal cues from a person, you will be able to recognize a pattern from which to assess their mood. You will also be able to evaluate the effect you are having without just relying on the words.

TIP

There are many cues to notice. Some you will already spot subconsciously and just know what someone is going to do or say before they do or say it. Notice the information available from someone's breathing, muscle tone or skin colour.

Rapport

If your communications always seem to be successful and without conflict, well done. It would seem that you are using all the information available and then adapting your representational style to suit the person with whom you are communicating. This is known in NLP terminology as being *in rapport*.

Rapport enables you to appreciate the other person's map of the world. If you make the effort to be like someone else, they will feel more comfortable in their dealings with you. They are more likely to trust you and do business with you. People tend to like people who are like them. You could also demonstrate rapport by seeing things from someone else's point of view, playing the same tune or getting under their skin in a positive way.

> **'Let me not judge my neighbour until I have walked a mile in his moccasins.'**
>
> Native American proverb

Matching

Rapport is partly established by *matching* the representational systems and body language of others. This might mean sitting down if they are seated, breathing slowly like them or speaking at a fast pace with them. They will have the sense that you are 'with and for' them rather than against them. The advantage of matching is that the other person recognizes at an unconscious level that you understand and value what they are communicating. It will also help you unconsciously to join in genuinely with their understanding.

It is worth noting that you can disagree with someone and still be in rapport: you are disagreeing from as close as you can be to their map of the world. You can also agree wholeheartedly with someone and not be in rapport because you are not 'speaking' the same language. With practice, matching can be performed elegantly and without detection. It is equally important that you match with integrity, not as a cynical means of tricking someone to your advantage.

Mismatching

There may be occasions when you no longer wish to be involved in a discussion or want to switch the focus. Imagine what would happen if you deliberately *mismatched* the other person(s) involved. In most cases, they will respond and move away or change direction. An extreme form of mismatching is turning your back.

Pacing and leading

Pacing extends rapport by respecting and responding to someone's emotional state. When we talk about a person's excitement or enthusiasm being 'infectious', we are merely describing our ability to pace and join in with them. You know what it is like if you go into work full of joy on a Monday morning: if colleagues pace your mood, you continue to feel good. If they say negative things, such as, 'It's all right for some,' or 'Don't know why you're so cheerful. Wait till you see your intray', you may feel deflated.

If you can match and pace someone's mood, then you can *lead* them away from it, too. For example, if someone is becoming increasingly angry at a meeting, you can help them calm down without 'losing face'. Alternatively, in an appraisal meeting, it would be helpful to understand and acknowledge the other person's nerves before creating a more conducive climate. The general rule is to pace a couple of times to make sure you have understood before leading to change. If you start to lead too soon, it will just seem like a mismatch and you will lose the rapport you have built.

Case study

A travel organization wanted to restructure its customer care programme. It called in an NLP expert who introduced a series of ideas including pacing and leading. Staff members were most challenged by irate, often anxious, customers who thought they had been let down by the organization, their main concern being delays and overlong travel times. They practised pacing the 'customer' by matching the energy of the mood and emotions displayed. For example, they talked more quickly, in staccato phrasing and with a sense of urgency.

After a couple of exchanges, they lowered their voice, and slowed their pace and breathing. They had moved to a more resourceful state and started to *lead* to solutions and options. They were overjoyed when their customers followed them and calmed down, too. Both parties had wanted a positive outcome. It was just that they had started from initially incompatible places.

Impact at work

Introducing change in the workplace is more acceptable if you can first match and pace the parties involved. Some basic research about how best to manage information saves time and conflict later on. People like and feel understood by people who are like themselves. So consider: would your colleagues want to see a written account of your proposals, would they rather talk them over, or would they prefer time to grasp and sense the nature of your ideas?

Think how you might approach the situations shown in the table below using each of the three main representational systems. Write or record a prepared statement for each, following the example shown.

	Visual	Auditory	Kinaesthetic
Recruitment interview	We've looked at your CV. Where do you see yourself in five years?	It sounds like you have wide expertise. Tell me about...	In which of your last jobs did you feel most settled?
Closing a meeting			
Staff briefing			
Appraisal			
Customer meeting			

Summary

The way people process information is crucial to communications both at work and elsewhere. When you think about it, it makes perfect sense that conflict can arise when people are processing information in different ways and don't recognize each other's preferences. As you increase your skill in interpreting the mismatches, you will go a long way towards creating more harmonious relationships.

Take your time and focus on the different cues and clues. It doesn't matter whether you start with eye patterns or other people's verbal or body language. You will soon find that you unconsciously understand the representational system being used.

By learning to recognize and understand other people's preferred systems, you can increase your rapport. Notice others who seem to do it naturally. What do they do and what can you learn from them? If there is someone with whom you don't see eye to eye, or with whom you feel out of tune, your challenge is to take your new-found skills, enter their world and change the relationship for the better.

Fact-check (answers at the back)

1. What are the three main senses referred to in NLP representational systems?
   - a) Smell ❑
   - b) Hearing ❑
   - c) Feeling ❑
   - d) Sight ❑

2. What do NLP predicates refer to?
   - a) Thoughts ❑
   - b) Ideas ❑
   - c) Words ❑
   - d) Phrases ❑

3. Which of these is in visual mode?
   - a) Record ❑
   - b) Examine ❑
   - c) Pressure ❑
   - d) Pinpoint ❑

4. Which of these is in auditory mode?
   - a) Word for word ❑
   - b) Strike a bargain ❑
   - c) Make a scene ❑
   - d) Hidden message ❑

5. Which of these is in kinaesthetic mode?
   - a) Loud and clear ❑
   - b) Weighed heavily ❑
   - c) Catch a glimpse of ❑
   - d) Too much to handle ❑

6. Which representational system is generally indicated by deep, low breathing?
   - a) Kinaesthetic ❑
   - b) Auditory ❑
   - c) Visual ❑
   - d) Gustatory ❑

7. What is rapport?
   - a) Recognizing a situation you've been in before ❑
   - b) Getting along with people ❑
   - c) Establishment of trust and harmony ❑
   - d) Entering into another person's world ❑

8. What can you match to establish rapport?
   - a) Body language ❑
   - b) Accents ❑
   - c) Breathing ❑
   - d) Perfume ❑

9. Why might you pace and lead someone's behaviour?
   - a) To increase their energy ❑
   - b) To change their emotional state ❑
   - c) To gain information ❑
   - d) To disguise your feelings ❑

10. What is calibration?
    - a) A way of recognizing behaviour patterns ❑
    - b) Cues detected through breathing and change in skin colour ❑
    - c) A way of regulating behaviour ❑
    - d) Something that fine-tunes your communications ❑

CHAPTER 24

Use precision questions to find out what people mean

In the previous chapter you worked out both someone's preferred way of accessing information and how to establish rapport. However, there may still be areas of misunderstanding. This is because the meaning of the words you use can be more complicated than they sound. You know what you want to say, and you know what the words mean. The challenge arises when you are speaking in your own 'shorthand', expecting the message to be understood, even acted upon, by someone else. It is unfortunate if, as far as the other party is concerned, you have given out only half the 'story', or one that has different interpretations. Words don't always transmit the intended meaning because the audience will interpret them in their own way.

Bandler and Grinder were particularly interested in the patterns of language and behaviour that effective psychotherapists used with their clients to effect change. They observed and modelled the interactions between Satir, Erickson, Perls and their patients that were successful. They concluded that certain types of questions worked and helped people to get better. These questions helped clients to recover 'lost' information, which enabled them to reconnect to their internal experience and so reconfigure their conscious mental processes.

The NLP communication model

The NLP communication model includes the notion that our five senses take in up to 2 million bits of information per second but that our conscious mind can only process 7+/-2 chunks of information at any one time. These can be internal thoughts and feelings or external events and activities.

Obviously there are many things that we do on a daily basis without having to think consciously about them. You weren't aware of the task of reading these words until I just wrote about it and you probably weren't thinking about the texture of the book or the sounds going on around you, until I raised your awareness. And this is as it should be. If we used all our conscious energy thinking about things we do 'naturally' and automatically, then we wouldn't have space to do anything else.

The meta model

Bandler and Grinder developed the NLP process known as the *meta model*. Its aim is to identify the ambiguities in our words and target them with a collection of questions to provide better understanding of the unconscious beliefs, values and decisions they represent. When you want to know clearly and specifically what the words mean, you can use the meta model.

> **Meta model** – a series of devices for achieving a better understanding of vague language patterns, including specific questions for added clarification.

There are times both at and outside work when it is crucial that we are clear and precise in what we say. If you are the health and safety officer who states that, 'There mustn't be too many people at this gathering because of the fire risk', it simply won't do. Equally, if you are talking in terms of a multi-million-pound deal and you suggest a profit share of 'around 10 per-cent-ish', or in an appraisal meeting you say, 'You're always out of touch with the rest of the section', you are not providing information in a form to which others can make a valid response. This is not a case of your being deliberately awkward but simply missing out information that you assume they know. At other times, it may be fine to be imprecise if we are with someone who understands our shorthand or we want to encourage creativity.

Linguistic research suggests that there is a difference between 'deep' and 'surface' structure levels of language. **Deep structure** describes the complete and whole experience you go through subconsciously before saying the words to convey your message. **Surface structure** represents the words you speak both internally to yourself (your own personal shorthand) and audibly to others. It is the conscious representation of your deep structure. If you put all your deep-structure thinking into words, the most basic narrative would take so long that you would lose your audience. Between deep structure and surface structure, we **delete**, **distort** and **generalize** our experience and verbalize the representation.

The meta model provides the techniques to enable you to recover information from another person which they have deleted, distorted or generalized en route from their deep structure. This prevents you wondering if you have guessed right. You can fill in the gaps and reconnect to the fuller meaning. When you are wondering, 'Why are you saying this?', 'What exactly are you trying to tell me?' or 'What do you want me to do?', the meta model provides a set of more elegant questions to help you find out. If we don't ask the questions, we may find we have moved a long way down conflicting paths because of an unnecessary misunderstanding.

Deletions

We delete all kinds of information when we presume that the other person will know what we mean, or when we consider it too trivial to include. Since we can't actively pay attention to everything our senses input, we omit certain parts of our current experience by selectively paying attention to certain other parts of it. That is, we focus on what seems most important at a particular moment and allow the rest to pass us by. The most common deletions occur when people use unspecified nouns, verbs or 'nominalizations', or make comparisons and judgements.

Unspecified nouns

In this pattern, you describe an action without clarifying *who* carried it out. This is sometimes used when the speaker wants to express their dissatisfaction and to avoid conflict by not naming names. It also depersonalizes situations where the speaker seems to be a passive bystander – so taking no responsibility for what is happening.

● 'He's not liked.'	● 'Who specifically doesn't like him?'
● 'They don't tell you anything.'	● 'Who, exactly?
● 'It's so difficult.'	● 'What, precisely, is so difficult?'

Unspecified verbs

In this pattern, you describe an action without clarifying *how* it was carried out. You may want to understand the behaviour behind a particular action, and you need to know how something was done.

● 'We will be the most efficient...'	● 'How exactly will we be the most efficient?'
● 'She's avoiding me.'	● 'How specifically is she avoiding you?'

Nominalization

'Any *communication* that includes lengthy *discussions* in an *organization* is likely to lead to *confusion!*' What on earth did you take that sentence to mean? It is unclear because it is full of nominalizations.

The word 'nominalization' is used to describe what happens when we take a verb or process which is dynamic and change it into a noun so that it becomes static. (These are also referred to as *abstract nouns*.) Meta-model questions enable us to find out the processes or actions that are missing.

● Any communication	● 'How do you communicate?'
● Lengthy discussions	● 'What are you discussing?'
● Organization	● 'What are you organizing?'
● Confusion	● 'How are you confusing yourself?'

Nominalizations are common in business and politics. They are often deliberately vague and abstract, meaning any number of different things to different people. Nominalizations become a challenge when they are mistaken for reality and we think they actually exist. Nominalizations delete so much information that we take the empty shell and fill it with our own ideas and assumptions. Compare 'raising the stakes' with 'development in investments'. The first describes an active process while the second is static and implies no active participation.

We can recognize a nominalization when the noun makes sense with the word 'ongoing' in front of it. An ongoing relationship or ongoing enterprise will probably relate to an abstract noun, while an ongoing dog won't. The other test is whether or not 'it' will fit into a wheelbarrow. You would struggle to put development or training into a wheelbarrow, whereas several cats, for example, would probably fit quite comfortably.

Comparisons

Sometimes, we can make a statement that implies a comparison but it is not clear what we are comparing. Our listener, rather than assuming that they know what we mean, will want the rest of the information.

● '...resulting in greater customer loyalty.'	● 'Greater compared to what?'
● 'She's better at organizing.'	● 'Better than whom?'

Judgements

> *'It is a truth universally acknowledged, that a single man in possession of a good fortune, must be in want of a wife.'*
>
> Jane Austen, *Pride and Prejudice*

If you heard these ironic opening words of Austen's novel spoken by someone, you might be inclined to reply: 'Says who?' Yet people often make these kinds of global statements, which can be very powerful and often received without question.

The speaker deletes the fact that this is their opinion, and expresses their belief as if it were an absolute fact. They are presenting their map of the world as the only one. In addition, they do not identify who is making the judgement. It may be important for you to know the source of the judgement before deciding on your response. It can also help the other person to consider: 'Who said this in the first instance?' and 'Is it still relevant or useful for me now?'

- 'That is the way to do it.'
- 'His incompetence is worrying.'
- 'According to whom?'
- 'Who thinks he is incompetent?'

Distortions

Distortion is a key component of imagination and a useful tool in motivating yourself toward your goals. When we plan, we use distortion to construct appealing imaginary futures, and we may choose to oversimplify or fantasize about what is possible or what has happened.

Distortions occur when a speaker draws conclusions that have no logical foundation, or assumes faulty connections between different parts of their experience. The skill is to discover what evidence you or the other person has to suggest that their distortion is fact.

Mind reading

These are the kind of interpretations people make when they presume that they know what someone else is thinking or feeling. It is important to check whether this intuitive response to someone is accurate or whether it could be affecting a relationship on the basis of guesswork.

● 'He's ignoring me.'	● 'How do you know?'
● 'I'm sure she loves surprises.'	● 'How can you be sure?'

You can also turn this mind reading around so that you give another person the power to read your mind. They then become responsible for your wellbeing or otherwise, and you can blame them for not understanding you. The classic 'You'd know if you really loved me' is a typical example of this. The meta-model question in response would be: 'What would I know?'

Complex equivalent

This often follows mind reading because it links two statements as if they have the same meaning – for example, 'You are frowning, and that means I'm in trouble.' Here, frowning is equated with being in trouble, which is not necessarily the case: some people frown when they are concentrating. The question for this pattern is: 'How does this mean that?'

● 'He's ignoring me.'	● 'How do you know?'
● 'He didn't wave back when I drove past this morning. He must be ignoring me.'	● 'How does his not waving mean he is ignoring you?'

Cause and effect

This pattern involves one thing having a causal relationship with another. Rather than the complex equivalent assuming that *x* means *y*, here the distortion is that *x* causes *y* and there is some sequence to the events. Use of the word 'but' is sometimes a clue to this pattern.

Presuppositions

These do exactly that and presuppose an underlying assumption about our beliefs and expectations. The classic question 'When did you stop beating your wife?' presupposes that beatings have happened and have now stopped. Whatever your answer, you are in a no-win situation. The responses to presuppositions are likely to include 'What makes you think...?', 'What leads you to believe...?' or 'How do you know...?'

> 'When you go to the meeting, are you voting for or against?' This presupposes that you are going to the meeting and have decided which way to vote. A useful response would be, 'What makes you think I am going? How do you know I'm voting?'

Generalizations

Generalizations involve interpreting one experience as an absolute truth, which applies in all circumstances. They also describe the rules or limits that govern our behaviour.

When these are operating as part of our beliefs, we can seem to be dogmatic and rigid in discussions. Often, there is an element of fear attached to the very idea of being able to change or release these strongly held views.

Universal quantifiers

The language of universal quantifiers is likely to include such words as 'always', 'every', 'never', 'no one', 'everyone', 'all' or 'nothing'. These words are all-inclusive and allow no room for manoeuvre. Using the meta model helps us recognize that our statement is not necessarily based on reality. We can then begin to expand and change our perceptions.

> One response you can make to someone using a universal quantifier is to repeat back the key words with emphasis and then exaggerate to show how inane it is:
>
> 'I'm always the last to know.'
> 'Always? You're right of course. Everyone else in the business world knows before you.'
>
> Take care how you use this or you may not get the outcome you want.
>
> Another response is to check for a counter-argument:
>
> 'Managers don't care about staff.'
> 'Has there been a time when they did?'

Modal operators of necessity

These relate to the conditions and rules by which we run our lives. They implicitly seem to call on an unseen authority or unwritten rules, often originating in childhood. Modal operators of necessity are indicated by words like 'should', 'ought', 'must' and 'have to' or their negative equivalents. These are all words that externalize responsibility. By asking the question 'What would happen if you did not do this?', you elicit the consequences of breaking the potentially constraining rule. This in turn enables the speaker to evaluate the present relevance of this rule.

> - 'I must be available for work.'
> - 'I shouldn't speak to strangers.'
>
> - 'What would happen if you weren't?'
> - 'What would happen if you did?'

Modal operators of possibility/impossibility

When a person says 'I can't' or 'It's impossible', they are talking about something that they perceive to be outside their ability or sphere of influence. In fact, it might just be

389

their perception that is limiting them, not their ability or their situation. If this pattern goes unchecked, it can impair personal development as well as interpersonal relating.

Whenever you find yourself saying 'I can't' or 'I'll never manage that', check whether it is more a case of 'I won't', 'I haven't learned yet' or 'I don't want to.' You can instantly broaden your possibilities. You might also ask yourself: 'What's stopping me?' This will give you many insights into your map of the world.

As with the operators of necessity, you can also ask the question 'What would happen if I did?' This is a very powerful question, and it can empower people to go beyond the barriers they build for themselves.

| ● 'I can't manage.' | ● 'What would happen if you could?' |

This statement suggests that the person has some notion of managing – or how else do they know they are *not* doing it? As they consider what would happen if they *could* manage, they imagine possibilities and shift their thinking.

Warning

The meta model can seem either an aggressive technique or overly pedantic. It is essential first to create rapport, so that your questions will be seen as a constructive way of extending your understanding. Take some time to practise the questions in your own way, so that they sound natural.

Summary

The meta model provides an invaluable set of precision questions for when you need or desire to be absolutely clear about what exactly someone is saying to you. Begin to notice any *deletions*, *distortions* and *generalizations* in your own internal dialogue.

Deletion occurs where you omit certain parts of your experience by selectively paying attention to certain other parts of it. By focusing on what seems most important at a particular moment, you allow the rest to pass you by.

Distortion is when you distort your experience of sensory data to make misrepresentations of reality. Distortion may cause you to oversimplify the meaning of events.

Generalization is the process by which you draw global conclusions based on your experiences or other people's rules. At its best, generalization is an efficient means of applying information globally. At its worst, it is taking a single event and turning it into a lifetime of experience.

Fact-check (answers at the back)

1. How many chunks of information does the NLP communication model suggest that the conscious mind can process?
   a) Five ❏
   b) Fifteen ❏
   c) Seven ❏
   d) Ten ❏

2. What is the meta model?
   a) A modelling technique ❏
   b) A set of precision questions ❏
   c) A series of statements ❏
   d) A system that works only with the conscious mind ❏

3. In linguistics, what does *surface structure* represent?
   a) Your complete internal representation as stored in the unconscious mind ❏
   b) The words you speak out loud ❏
   c) The words you speak internally to yourself ❏
   d) The meaning of your words ❏

4. What does transforming deep structure experiences to surface structure communication involve?
   a) Deletion ❏
   b) Creation ❏
   c) Generalization ❏
   d) Distortion ❏

5. Which of the following are examples of deletion?
   a) Mind reading ❏
   b) Modal operators ❏
   c) Unspecified verbs ❏
   d) Judgements ❏

6. Which of the following are examples of distortion?
   a) Mind reading ❏
   b) Cause and effect ❏
   c) Universal quantifiers ❏
   d) Nominalizations ❏

7. Which of the following are examples of generalization?
   a) Mind reading ❏
   b) Presuppositions ❏
   c) Modal operators ❏
   d) Universal quantifiers ❏

8. How can you challenge the deletion 'He's better at managing'?
   a) 'How do you know?' ❏
   b) 'Better than whom?' ❏
   c) 'Better at managing what?' ❏
   d) 'Better than before?' ❏

9. How can you challenge the distortion 'It's bad to be late'?
   a) 'Who says it's bad to be late?' ❏
   b) 'How do you know it's bad?' ❏
   c) 'When were you last late?' ❏
   d) 'When is it good to be late?' ❏

10. How can you challenge the generalization 'She's never on time'?
    a) 'Never?' ❏
    b) 'Not even once?' ❏
    c) 'How else does she let you down?' ❏
    d) 'Have you ever not been on time?' ❏

CHAPTER 25

Identify different communication filters

At work, do some of your colleagues look forward to the finishing line in a project while others just do not want to be left behind? Do some prefer to check what is wanted through consultation, while others just seem to know what is required and get on with it? Different people in your team will process the information they receive in different ways. Those who operate in the same way as you will seem much easier to motivate, while those who do not may come across as awkward.

The key is to recognize that we each have our own way of filtering and sorting the information around us: none is inherently right or wrong; it is simply the way we do it. In NLP, these filters are called *metaprograms*. When you recognize which filters are being used, you can adjust your communications to fit in with them. Once you recognize someone else's filters, you can work with them from a position of rapport rather than conflict. One of the best ways to motivate others is to recognize and understand how they motivate themselves.

In this chapter you will learn how you respond to information you are given (your filters) and how you programme it. You will also consider other people's filters and how to create rapport with them.

What are metaprograms?

Metaprograms are the internal filters that we use to sort the information we receive in a systematic way, and which then determine our behaviour. They help us deal with the huge amount of sensory-based information in the external environment, organize our thinking and decide where to focus our attention.

If you won a large amount of money tomorrow or were made redundant with a healthy severance package, what changes would it make to your life? Would your answers relate to all the things you could do – sail around the world, set up your own business, write a novel – or to those things you would not need to do any more – stop worrying about bills, not have to go to work, not be cautious when shopping? The way you respond to such questions will give you an idea about the way you filter experiences and information – your metaprograms.

Metaprogram filters

It is important to recognize how flexible people are when they filter or sort their experiences. We all habitually notice some experiences and screen out others, which leads to consistent patterns in the way we think and work.

The reason for identifying someone's metaprogram is to appreciate and understand differences. Once you have recognized the metaprogram, you can work with the person from a position of rapport rather than conflict. The implications at work are immense: rather than being frustrated by someone else's 'pig-headed' disagreements with you, you adapt your interaction to compensate once you identify their metaprogram. You may find you understand them better, too.

Towards/away from

An example of a question to help determine this metaprogram could be the one already quoted: 'If you took voluntary severance tomorrow, what changes would it make to your life?'

Your answer to this question will give you a good indication of whether you move *towards your goals* or *away from unpleasant consequences*. A towards person talks about benefits and knows what they want. An away-from person talks about problems and is more focused on what to avoid than on what to aim for.

At work, a towards person will be a risk taker and will have a 'go for it' approach. They may need an away-from person to anticipate possible pitfalls. An away-from person will put off doing something until the last minute, or until the disadvantages of not doing it become great enough to spur them on. Such a person may also respond better to threats than to rewards. They may need a towards person to give them a push-start.

Sameness/difference

An example of a question to help determine this metaprogram is: 'What is the relationship between the work you are doing now and the work you did last year?'

The answer to this question gives you an indication of whether a person considers information to find similarities and familiarity – 'still looking at' ... 'the same as before' – or whether they do so to find difference and exception – 'changed projects', 'new clients with a different slant'. A person who prefers *sameness* will probably be happy to stay in the same or similar type of job and not look for changes. They can often find areas of mutuality. A *difference* person, on the other hand, wants variety at work and is more likely to make a number of career changes. The latter are often the rule breakers.

In addition, there are people whose attention is focused primarily on sameness, with a secondary emphasis on the differences, or people who look for the differences first before considering the similarities. Together, they form a large enough proportion of the population to be the main target for many advertisers. They will reject 'new' unless it is an improved version of the existing model, and will reject 'improved' unless it still has some of the original qualities. What could be better than the familiar with some extra spice?

Internal/external

An example of a question to help determine this metaprogram is: 'How do you know when you have done a good job?'

This is sometimes called the **frame of reference** filter because it refers to the way people make judgements about their actions. An *internally* referenced person would be likely to answer the above question with words like 'I just know' or 'I feel good inside.' On the other hand, the responses 'When someone tells me,' or 'When people use my ideas,' both represent an *externally* referenced person.

Internals are self-motivating people who want to make their own decisions. They work best with minimal supervision, which recognizes their preference to think for themselves. Externals want someone else to set the standards against which to assess themselves. They like to receive clear, positive feedback, and appreciate accessible management.

General/detail

An example of a question to help determine this metaprogram is: 'Tell me about the last film you saw.'

A *general* person would probably give you a broad overview and describe the film as 'a comedy, sci-fi film with excellent special effects', whereas a *detail* person might tell you about the different characters, the subplots, the music and the costumes. A general person thinks about the big picture and overall concepts. They will often leave out the 'small print' and encourage you to 'get to the point'. Their detail counterpart likes to deal with small pieces of data and works well with 'step-by-step' information. They often assess a situation in terms of all the pieces that make up the whole.

Case study

The members of a small amateur dramatics company were all losing patience with one of the actors. She insisted that when the table was laid, the spoons and plates must be in the same place every time, and that someone kept moving them. Operating from a detail perspective, she needed to know that the table was set correctly. The director calmed her down by suggesting that the really important thing was to have the correct number of everything on the table, and that the other actors could use their dramatic abilities to move things around.

This seemingly trivial intervention changed a potential lynching into a smoother-running production.

Options/procedures

An example of a question to help determine this metaprogram is: 'Why did you choose your last job?'

Options people would give reasons for their choice such as 'The terms and conditions suited me,' or 'They gave me scope to develop my own style.' A *procedures* person would more likely describe how they chose – for example, 'I bought all the relevant trade journals, selected vacancies in the areas I would move to...' – thus giving you the procedure they followed.

Options people may follow a procedure to begin with and then add variations to suit. They are motivated in a setting where they have freedom of choice to expand the possibilities available to them. The procedures person likes to follow the set task sequence and enjoys doing things to meet the 'standard'. They like a clearly defined course of action and detailed instructions.

Proactive/reactive

An example of a question to help determine this metaprogram is: 'How do you take the initiative?'

Proactive people take the initiative by getting on with things at their own prompting. They are self-starters who shoot first and ask questions later. *Reactive* people wait and respond to others who ask for help. They are good at analysing tasks and gathering information before taking action. Proactive people can make mistakes by ignoring the analysis and planning stages in decision-making. Reactive people may slow things down by too much analysis or because they are waiting for someone else to take responsibility.

Metaprograms in practice

The following table gives an overview of the different metaprograms covered so far. The 'Language' column briefly describes the words associated with each. The 'Work pattern/role' column indicates the areas and types of work that would be suitable for people with those metaprograms. The final column, 'Response', suggests the words you might use to establish rapport with each.

You may want to consider the different combinations and how they work together. You may find you are mainly a towards person who is externally referenced and proactive. Does that suit the job you do? It is worth remembering that your metaprograms are likely to be contextual.

Metaprogram	Language	Work pattern/role	Response
Towards	Get, have, gain, attain, achieve	Sales, innovation	Goal-oriented, incentives
Away from	Avoid, steer clear, exclude, prevent	Problem-solving, auditing health & safety	Point out dangers of not doing
Same	Usual, familiar, always, similar	Mediation, trends, negotiation	In common, traditional
Difference	New, change, one-off, different	Marketing, consultancy	Unique, special, revolutionary
Internal reference	'I decide', 'I made the decision...'	Self-employed, MD	'Only you can decide/will know'
External reference	'What do you think?' 'Is that OK?'	Team player, certificates	'Others think...', 'The facts show...'
General	Overall, big picture, globally	Explorer, policymaker	Basically, framework
Detail	Specifically, precisely	Pilot, architect, finance	Structure, exactly, 'Let's be clear...'
Options	Choice, possibility	Teacher	Brainstorm, variety
Procedure	Necessity, must	Filing, accounts	Known way, proven
Proactive	Initiative, action, future plans	Sales, fundraising, journalist	Independent, direct
Reactive	Respond, reaction, past achievement	Help desk, receptionist	Analysis, waiting

Company metaprograms

It is possible that the company you work in or the managers and staff you work with have similar metaprograms to you. However, if you feel like an outsider, this may suggest that your metaprograms are different in significant ways. It can be very frustrating if you are proactive and your employers are reactive, using crisis management as their norm. Your company may be externally referenced, wanting to know what is going on and what can be learned throughout the industry, rather than just being committed to excellence from within.

Different departments will need people with different meta-programs to be most effective: options people who mismatch will work well in research and development, while detail and procedures people will create an efficient finance section. Teams that have a balance of metaprograms among their members will be more effective.

Sorting categories

Think about your first day at work. The elements you remember will depend on the sorting categories you use. Knowing that none is right or wrong, recognize the way you sort information.

First-day memories might focus on:

- **people** – the person who showed you around, your immediate manager, your team members, new friends
- **places** – the location, your office, the restaurant, the main reception area
- **things** – your desk, chair, computer, paintings, coffee-making facilities
- **activity** – induction, team meeting, staff briefing, phone calls
- **time** – when it happened, dates, what you did hour by hour
- **information** – how you chose the job, why you joined the company.

It is useful to recognize another person's focus of interest in a particular context. Being people-focused is important for staff at the customer interface as they will respond better to the customer's needs. An activity focus will be helpful to someone who is organizing the weekly rotas.

Which focus is important in your job? Which is your favourite sorting category?

Time travel

The way we relate to time also has implications for the way we communicate:

1 Some people seem to live in the past, remembering the way things were. They might talk about how things were done in their last job.
2 Others live for now and their attention is on the present moment. They talk about the here and now and 'Let's do it.'
3 Future-oriented people tend to plan and to be thinking about the future. They are the sort of people who want to know what they will be having for dinner just as they finish their lunch.

Consider which way you and those around you relate to time. What could you change to take you closer to them? There are benefits to any team if you have all three of the above types available, as long as they appreciate each other's value to the team.

Timelines

People code time in different ways. We may use the same words, 'past', 'present', 'future', but we will place them differently in the way we represent them in our minds. How do you know whether something is a past memory or a plan for the future? In NLP, the term *timeline* is used to explain where people position their concepts of time.

Find your timeline

● **Past** Think about four events from your past. Where were those memories positioned? If you were to point to their location, would they be behind you, in front, to the left or to the right of you?

In time

The timeline known as 'in time' is so called because in this representation a person has time passing through them: their past is behind them, their future is ahead of them and their present is inside them. They are *in* their timeline.

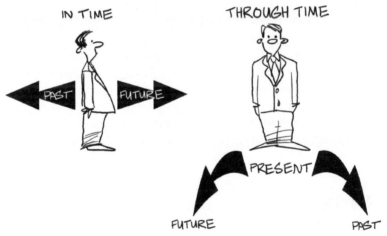

IN TIME   THROUGH TIME

PAST   FUTURE

PRESENT

FUTURE   PAST

Through-time and in-time timelines

These people tend to concentrate on the present and may be less good at planning and setting deadlines. Their idea of 'urgent' may be quite flexible because they do not strongly connect what they are doing now with what will happen in the future. They can tend to be late because they are so involved in 'now' and easily lose track of time.

Through time

When someone is operating on a 'through time' timeline, they have their past, present and future in front of them. They think of events as a series of related episodes, where time is linear, continuous and uninterrupted. It is likely that through-time people are the designers of time-management schemes, and cannot comprehend how they might be unclear to in-time people. Through-time people tend to arrive on time and place a high value on punctuality. They are also excellent at forward planning.

Chunking

We manage information at different levels and in different-sized *chunks*. You can change the way someone is thinking about an issue by *chunking up* – taking a broader, more general perspective – or *chunking down* – discussing a set of tasks necessary for the success of a key project – or *chunking sideways* – into a related or comparative area of research. Managers need to be able to chunk down high-level projects and purposes into specific, manageable and delegated tasks. They will also have to chunk up the collective goals of their individual staff to form unit and departmental plans. The concept of diversification represents sideways chunking.

Warning

Timelines and metaprograms are generalizations of how people process information and of their resultant behaviour. They are not absolutes, and they will alter with the context. As with all NLP concepts, their purpose is to enable you to think about patterns that help you to understand and communicate better.

Summary

The fact that we all habitually notice some experiences and screen out others leads to consistent patterns in the way we think and behave. In this chapter we have seen how metaprogram filters determine how we unconsciously select what we attend to, which then determines our behaviour. We each have our own way of filtering and sorting the information around us.

Metaprograms are context-specific. The patterns you use may vary in different circumstances: with colleagues, at home, with management and in the family – as a child, parent, sibling or partner. At work you might enjoy taking the initiative and driving things forward, whereas socially you might prefer to react to others' suggestions for an evening out. Nonetheless, you are still likely to have dominant patterns and preferences.

While it is a good idea to resist the temptation to label or stereotype people's metaprograms and resultant behaviour, notice the patterns they regularly use across a wide range of contexts.

Fact-check (answers at the back)

1. What characterizes metaprograms?
   a) They are fixed, not contextual ❏
   b) They help to organize your thinking ❏
   c) They are unconscious filters ❏
   d) They improve your ability to establish rapport ❏

2. What is a 'towards' motivated person?
   a) Someone who puts energy into getting what they want ❏
   b) A risk taker ❏
   c) A person who steers clear of problems ❏
   d) Someone who knows what they don't want ❏

3. What is an 'away from' motivated person?
   a) Someone who anticipates pitfalls ❏
   b) A goal-oriented person ❏
   c) Someone who talks about problems ❏
   d) A person with a 'go for it' attitude ❏

4. What words describe a 'difference' filter?
   a) Familiar ❏
   b) Still looking at ❏
   c) Change ❏
   d) Reorganization ❏

5. What characterizes people with an externally referenced filter?
   a) The need for approval ❏
   b) They are good team players ❏
   c) They prefer minimal supervision ❏
   d) They just know when something has worked well ❏

6. What does the general filter describe?
   a) The small print ❏
   b) The big picture ❏
   c) Broad brush strokes ❏
   d) All the pieces ❏

7. How will a person with a procedures filter behave?
   a) They will stick to the rules ❏
   b) They will describe how they make choices ❏
   c) They will enjoy detailed instructions ❏
   d) They will seek variety ❏

8. What words describe a proactive filter?
   a) Responsive ❏
   b) Self-starter ❏
   c) Wait for instruction ❏
   d) Initiative ❏

9. What characterizes 'in time' people? ❏
   a) They have their past in front of them ❏
   b) They have their past behind them ❏
   c) They concentrate on the present ❏
   d) They tend to be late ❏

10. What characterizes 'through time' people?
   a) They have their present time inside them ❏
   b) They have their present time in front of them ❏
   c) They like to establish deadlines ❏
   d) They consider time as linear ❏

CHAPTER 26

Use the six levels of change and reframing

We have already considered how our representational systems, language and thinking patterns and filters can explain some of the differences in the way we communicate and process information. Now we will extend that thinking beyond these different perspectives to the different levels of experience that influence the way we live our lives.

We will consider the so-called *neurological levels*, also known as the logical levels of change. Devised by Robert Dilts, this neurological levels model helps individuals and teams align their environment, behaviours, competencies, beliefs and values, identity and purpose, challenging them also to consider a higher purpose – whether work based, family, social or spiritual – in which they make a contribution outside the day-to-day demands of life.

We will also look at the NLP technique of *reframing*, as another way to facilitate change. Reframing enables you to put a new or different frame around an image or experience. What seems to be an extremely challenging situation in the present can be reframed to have less impact when considered as part of your whole life experience.

Neurological levels of change

Robert Dilts, one of NLP's leading thinkers, suggests that there are six levels of learning, communication and change. He terms these *neurological levels* because they fit together in a logical, hierarchical way.

The six levels of change

From the highest to the lowest, the levels are:

- Connectedness and higher purpose – who else?
- Identity and mission – who?
- Beliefs and values – why?
- Capabilities – how?
- Behaviour – what?
- Environment – where and with whom?

Dilts suggests that any changes made at the higher levels will have a greater influence on you than those made at the lower levels. The most important factor for effective change is to recognize the level at which you are stuck in any particular context.

If you have recently been promoted, do you need to change your behaviour to become a more effective manager? Perhaps you still think of yourself as a team member. This is an identity-level issue. Have you ever heard anyone say, 'I can't believe they've promoted me'? This would suggest they are challenged at the belief level and will need to find ways of being convinced that their promotion is totally believable and deserved.

There are some aspects of your life that are so much easier to change than others. One person will think nothing of relocating regularly to progress in their job – an *environmental* change. Another is just as happy to keep changing the job they are doing – a *behavioural* change. A third might want to be a perpetual student collecting qualifications and competencies – a change at the *capabilities* level. Your ability to make these changes easily depends on your beliefs, your identity and the broader systems to which you belong.

Once you can do that for yourself, you will be able to understand and match other people's levels, too. The neurological levels are also relevant to companies.

Case study

When the directors of Markys introduced an appraisal system across the board, they encountered fierce opposition from their first-line supervisors. This imposed change at the behaviour level did not fit in with the supervisors' views at the identity level. 'We're not managers' was their first response, followed by a capabilities concern: 'We're not trained to do this.' A little research and discussions with the supervisors would have saved Markys from the struggle it went through.

Neurological levels can help you develop greater flexibility in the way you think about all aspects of your life. If you seem to be in an unsatisfactory situation of any kind, you may find that applying neurological-level questions will help you locate and alter the source of your unease. You can use the levels to extend your awareness of what in your life is working for you. The descriptions below explain each neurological level and then offer some applications for individuals and companies.

Connectedness and higher purpose

This level refers to the larger system of which you are a part. In a metaphysical sense, it involves understanding your purpose in whatever you do in the world around you. This is *your* innermost sense of yourself, and it is sometimes called your 'higher purpose'. This level gives you a sense of whether or not you are fulfilled in what you are doing. If your feelings are strong at this level, you may only need to make minor adjustments elsewhere. If this is where you feel unease, then you might need to make changes across the board.

At this level, you would be answering the question: 'Why am I here?'

- **Individual implications:** 'No man is an island', and so whatever changes you make in your life are likely to affect those around you and will include a consideration of your higher purpose. Your decisions about the type of work you would prefer to do will be influenced by the systems to which you want to belong. Given the choice, most people work in settings that complement their ethical position; otherwise they can find themselves at odds with the company mission.
- **Company implications:** companies that attend to their bigger system are concerned about the world in which they do business. To this end, some insurance companies have 'ethical portfolios' which are committed to investing only in projects that make minimal demands on the world's resources.

Identity and mission

Your identity is a description of *who* you think you are, at any given time and in any given role. It is often conveyed in the labels you give yourself. In many cases, these have a qualitative element, for example: 'I am a financial wizard.' As you travel through life, your sense of yourself changes at this identity level and influences some of the options to which you allow yourself to be open. Your identity level can therefore be empowering or restricting of your development. You can enhance someone else's self-esteem by giving them positive feedback at the identity level: 'You are a brilliant organizer.'

At this level you would be answering the question: 'Who am I when I am doing this?'

- **Individual implications:** you will have a number of different identities depending on the context. Think about your identity when you attend a meeting. Are you the chairperson, the minute taker, an expert, a representative, a participant, an observer, an *ex officio* member, a volunteer, or a combination of some of these? When you go to a family gathering, are you a parent, child, brother, sister, aunt, uncle, etc.? The way you describe yourself passes on a message to those around you. It is important that your identity includes a number of different activities.

'It's just the way I am.' 'This is how God intended me to be.' There is often a quite fixed sense of self behind these statements. Some people are frightened that a new identity might fundamentally alter their perception of themselves or others' perceptions. This, of course, ties in with their beliefs, too.

● **Company implications:** the company identity gives employees and customers a clear idea of what to expect from the organization. Where there is a strong figurehead as founder, that person will often incorporate their identities and values into the company.

There is sometimes a challenge when an identity presented to the customer is not applied to staff. 'A company that cares...' may not be consistent in its treatment of its staff. This can percolate through to the way staff treat customers, and the company identity then becomes meaningless. Working with neurological levels can uncover these inconsistencies. There are obvious implications in mergers and takeovers. The new company needs to have a clear identity to share with the amalgamating groups. Staff at all levels can fear being 'taken over' and pushed into an alien identity. If the new identity is discussed and considered as part of the merger package, it can make the transition much smoother.

Beliefs and values

In Chapter 21, we considered the influence of *beliefs* on the way you think, your feelings and how you behave as a result. At the neurological level of beliefs, you are working with what you believe to be true, and this forms the basis for daily action. Some beliefs are handed down through families and go unchallenged from generation to generation. These can take the form of 'sayings', and they are very powerful: 'You can't teach an old dog new tricks', 'If it tastes bad, it's doing you good', 'Learning happens everywhere', 'Life begins at 40.' Can you think of any that are still around for you? Are they helpful or ready to be jettisoned?

Your *values* are the criteria against which you make decisions. They are the attributes that are important to you in the way you live your life. These could include loyalty, liberty and honesty. Your beliefs support and reinforce your values. You have to believe that you can change in order to make changes at any of the neurological levels.

At this level, you would be answering the question: 'Why am I doing this?'

- **Individual implications:** beliefs can promote or inhibit personal growth. Many beliefs are conveyed in thoughts, and they represent your opinion more than firm facts. You tend to notice information that reinforces them and to delete the opposite view.
- **Company implications:** have you ever noticed the passion and zeal in brand-new companies? People here may work exceptionally long hours for relatively little financial gain. The rewards they are getting stem from the firm and shared belief in what they are doing. There is a captivating energy that maintains momentum. As with identity, it is important that the company's beliefs about customers as human beings should also be reflected in the beliefs about staff.

> **'Whether you think you can or whether you think you can't, you're probably right.'**
>
> Henry Ford

There were many limiting beliefs around in the area of new technology. People who for years would have managed their data with a typewriter or secretarial assistance now suddenly found a PC on their desk. The beliefs that might stop them from using the machinery – a PC, a smartphone, a tablet computer or an ebook reader – were based on a lack of confidence or fear of the new: 'I can't work machines', 'It's too complicated, I'll break it' and 'I'm too old to learn.' Contrast these with: 'I thrive on anything new' and 'I can handle it.'

A company's values provide the codes of practice for the workforce, for example equal opportunities and environmental policies. There is obvious discord when the company displays such policies but doesn't believe or practise them.

Capabilities

Your capabilities are the resources that you have available to you as skills and qualities. These may be formally recognized through standards, qualifications and competencies, and will be demonstrated by the strategies you use. Many of your capabilities are processes that you perform regularly, and in many cases they are automatic and habitual.

At this level, you would be answering the question: 'How am I doing this?'

- **Individual implications:** having learned a new set of skills, you might want to consider how you incorporate these. It is great to return from a counselling skills course fired with enthusiasm. If you insist that everyone tells you how they feel all the time, they may react in a negative way. You are only part of the way to absorbing the capability that ensures appropriate use of your counselling skills.
- **Company implications:** companies that want to restructure in some way will succeed if they have considered and attained the necessary capabilities on the way. It may seem a small jump to go from being a photographic studio specializing in portraits to an internet supplier. You will need to know how to create a web page with ecommerce and handle the needs of quite different customers. Your accounting skills and staffing needs will be different, too.

Behaviours

Your behaviours are what you do, what you say and what those around you observe or hear. They are the external representation of your capabilities, beliefs, identity and connectedness. In Chapter 21, you considered outcomes and how to achieve these. One section described being specific. This is very important at the behaviours level. If you have an outcome to aim for, you will be greatly helped by considering the actions you will take to get there.

Behaviours can be easily learned through copying significant *role models* around us. *Modelling* is one of the key NLP skills, and played an important role in NLP's creation. Bandler and

Grinder wanted to know what the key therapists did that made them excellent.

At this level, you would be answering the question: 'What am I doing?'

- **Individual implications:** what do you do to achieve your outcomes, both personal and work-related? You can set yourself behavioural tasks that will enhance your development. You might decide to volunteer to take the minutes at the next team meeting, or to make a tricky phone call that everyone else is avoiding.

  Behaviours are sometimes confused with identity and capability, which can damage a person's confidence and competence. Failing an exam doesn't mean that you are stupid or useless at studying, but, if it is taken at those levels, you are unlikely to seek feedback as to how you can improve. When you are giving or receiving feedback, consider it at the level of *what you do*, not at the identity level – *who you are*. 'You failed this exam but you have passed many other testing situations in your life.'

- **Company implications:** companies behave in many different ways to let the outside world know they exist. They conduct market research surveys and advertising campaigns, they sponsor local charities and send out promotional material to prospective and existing customers. There are set or agreed behaviours that need to be actioned for many company procedures, from allocating petty cash to promotions. These behaviours are lovingly referred to as *red tape*.

Environment

Environment refers to everything that is *outside* you: where you are, the people you are with, your home, your work – your surroundings.

At this level, you would be answering the questions 'Where?' and 'With whom?'

- **Individual implications:** your choice of where to live will be influenced by your identity. If you have to move, you would also consider environmental-level factors such as schools, public transport, green space, distance from friends, etc. Where you go and what you do socially can all be considered at the environment level.

- **Company implications:** the comfort and safety of your surroundings make a big difference to how well you work and how satisfied you are. Considerations at this level could include who you lunch with, how you are as a co-worker and your effectiveness in an open- or closed-plan office. Many people will tolerate a poor working environment if they have good relationships with their work colleagues.

Describing change

The following sample table illustrates how someone may describe their desire for change. Read the words and note the implications: these give you a broad idea of which levels would benefit from change. In the table, a nurse is describing his dissatisfaction with work at each level. The questions in italics are ones that might facilitate his change.

In this example, you could help the nurse at any of the neurological levels. The six levels are interactive and influence each other. Changes at one level will effect change at the levels below, but changes on the lower levels will not automatically cause change at the higher levels. If he were to change and believe he was good enough, he would acknowledge that his skills were valid, he would behave differently and he would be able to move on in the way he needed.

Neurological level	I don't enjoy nursing any more.
Purpose	I don't know why I am doing this any more.
	What were your reasons for becoming a nurse?
Identity	I don't like the person I become when I'm nursing.
	Who do you want to be when you are nursing? How might you become a person you do like?
Belief	I don't believe I'm good enough any more.
	How were you good enough in the past? What would make you believe you are good enough now?

Neurological level	I don't enjoy nursing any more.
Capability	I need to update my training.
	How could you do that? How do other qualifications and experience count?
Behaviour	I don't have enough time to do all I need to.
	What do you have enough time for? What do you do well?
Environment	It might just be this area.
	Is it this specialism, this ward or this hospital? What are the hospitals like in other areas?

Think about an issue that is not right for you at present. In which level is it based? Where might you start to intervene? Once you start to ask yourself the right questions, you may find you move around the levels. How much change or development do you want? Take time to notice whether you have certain levels at which you prefer to operate – how do these compare with colleagues'? If you work in a team where there is friction, it may be that each team member has different ideas at the values or beliefs levels, and that these need to be addressed.

Reframing

In NLP terms, a *frame* is the focus of attention you give to something. If you look at a picture from one side, it may appear quite different than from another perspective. The value of reframing is in being able to consider an issue from many different angles. If you have ever put a picture or photograph into a new frame, you will know how much that can alter it. That is what you can do with behaviours or thoughts that seem stuck.

Reframing is a way of getting people to say: 'How else can I do or consider this?'

Context reframing

Context reframing enables you to recognize that there is a positive place for almost any behaviour – doing the right thing in the right place at the right time. Embarrassment is sometimes the result of just getting the time or place wrong. Next time you find yourself or someone else limiting themselves with phrases like 'I'm too sensitive, too careless, too slow', or 'I wish I could stop doing...', use reframe questions to find a context in which the behaviour is appropriate and positive:

> **Question:** 'When would it be beneficial to be sensitive?'
>
> **Answer:** 'When I notice someone in the office who is nervous or unsure.'
>
> **Question:** 'Where would being slow be an advantage?'
>
> **Answer:** 'In a meeting that is making decisions about budgets.'

Content reframing

Content reframing is where you change the meaning of a seemingly limiting behaviour. You might want to use content reframing next time you hear statements like 'My mind goes blank when I stand up to make a presentation,' or 'I get upset when I make mistakes.' Your aim is to find another, more useful meaning.

> **Question:** 'What else could going blank mean?'
>
> **Answer:** 'It could mean I'm clearing my mind to concentrate on what I want to say.'
>
> **Question:** 'What is the value of getting upset?'
>
> **Answer:** 'It shows how much pride I take in doing a job well.'

Remember that, in Chapter 22, Hannah used perceptual positions to reframe her description of her role at work. She changed from the frustration of being 'piggy in the middle' to become a more acceptable skilled mediator.

Checklist for change

The following table gives you an idea of the questions that will help you to check which level or levels are problematical and how to address the issues they reveal. Where things are already going well, you can use the levels as a guide to making your situation even better as they extend your awareness of what in your life is working for you.

Neurological level	Meaning
Connectedness and higher purpose	Why you are who you are. What you are here for. How you can be fulfilled. Is there more involved than the obvious? Your contribution to society.
Identity	Who you are – i.e. what role(s) do you play in this context? What is your identity relative to those around you?
Beliefs and values	Your values, what you believe. Your expectations about this situation. What is important to you.
Capabilities	What you can do. What are your skills? How are they relevant? How do you apply them?
Behaviour	What you do and how you behave.
Environment	Where you live, work and play. The physical, social and emotional environment.

Summary

This chapter focused on *change.* With the neurological levels model, you were able to understand how the different levels of thinking interact. The model gives you a framework with which to organize and gather information in order to identify the best point for intervention and to make or suggest changes. The levels can help you develop greater flexibility in the way you think about all aspects of your life.

In addition, we considered the technique of reframing challenges, limiting thoughts and behaviours, working from the premise that 'choice is better than no choice'. For example, the arrival of rain is joyful in a drought-ridden environment and most unwanted on a camping trip, outdoor wedding or much-awaited barbecue. It is all a matter of which frame you use.

Fact-check (answers at the back)

1. Which of these are NLP's models and techniques for change?
   a) Representational systems ❑
   b) Reframing ❑
   c) Seeing life as a journey ❑
   d) Rapport ❑

2. In the neurological levels hierarchy, which levels are below the identity level?
   a) Capabilities ❑
   b) Higher purpose ❑
   c) Environment ❑
   d) Beliefs and values ❑

3. What would you ask at the level of higher purpose?
   a) How does this contribute to the greater good? ❑
   b) Why am I here? ❑
   c) Who else may be involved? ❑
   d) Whose fault is it? ❑

4. What would you ask at the level of identity?
   a) Why me? ❑
   b) Who am I? ❑
   c) What roles do I have? ❑
   d) What kind of organization are we? ❑

5. What would you ask at the level of beliefs and values?
   a) Why am I doing this? ❑
   b) How do I know what to believe? ❑
   c) What is important to us? ❑
   d) How do I affect others? ❑

6. What would you ask at the level of capabilities?
   a) What do I need to do here? ❑
   b) Who can help me do this? ❑
   c) What skills do I have? ❑
   d) How am I doing this? ❑

7. What would you ask at the level of behaviour?
   a) What am I doing? ❑
   b) How could I do this better? ❑
   c) How does this behaviour limit me? ❑
   d) How can I change your behaviour? ❑

8. What would you ask at the level of environment?
   a) What are the external influences on me? ❑
   b) Where does this happen? ❑
   c) Who is involved? ❑
   d) How does this affect global warming? ❑

9. How can context reframing be described?
   a) Almost all behaviours are useful or appropriate in some context ❑
   b) Doing the right thing in the right place at the right time ❑
   c) Changing the location of a seemingly limited behaviour ❑
   d) Providing a focus for your thoughts and actions ❑

10. What does content reframing mean?
   a) Changing the meaning of a seemingly limited behaviour ❑
   b) Having more resources through having more perspectives ❑
   c) Having a major influence on how you interpret and react to your experiences ❑
   d) The meaning of a situation is determined by what you choose to focus on ❑

CHAPTER 27

Increase
your options

Wouldn't it be good if you could change the way you approach and react to a variety of different situations, instead of feeling there is nothing you can do about them and telling yourself, 'That is just the way things are'? One way to increase your options is to give more attention to what works in your life rather than being stuck with what doesn't work. If you have been successful, confident and motivated in any aspects of your life, you can use those experiences to be so again in many situations. This is another opportunity to use the presupposition, 'We have all the resources we need,' and act as if it were true.

In this chapter we look at three techniques to enhance your flexibility before outlining where you might go next:

1 Submodalities can help change the way you code your memories. You cannot change what happened, but you can change the way it affects you now.

2 Anchors are naturally occurring stimulus– response connections. You can create your own anchors to trigger a particular state or emotion in a specific future context.

3 Modelling is based on the NLP presupposition, 'If one person can do something, anyone can learn to do it.' You will have the chance to observe and recreate someone else's successful behaviours or attitudes.

Submodalities

In Chapter 23 we considered representational systems and how these are an expression of the way we think and process information. Within each of these systems we can now make finer distinctions, which give us more data about the quality of our experiences. These distinctions – called *submodalities* in NLP – describe how we refine our sensory experiences. They are the foundation stones of the senses, characterizing how each picture, sound and feeling is composed.

> **Submodalities** – how we code experiences and distinguish different sensory systems.

If you're thinking *visually*, the pictures in your mind's eye will, for example, include colour, movement, shape or dimension. Thinking in *auditory* could have sounds – melody, rhythm or tonality. *Kinaesthetic* thinking could include temperature, texture, weight or location.

Submodalities make the difference between an experience you remember as positive and one that you would rather forget or that makes you cringe when you recall it. Once you recognize your preferred method of coding, you can choose whether or not to change the code. This is particularly useful when you want to replace an unmotivated state with a more motivated one, or to lessen the impact of a painful past event. Some people tend to store their memories in a way that leads to negative, low-energy reactions, or to anticipate future events with worry and anxiety. By changing their submodalities, they can alter their whole experience.

What is different about those days when you just can't seem to get out of bed and those when you're up bright and early, raring to go? Some people see the day ahead as dark and cold, and all they can hear is a morbid drone. On the other hand, on their good days, everything is brighter, they feel full of energy and they enjoy listening to the birds singing sweetly. Once you recognize the words that describe your 'good' days, you can choose how to use them.

Find your preferred submodalities

1 Think about a task that you don't like. As you do so, notice whether you recall pictures of the task, the words or sounds associated with it or the accompanying feelings.

- Write down or record a description of what came into your mind, and be as detailed as you can.

- Stop thinking about that experience, move around and think of something else.

2 This time, think about a task you really enjoy and take on with vigour. As you do so, notice whether you recall pictures of the task, the words or sounds associated with it or the accompanying feelings.

- Write down or record a description of what came into your mind, and be as detailed as you can.

- Stop thinking about that experience, move around and come back to now.

3 Compare the lists and notice what kind of words you have used to describe your motivated and unmotivated states.

Which submodalities are the difference that makes the difference?

What you have now is an indication of the way your thinking about a situation can make it pleasurable or not. If you accept that a memory is simply that – an event that happened and cannot be changed – why spend time wallowing in the bad moments and letting them influence the way you run your life? By changing your submodalities, you can change the impact and meaning of your thoughts. You can also change your approach to any outstanding tasks. Your submodality distinctions may have been visual, auditory or kinaesthetic.

Visual

- in colour, black and white or shaded
- brightness: dull or shiny
- clarity: dim and hazy, or sharp and in focus

- size: larger than life, life-size or smaller
- framed or panoramic
- location: in front, to one side or behind you
- clarity: blurred or in focus
- associated, i.e. seen through your own eyes, *or*
- dissociated, i.e. watching yourself in the picture.

Auditory

- volume: loud or quiet
- words or sounds
- stereo or mono
- distance: close or from afar
- tone: soft or harsh, and whose voice(s)?
- speed: faster or slower than usual.

Kinaesthetic

- pressure: hard, soft or a sense of being pushed
- texture: rough or smooth
- weight: light or heavy
- location: where in your body do you experience sensations?
- shape: angular or curved
- intensity: strong or weak
- temperature: hot or cold.

Change your submodalities

1 Go back to a task that was not one of your favourites.

2 As you think about it this time, consciously make it bigger, brighter, more colourful and closer to you. Imagine yourself doing it rather than looking on from the outside. Use a positive tone of voice to tell yourself how good it will be when you have done it. Imagine feeling satisfied, with a great sense of achievement.

3 Play around with your submodalities and notice the way they change the impact on you.

You can make changes in any situation. If you don't like the result, change the submodalities back or try something different.

There are some general trends in the submodalities connected with feeling confident and motivated. Pictures here tend to be associated, big and bright. Sounds are clear and normal pace. Feelings will be solid and warm. The way we talk about our inner thoughts also reflects our mood, and thus 'I always look on the bright side', for example, is preferable to 'The future looks black.'

Next time you are thinking about a painful or unpleasant memory, make the picture dark, small and far away from you. Change the voices to comic ones like Donald Duck's, and change the music to honky-tonk. Then notice the difference in the way you relate to it.

Anchors

In NLP terms an anchor is any stimulus which evokes a consistent response. This can be practical (e.g. the sound of a fire alarm, which means 'Stop what you are doing and move outside') or emotional (e.g. a photograph of a loved one, which makes you feel happy and valued). The power of anchors is based on our ability to learn by making links and forming associations. Once established, they become automatic responses that can be beneficial or detrimental to you. The *beneficial* anchors are those that trigger resourceful states such as confidence, energy and creativity. The *detrimental* anchors activate unresourceful states such as depression, frustration and lethargy.

The power of anchors

You've had a stressful day at work. You get into your car or on to the bus or train and listen to your 'soothing' music or take a favourite route home. This will calm you down, possibly slow you down and alter your stressed state into a more congenial one. On the other hand, you could get into your car, bus or train, and go over in fine detail all the elements of the meeting that stressed you. You might sit down with a thud, grip the steering wheel tightly, or clutch your briefcase and newspaper tightly and glare at anyone who considers sitting near you. This will keep you fired up and speeded up. I wouldn't want to be the next person to meet you!

By choosing affirmative anchors, you can calm yourself down and ensure that the stress is left behind where it belongs and you can carry on more positively with the next part of your day.

What works for you?

If you are nervous or apprehensive about making a presentation or team briefing (or anything you still have to do), you can now choose resourceful anchors to change your approach. The good news is that if you accept the NLP operating principle that we've discussed – 'We have all the resources we need' – then you can transfer what you do well and resourcefully from one part of your life to any other part of your life that you choose. You may feel highly creative when decorating your home, and now you can take that creativity into presentations, report writing or negotiations.

> *Think of a situation at work or outside where you would like to be more resourceful. Then decide which resource(s) you need to become so (e.g. confidence, calmness, energy, concentration or humour).*

Locate the resource

Think about a time in the past when you have fully experienced that state you wish to draw upon. It doesn't matter how long ago it was or whether it was in your professional or personal life. Relive the experience now, seeing the people and things around you as you did at the time. Hear the sounds again, the voices, other noises or maybe the silence. Savour the positive feelings that accompany the experience. Make sure that you are fully associated into the experience, not an onlooker. As you recall the resourceful time, you may also notice physiological changes that indicate a sense of wellbeing. Enjoy this intense feeling of being in your chosen state.

Choose your anchor(s)

You may prefer a *visual* anchor like a particular scene, person or object. An *auditory* anchor would include sounds, music or voices, and a *kinaesthetic* anchor could involve a gesture to recreate the emotions, sensations and feelings. To create a very powerful trigger, you may choose to have all three available. You may see a riverside scene, hear the word 'relax' and squeeze your fingers together to switch yourself instantly into a relaxed state. Do you have a lucky outfit or interview suit? These are anchoring you kinaesthetically because you feel confident and comfortable in them. They are also visual anchors because you like the way you look in them. If they are very bright, they could also be 'loud' auditory anchors!

Decide what your anchor will look, sound or feel like. Make it different from your regular behaviour so that you don't confuse it with other states and resources. Also, choose something discreet that no one else will notice.

Put them together

Return to the resourceful time in the past. Re-experience it again and connect with being there. When the feeling is strong and reaching its peak, implement your anchors. See the picture, hear the sound and feel the gesture. Hold them for a few moments and then release them. Then shake yourself or move in some way to bring yourself back to the present.

Test it

Remember the initial situation in which you wanted to be more resourceful? Think about it now and, as you do so, fire your anchors when they will be most useful as you go through the situation. How did you react? Has your thinking about the original situation changed? Notice that you can now switch to a more resourceful state instantly.

Anchoring is a skill that needs practice. It becomes easier and more effective the more you use it. The more you use it, the more it will become part of your unconscious behaviour. Notice those that already work for you and aim to use them more. Notice also how you anchor 'unresourceful' states such as bad moods and debilitating anxiety. Change the anchors and observe what happens. With resource anchoring, you can increase your emotional choices.

Modelling

As we noted previously, NLP itself was conceived by working out how excellent therapists communicated with their clients. Bandler and Grinder did not 'become' Satir, Erickson or Perls; they learned how to think like them, *modelled* them and then applied that thinking to NLP.

> **Modelling** – the process of understanding the thoughts and actions of successful people that enable someone to accomplish a task excellently.

Children learn much of their early behaviour through modelling the people around them. It is not surprising that many will share any key interests or hobbies that their parents enjoy. There is a saying, 'Imitation is the sincerest form of flattery', and people do indeed want to be like the people they admire. NLP is not suggesting you can become someone else, just that, if you can understand what makes them achieve so much, you can model it yourself and then apply your learning to increase your effectiveness.

Great achievers, particularly in sport, will often claim that they modelled themselves on a childhood hero in the same field. They watched how they perfected their game, noticed how they walked or ran, and imagined how it would be when they were like their hero.

The modelling process

There are three parts to the full NLP modelling process:

1 **Using the second of the perceptual positions.** This involves studying the behaviours of the person you want to model and understanding as nearly as possible their map of the world.

Ask the question: 'What would I have to do to think and behave like you – as if I were you?'

2 **Testing the model.** Do this by taking out one element at a time as you use it. Notice the effect: does its removal make any difference? If 'no', you don't need it. If 'yes', then you have identified an essential element.

3 **Designing a way to teach the skill to others.** This has clear implications in an organizational setting. You can study the excellent staff in any section and, through coaching and mentoring, pass on the relevant strategies to enhance the skills of the relevant personnel.

Modelling exercise: key questions

1 Identify the skill you want to model and reproduce. (You can model yourself and transfer an effective strategy of your own into different settings.)

2 Select a person or people who demonstrate excellence in this skill.

3 Observe and identify:

● their behaviour – what they do and how they do it

● their representational systems and body language

● their filters and metaprograms

● their neurological levels.

4 Where possible, it is useful to interview your model to obtain a clear understanding of what they do. Don't be surprised if they are not clear: they will probably do a lot of it unconsciously. If, for example, you wanted to know how someone successfully negotiated a pay rise, ask:

● 'What do you think about before you go to see your manager?'

● 'How do you help yourself feel confident?'

● 'What sorts of questions do you prepare, and how many do you have?'

● 'How would you describe yourself in the situation?'

● 'How do you prepare to compromise?'

Next steps

This section has given you the basic tools for understanding neuro-linguistic programming and an overview of some of the main themes and thinking that make up NLP. It is a vast area of study and people are finding new applications all the time. Although the techniques and models are derived from a combination of NLP thinkers, by definition, they represent *my* map of the NLP territory. Follow up the bits that have most interested you and enjoy where they take you. Practise establishing rapport in your communications and understanding which representational systems are being used. Use the submodalities to change your responses to past events and, along with anchoring, to positively prepare for the future.

With NLP, you can increase your choices about how you feel and react in any situation and extend your repertoire in communications with others. It is up to you where you go next.

You may want to go back and assimilate the ideas you have read about, or experiment further with the exercises. Please change any of them so that they make best sense for you. You might decide that you would like to take a course or study further.

Know your outcome

If you have some ideas about your future with NLP, this is also an opportunity to revisit the questions related to outcomes. What do you want to do with NLP? Is it something you think will help with family, friends, at work or purely to enhance your own development?

Be flexible

Flexibility is a key element of NLP, as you will have realized. It encourages you to be open to options in the way you behave and communicate. Try out lots of different behaviours and techniques to find out the kind of responses you get. Notice the way other people are thinking and the words they use. Practise the exercises with friends or colleagues. Some may take longer than others to comprehend fully. Start with those that first caught your eye, sounded good or just felt right.

Instead of staying stuck in any situation that isn't working for you, repeat the following sentence:

'If what I'm doing isn't working, I'll try something, anything else.'

Summary

A key aim of NLP is to help you move from situations you don't like or that aren't working for you to ones that are. In this chapter we've examined three ways of increasing your ability to make positive changes.

Using submodalities, we learned that we can keep our pleasant thoughts and memories uppermost and dynamic in our mind and move our unwanted thoughts and memories far away into some distant, less central place.

We all create and respond to positive and negative anchors, but once we recognize them and their effect on us, we can keep or change them. What are your significant anchors? For example, what pictures form the background on your computer or phone? Make sure you choose anchors that make you feel good, happy, relaxed and confident.

Modelling suggests that we can learn how a successful person achieves their success. They become our model. Replicating a particular behaviour involves more than just imitating that behaviour. It involves releasing our limiting beliefs and identifying the values and beliefs that drive their behaviour and the specific skills that enable those behaviours to happen – the 'why and how' of something a person does well.

Fact-check (answers at the back)

1. What do the submodalities do?
   a) Give you more information about the quality of your experiences ❏
   b) Help you differentiate between 'good' days and 'bad' days ❏
   c) Describe your unconscious thoughts ❏
   d) Relate to representational systems ❏

2. What do submodality distinctions in visual mode include?
   a) Volume ❏
   b) Weight ❏
   c) Clarity ❏
   d) Size ❏

3. What do submodality distinctions in auditory mode include?
   a) Volume ❏
   b) Rhythm ❏
   c) Clarity ❏
   d) Intensity ❏

4. What do submodality distinctions in kinaesthetic mode include?
   a) Volume ❏
   b) Temperature ❏
   c) Clarity ❏
   d) Texture ❏

5. What generally happens when we feel confident?
   a) Pictures are associated and bright ❏
   b) Sounds are muffled ❏
   c) Feelings are cool ❏
   d) Inner thoughts are of a bright future ❏

6. What characterizes anchors?
   a) They keep you stuck in one place ❏
   b) They are automatic responses ❏
   c) They occur naturally ❏
   d) They are different in different situations ❏

7. What is the purpose of establishing an anchor?
   a) To trigger a particular state or emotion ❏
   b) To make you a better communicator ❏
   c) To access a particular state or emotion ❏
   d) To change other people's behaviour ❏

8. Why does NLP use modelling?
   a) To enable you to become someone else ❏
   b) To increase your behavioural repertoire ❏
   c) To understand someone else's behaviour ❏
   d) To model human excellence ❏

9. When modelling, what can you observe and identify?
   a) Behaviour ❏
   b) Emails ❏
   c) Body language ❏
   d) Musical preferences ❏

10. How can you improve your NLP skills?
    a) Television programmes ❏
    b) Workshops ❏
    c) DVDs ❏
    d) One-to-one coaching ❏

7 × 7

1 Seven key themes

- **Know what you want (goal setting):** Well-formed outcomes are an important tool for ensuring that you get more of what you want in your life.

- **Know whether you're getting what you want (sensory acuity):** Once you know where you want to go, you need to be able to notice – using one or more senses – whether or not you are going there. Sensory acuity trains our minds to see and listen to non-verbal communication.

- **Get the attention of the unconscious mind (rapport):** Rapport – the process of building and sustaining a relationship of mutual trust, harmony and understanding – happens when two people's behaviours match.

- **Adjust what you're doing accordingly (behavioural flexibility):** When you notice that you are not getting what you want, or when what you're currently doing isn't working, you need the flexibility to change what you are doing in order to get a different result.

- **Model excellence:** A NLP presupposition is that 'if one person can do something, anyone can learn to do it' (within physical, practical and psychological limits). With that person as our model, all we have to do is release our own limiting beliefs, work out how they do the thing we want to do and start to apply their methodology.

- **Identify limiting beliefs:** Often based on emotions rather than facts, beliefs are the assumptions we make about ourselves and others and about how we expect things to be. These assumptions determine the way we behave and shape our decision-making processes. We tend to notice 'facts' that reinforce the beliefs. It is almost as if we attract only ideas that feed rather than contradict our beliefs.

- **Use the bell jar distraction technique:** Imagine you have an inverted bell jar surrounding you. This container acts as a barrier and stops other people's negative thoughts and feelings from reaching or touching you. Let the past go and forgive. Dragging your past with you only slows you down.

2 Seven assumptions to live by

- **The meaning of your communication is the result you get.** In other words, it's up to you to get others to understand your message. You have to take responsibility for your communication.

- **We are all unique.** Every human being – even an identical twin – has their own unique way of understanding and interpreting the world. We all think differently.

- **There is no such thing as failure – only feedback.** Information you receive about something you did is simply that, information or feedback. It's about your actions and has nothing to do with you personally.

- **Behaviour speaks louder than words.** Listen to what people say, but pay more attention to what they do. If there is any contradiction between the two, look for behavioural evidence of change and don't just rely on people's words.

- **We cannot *not* communicate**. As long as you are awake, you are communicating things about yourself without using words, simply by the way you stand or sit or even breathe.

- **You have within you all the resources to achieve what you want.** Most of us can do most things that we want. Sometimes we just need to be reminded how to do it.

- **Behind every behaviour there is always a positive intention.** Whatever a person's behaviour may be, they have a positive purpose for behaving in that way.

3 Seven great quotes

- 'Keep your thoughts positive because your thoughts become your words. Keep your words positive because your words become your behaviour. Keep your behaviour positive because your behaviour becomes your habits. Keep your habits positive because your habits become your values.

Keep your values positive because your values become your destiny.' Mahatma Gandhi

● 'I've learned that people will forget what you said, people will forget what you did, but people will never forget how you made them feel.' Maya Angelou

● 'You can conquer almost any fear if you will only make up your mind to do so. For remember, fear doesn't exist anywhere except in the mind.' Dale Carnegie

● 'If you don't make decisions about how you are going to live in years to come, then you have already made a decision – to be directed by environments instead of shaping your own destiny.' Anthony Robbins

● 'I never hit a shot, not even in practice, without having a very sharp, in-focus picture of it in my head ... the final scene shows me making the kind of swing that will turn the previous images into reality.' Jack Nicklaus

● 'Nothing can stop the man with the right mental attitude from achieving his goal; nothing on earth can help the man with the wrong mental attitude.' Thomas Jefferson

● 'The best thing you can do is the right thing. The next best thing you can do is the wrong thing. The worst thing you can do is nothing.' Theodore Roosevelt

4 Seven tips for using NLP

● **Anchor great emotional states** in people, such as: learning is easy; a curious state of mind; enjoyment; contentment and so on.

● **Use stories and metaphors** to change content, context and meaning. The unconscious mind loves to hear stories. They're a powerful form of change.

● **Be flexible:** remember to use your immense flexibility to get your desired outcome. If what you're doing isn't working, do something different.

● **Always be in rapport** with the other person when using NLP.

- **Use perceptual positioning** to work out what's going on between you and another person. You can't really understand someone until you 'walk a mile in their shoes'.
- **Reframe to accept or change behaviour.** Behaviours are rarely wrong in themselves: they just occur in the wrong context.
- **Focus on what works.** NLP asserts that the conscious brain carries a maximum of nine pieces of information at any one time.

5 Seven principles from NLP

- NLP has four pillars on which to build success: know what you want; understand others and let them know you understand; be prepared to change what you're doing and your goals; experience the world and process information, using all your senses. Use these pillars to support you to be open to previously unexpected possibilities.
- Your mind is your internal powerhouse that steers your thoughts and subsequent actions. The messages and thoughts from your mind influence the way you feel and the actions you take.
- It's not what people say to you that affects you but what you say to yourself afterwards that makes the difference. NLP recognizes the impact our language has on our lives. Use language that helps and inspires you.
- You always have a choice, though you may not seem to. NLP suggests you find at least three ways of doing something.
- Change your physiology to change your state. If you're feeling stuck, angry, unhappy or unmotivated, do one or more of the following to change your mood: walk around; dance to some jazzy music; jump up and down; relax; sing out loud.
- Mental rehearsal – also known as visualization – is practice in the imagination, which prepares and primes the body for an actual situation. Use it to help you run through what you want in your mind before experiencing the actual event.

- Recognize your own and other people's motivation direction. A 'towards' person will be a risk-taker and have a 'go for it' approach. They may need an 'away' person to anticipate possible pitfalls. An 'away' person will put off doing something until the last minute, or until the disadvantages of not doing it become great enough to spur them on. 'Towards' people respond better to rewards, 'away from' people to threats.

6 Seven great coaching questions

- **What do you want?** This is the ultimate NLP coaching question. Many people only know what they don't want. Once you help someone state their goals in positive terms, you can both work out the steps needed to get there.

- **What would happen if you did?** When a person says, 'I can't' or 'It's impossible', they are talking about something that they perceive to be outside their ability or sphere of influence. In fact, it might be just their perception that is limiting them, not their ability or their situation.

- **What's the best question I could ask you now?** Rather than scrambling around to ask the 'right' question, trust the other person to know what is best for them.

- **How do you stop yourself?** It takes a lot of energy for someone to keep a problem in place. This question subtly suggests that they are the one with the power to move it.

- **Always?** Generalizations involve taking one experience and making it an absolute truth in all circumstances. They also describe the rules or limits governing our behaviour. These words are all-inclusive and allow no room for manoeuvre. This question is designed to identify and challenge the thinking.

- **Where, when and with whom (do you want)?** It's important to put goals into context and describe a goal in as much detail as possible, for both the conscious and the unconscious mind of the person.

- **If you did know, what would be the answer?** This is a great question to use when people say, 'I don't know.' It's imperative to be in rapport with them, otherwise the question can seem glib and provoke a defensive response.

7 Seven influential people

- **Richard Bandler:** Bandler, the co-founder of NLP, has changed therapy, education and medicine for ever. His record of helping patients deemed incurable is unsurpassed.

- **John Grinder:** The co-founder of NLP, Grinder has devoted his life's work to his quest to uncover and present human patterns of excellence, modelled from geniuses in different fields. He created NLP with Bandler as a means to investigate and replicate human excellence.

- **Milton Erickson:** Erickson believed the unconscious mind was self-generating, positive, and key to successful change. The purpose of therapy is to access unconscious resources.

- **Virginia Satir:** Satir was one of the pioneers of family therapy, and a major source of NLP patterns and distinctions.

- **Shelle Rose Charvet:** Known in the NLP community as the 'Queen of LAB Profile' (Language and Behaviour Profile), Charvet developed an in-depth insight into metaprograms.

- **Anthony Robbins:** One of the foremost authorities on the psychology of peak performance, Robbins is the guru of personal, professional and organizational turnaround.

- **Sue Knight:** Knight is the author of *NLP at Work*, the book that pioneered the application of NLP to business.

Find out more

If this Part has whetted your appetite and you want to take it further, there are many resources for you to do so. You can learn from one-day taster courses, weekend workshops or NLP practitioner courses. Check that your trainers are accredited and have trainer or master trainer qualifications. Take time checking that their way of thinking and training works for you.

Read some of the other authors listed at the end of the book to broaden your map. Watch DVDs or YouTube clips, listen to CDs or take a training course. To find training courses and practitioners, visit:

● Association of NLP – www.anlp.org
● International NLP Trainers Association – www.inlpta.co.uk
● The Professional Guild of NLP – www.professionalguildofnlp.com

Whatever you do next… enjoy getting to know yourself and making sense of what makes you the unique person you are.

Answers

Part 1: Your Negotiation Skills Masterclass

Chapter 1:
1. a) 0 b) 1 c) 2 d) 0
2. a) 1 b) 0 c) 0 d) 2
3. a) 1 b) 0 c) 2 d) 0
4. a) 1 b) 2 c) 0 d) 0
5. a) 2 b) 0 c) 0 d) 1
6. a) 0 b) 0 c) 2 d) 1
7. a) 0 b) 0 c) 1 d) 2
8. a) 2 b) 0 c) 1 d) 0
9. a) 1 b) 2 c) 0 d) 0
10. a) 0 b) 2 c) 1 d) 1

Chapter 2:
1. a) 1 b) 1 c) 1 d) 2
2. a) 0 b) 1 c) 2 d) 1
3. a) 0 b) 2 c) 1 d) 0
4. a) 1 b) 1 c) 1 d) 2
5. a) 1 b) 1 c) 1 d) 2
6. a) 1 b) 2 c) 0 d) 0
7. a) 0 b) 1 c) 2 d) 0
8. a) 2 b) 0 c) 1 d) 0
9. a) 0 b) 0 c) 2 d) 0
10. a) 1 b) 0 c) 2 d) 1

Chapter 3:
1. a) 1 b) 1 c) 2 d) 3
2. a) 0 b) 0 c) 2 d) 1
3. a) 2 b) 0 c) 0 d) 0
4. a) 2 b) 0 c) 0 d) 1
5. a) 1 b) 2 c) 3 d) 1
6. a) 3 b) 1 c) 0 d) 0
7. a) 0 b) 2 c) 3 d) 0
8. a) 0 b) 0 c) 0 d) 2
9. a) 0 b) 2 c) 1 d) 3
10. a) 1 b) 0 c) 1 d) 2

Chapter 4:
1. a) 2 b) 2 c) 0 d) 0
2. a) 0 b) 1 c) 0 d) 2
3. a) 1 b) 2 c) 0 d) 1
4. a) 2 b) 0 c) 1 d) 1
5. a) 0 b) 1 c) 2 d) 0
6. a) 1 b) 1 c) 2 d) 0
7. a) 0 b) 2 c) 1 d) 0
8. a) 1 b) 2 c) 0 d) 0
9. a) 2 b) 0 c) 1 d) 0
10. a) 1 b) 0 c) 2 d) 1

Chapter 5:
1. a) 0 b) 0 c) 2 d) 1
2. a) 0 b) 0 c) 1 d) 2
3. a) 0 b) 1 c) 1 d) 2
4. a) 2 b) 2 c) 0 d) 2
5. a) 1 b) 0 c) 2 d) 1
6. a) 2 b) 1 c) 1 d) 0
7. a) 2 b) 0 c) 0 d) 1
8. a) 0 b) 1 c) 2 d) 0
9. a) 1 b) 2 c) 0 d) 0
10. a) 1 b) 0 c) 0 d) 2

Chapter 6:
1. a) 0 b) 0 c) 2 d) 1
2. a) 1 b) 2 c) 0 d) 0
3. a) 0 b) 0 c) 1 d) 2
4. a) 1 b) 0 c) 2 d) 0
5. a) 1 b) 2 c) 1 d) 0
6. a) 2 b) 3 c) 1 d) 1
7. a) 0 b) 2 c) 0 d) 1
8. a) 0 b) 0 c) 1 d) 2
9. a) 2 b) 0 c) 1 d) 0
10. a) 0 b) 2 c) 0 d) 1

Total score out of a possible 126:

Part 2: Your Advanced Negotiation Skills Masterclass

Chapter 8: 1d; 2c; 3d; 4c; 5c; 6d; 7a; 8d; 9a; 10d

Chapter 9: 1d; 2c; 3c; 4c; 5d; 6b; 7a; 8a; 9c; 10c

Chapter 10: 1d; 2d; 3c; 4b; 5d; 6d; 7a; 8a; 9a; 10a

Chapter 11: 1d; 2d; 3c; 4b; 5d; 6d; 7a; 8a; 9a; 10a

Chapter 12: 1d; 2d; 3c; 4b; 5d; 6d; 7a; 8a; 9a; 10a

Chapter 13: 1c; 2d; 3b; 4a; 5a; 6b; 7b; 8c; 9b; 10d

Chapter 14: 1a; 2d; 3c; 4a; 5a; 6c; 7b; 8d; 9b; 10c

Part 3: Your Persuasion and Influence Masterclass

Chapter 15: 1b; 2a; 3d; 4b; 5a; 6b; 7a; 8c; 9b; 10a.

Chapter 16: 1c; 2a; 3d; 4b; 5a; 6a; 7a; 8b; 9c; 10a.

Chapter 17: 1c; 2a; 3d; 4a; 5a; 6d; 7c; 8b; 9b; 10b.

Chapter 18: 1a; 2d; 3c; 4a; 5d; 6a; 7b; 8c; 9a; 10c.

Chapter 19: 1c; 2c; 3a; 4b; 5a; 6b; 7b; 8d; 9c; 10a.

Chapter 20: 1c; 2a; 3d; 4a; 5a; 6b; 7d; 8c; 9b; 10b.

Part 4: Your NLP Masterclass

Chapter 21: 1b & d; 2b; 3a, b & c; 4d; 5c; 6b; 7d; 8b & c; 9c & d; 10d.

Chapter 22: 1a & d; 2b; 3a & c; 4b & d; 5c; 6a & b; 7c; 8b & c; 9b; 10b, c & d.

Chapter 23: 1b, c & d; 2c & d; 3a & d; 4a; 5b & d; 6a; 7c & d; 8a & c; 9b; 10a & b.

Chapter 24: 1a & c; 2b; 3b & c; 4a, c & d; 5c & d; 6a & b; 7c & d; 8b & c; 9a & b; 10a & b.

Chapter 25: 1b & c; 2a & b; 3a & c; 4c & d; 5a & b; 6b & c; 7b & c; 8b & d; 9b; 10b & d.

Chapter 26: 1b, c & d; 2a, c & d; 3a & c; 4b, c & d; 5a & c; 6c & d; 7a, b & c; 8a, b & c; 9a & b; 10a, b & c.

Chapter 27: 1b & d; 2c & d; 3a & b; 4b & d; 5a & d; 6b & c; 7a & c; 8b, c & d; 9a & c; 10b, c & d.

Further reading

Alder, H., *NLP for Managers: How to Achieve Excellence at Work* (Piatkus, 1996)

Andreas, S. & Andreas, C., *Change Your Mind and Keep the Change* (Real People Press, 1988)

Bandler, R., *Using Your Brain – for a Change* (Real People Press, 1997)

Bandler, R. and Grinder, J., *Frogs into Princes* (Eden Grove, 1990)

Bavister, S. and Vickers, A., *Essential NLP* (Hodder Education, 2010)

Charvet, S., *Words That Change Minds: Mastering the Language of Influence* (Kendall/Hunt Publishing, 2010)

Knight, S., *NLP at Work: The Difference that Makes a Difference in Business* (Nicholas Brealey Publishing, 2002)

McDermott, I. and Jago, W., *The NLP Coach* (Piatkus, 2002)

McDermott, I. and O'Connor, J., *Practical NLP for Managers* (Gower, 1997)

Molden, D., *Managing with the Power of NLP for Competitive Advantage* (Pitman Publishing, 1997)

Molden, D., *NLP Business Masterclass*, 2nd edn. (Financial Times/Prentice Hall, 2007)

O'Connor, J. and Seymour, J., *Introducing NLP*, 2nd edn. (Thorsons, 2003)

Overdurf, J. and Silverthorn, J., *Training Trances* (Metamorphous Press, 1995)

Quilliam, S., *What Makes People Tick?* (Element Press, 2003)

Robbins, A., *Unlimited Power* (Simon and Schuster, 2001)

Shapiro, M., *Shift Your Thinking, Change Your Life* (Sheldon Press, 2001)

Shapiro, M., *Presenting: Bullet Guide* (Hodder Education, 2011)

Steinhouse, R., *How to Coach with NLP* (Pearson Education, 2010)

Notes

Notes

Notes

Notes

Notes